Visions of European Unity

Visions of European Unity

EDITED BY
Philomena Murray
and Paul Rich

LONDON AND NEW YORK

To John and Stephen, with love
—P.M.

To Caroline Swain
—P.R.

First published 1996 by Westview Press, Inc.

Published 2018 by Routledge
52 Vanderbilt Avenue, New York, NY 10017
2 Park Square, Milton Park, Abingdon, Oxon OX14 4RN

Routledge is an imprint of the Taylor & Francis Group, an informa business

Copyright © 1996 Taylor & Francis

Library of Congress Cataloging-in-Publication Data
Visions of European unity / edited by Philomena B. Murray and Paul B. Rich.
  Rich.
    p. cm.
  Includes bibliographical references and index.
  ISBN 0-8133-8965-8 (hardcover)
  1. European Federation. I. Murray, Philomena B. II. Rich, Paul
B., 1950– .
D1060.V57 1996
341.24'2—dc20   95-42498
                                              CIP

ISBN 13: 978-0-367-21321-3 (hbk)
ISBN 13: 978-0-367-21602-3 (pbk)

Contents

Preface

This book was born of a desire to explore visions and ideals of European Unity at a time of debate on the aftermath of the Maastricht Treaty on European Union. We would like to thank the University of Luton for financial assistance towards the camera-ready production of the book. We would like to thank Lilian Topic for her excellent assistance in reading the first version of the book and rendering it presentable to Westview. We thank Christine Agius, Iona Annett, W. E. Paterson, John Polesel, and Lilian Topic for reading parts of the book and offering helpful comments and suggestions. We thank Leslie Holmes for his encouragement of this project. We thank Craig Lonsdale, professional officer of the Department of Political Science of the University of Melbourne for help with printing difficulties and final camera-ready corrections. We would also like to acknowledge Wendy Ruffles for word-processing assistance. Special thanks are also due to Joanne Kummrow for her excellent work on the camera-ready version of the book. We thank our partners, John Polesel and Isabelle Rich, for their support throughout the period of gestation of the book. We are especially grateful to Susan McEachern of Westview Press for her patience and encouragement at all times.

Philomena Murray
Melbourne, Australia

Paul B. Rich
Luton, U.K.

Abbreviations and Acronyms

CAP	Common Agricultural Policy
CD	Christian Democratic Party
CDU\CSU	German Christian Democratic Union
CERES	Centre d'Etudes, de Recherches et de l'Education Socialiste
DG	Directorate General
EC	European Community
ECJ	European Court of Justice
ECSC	European Coal and Steel Community
ECU	European Currency Unit
EDC	European Defence Community
EDG	European Democratic Group
EEA	European Economic Area
EEC	European Economic Community
EES	European Economic Space
EFTA	European Free Trade Association
EMS	European Monetary System
EMU	European Monetary Union
EP	European Parliament
EPA	European Political Assembly
EPP	European People's Party / Federation of the Christian Democratic Parties of the European Community
EPU	European Political Union
ETUC	European Trade Union Confederation
EU	European Union
EUF	European Union of Federalists
EURATOM	European Atomic Energy Community
EUT	Draft Treaty establishing the European Union
FN	National Front of France
IGC	Intergovernmental Conference
IMF	International Monetary Fund
MEP	Member of the European Parliament
TEU	Maastricht Treaty on European Union

MFE	European Federalist Movement
NATO	North Atlantic Treaty Organisation
OJ	Official Journal of the European Communities
PCI	Italian Communist Party
POSL	Parti Ouvriere Socialiste de Luxembourg
PSB	Parti Socialiste Belge
SACEUR	Supreme Allied Commander Europe
SEA	Single European Act
SFIO	Section Francaise de l'Internationale Ouvriere, former name of the French Socialist Party, now known as the PSF
SPD	German Social Democratic Party
UK	United Kingdom
UNICE	Union of Industries in the European Community
WEU	Western European Union

1

Introduction

Philomena Murray and Paul Rich

This book addresses the variety of ideals and theories behind the idea of a united Europe. Taken as a whole, we see these ideals and theories forming a series of "visions" of European unification that served as mental maps for those politicians and intellectuals who hoped Europe could develop as a powerful and cohesive political entity, including, for some, strong federal institutions and a common foreign and security policy. The ideals were inspiring and often utopian. What is remarkable is that few have been achieved as they were originally envisaged, even though they continue to influence the course of political debate on European unification. Indeed some analysts such as Simon Serfaty have suggested that European integration has occurred without any real vision at all and more in a fit of absent-mindedness.[1] This is a considerable exaggeration. As the chapters in the volume show, the diplomatic moves towards closer European union from the early 1950s onwards were rooted in a long-term set of political ideals, even though there was not always an immediate consensus on what these necessarily were.

This book attempts to fill in a gap in our understanding of the politics of European Union by carrying out an analysis from international specialists on these ideals and theories. It combines the examination of actual ideals and idealists with theoretical approaches to the study of the central body in the history of European unification the European Community (known since 1 November 1993 as the European Union). These theoretical approaches have often been called, for convenience, integration theory, though, as some chapters make clear, there is a teleological danger in this term. The interesting aspect of the visionaries of European unity is that they were often the early theorists of integration as well as being intellectuals, politicians or bureaucrats. Their visions differed, according to their respective experience, nationality and ideological background. What they had in common was a belief that there could be created, from the ruins of post-World War Europe, a cohesive society of nations which might ultimately transcend the nation state. Where they differed was about both aims and means, reflecting the diversity of ideas on European unification at the end of World War II and the wide social base of those involved in the debate.

The issue of European unity started as an intellectual debate, especially in the years before and after World War II. In more recent years, it is possible to see a populist political reaction in many European countries (particularly at the time of the Danish and French referenda in 1992-1993 on the Maastricht Treaty) to this earlier, rather elitist, debate as many politicians started to play the nationalist political card in reaction to the perceived growing powers of the European Commission and the Brussels bureaucracy. There have been, nevertheless, major historical reasons for this earlier commitment by many intellectuals in Europe to the idea of continental unity. The decade of the 1940s acted in many respects as a watershed in the thinking of the European intelligentsia as earlier hopes in the internationalism of the League of Nations became dashed as Europe drifted into war. Many European intellectuals at this time began to explore the possibilities not only for a wider European political union in some form but also of a common European culture. Indeed, it is possible to see emerging during this period a distinct "Europe of the intellectuals" as numerous seminars, symposia, conferences and discussion groups were held in both Europe and the United States to debate the idea of "European integration."[2] The full intellectual history of this period from the mid to late 1940s to the late 1970s and 1980s remains to be written and this volume is in many ways an incursion into a huge area requiring extensive collaborative research.

Functionalism, Federalism and Neofunctionalism

The debate on Europe quickly became infused with the passion in the postwar social sciences for behaviourism. Broadly speaking, three distinct schools of thought had emerged by the 1960s on the possible trajectory of European "integration." The first school has been termed functionalist and stretches back to the ideas on progressive functional integration espoused by the Romanian scholar David Mitrany at the London School of Economics in the 1930s and 1940s. This approach was economistic and technocratic in nature and reflected the phase of Keynesian thinking in economics. It assumed that through the progressive harmonising by rival nation states of economic and trade policies an eventual "spillover" would occur into the area of political unification. The approach was gradualist and pragmatic and placed great faith in the benign rationalism of the managers of nation states.[3]

In some respects, functionalism underpinned the thinking of post-war advocates of closer European unification such as Jean Monnet, Robert Schuman and Paul Henri Spaak, leading to the creation of the European Coal and Steel Community (ECSC) in the early 1950s.[4] However, it was also challenged by the more idealistic advocates of a more far-reaching federalism in Europe who had been inspired by many of the idea of the European resistance in the early 1940s. Federalism has a long history in European political thought and is based on a division of powers between central federal governments on the one hand and regional or provincial states on the other. Federalists sought a far more wide-ranging pooling of sovereignty by European powers compared to the functionalists. They have also usually sought greater democratic participation by electorates in the unification process, despite attacks made by contemporary "Eurosceptics" in Britain against a federalism that is simplistically associated with an undemocratic Brussels bureaucracy.

Federalism, though, largely failed to become the dominant political model in European unification; it was far too wide-ranging and assumed a much greater willingness by national governments to pool their sovereignty than actually existed in postwar Europe. The study of federalist thought and federalism as a theory of European integration, has been given a new lease of life after a moribund decade or two by the work of Michael Burgess, Alain Gagnon, Francois Duchene and John Pinder.[5] They have succeeded in rigorously examining the nature of federalism as ideology and as political thought and visions in Pinder's *The European Community; The Building of a Union* and the Burgess and Gagnon edited volume which acts as a means to raise necessary questions about the nature of federalism in the political agendas of the founders of the EC, the role in the current Community/Union. There is also an examination of the case, put forcefully by Pinder, for a neofederalism, consisting of a federalism which takes on board some of the tenets of the neofunctionalists' logic of integration. In many ways this book complements these studies as it examines the role of theory and also the role of visions in the course of the twentieth century.

By the 1960s a third school had begun to develop of neofunctionalists led by scholars such as Karl Deutsch and Ernst Haas and Leon Lindberg. This third school has sought to modify the original functionalism of Mitrany to incorporate the autonomous activities of political institutions in the "integration process" in Europe. Haas in particular pointed out in a major book *The Uniting of Europe* that when some sectors of sovereign nation states are integrated this sets in motion a cumulative political process in which political parties and interest groups become progressively involved. The "integration process" thus becomes inherently expansive and extends into further and further areas until it encompasses most of the major policy areas that had hitherto been solely controlled by national governments.[6]

This book thus attempts to draw out in particular the theme of the tension of federalism and functionalism in its many appearances over the last five decades. It is clear that this tension is expressed in the theoretical approaches to the study of European integration as well as in the conflicts between the functionalist and federalist idealists since the beginning of the postwar desire for the United States of Europe, in whatever political form that that may take. The book also illustrates that federalism has been both an aim and a theory of the united Europe and that it is important to be keenly aware of federalism as a motivating force, a desired outcome and sometimes as a trend. All of these issues are explored in the book. The fascinating character of European unity ideals has thus been the fact the that the theories and actual programmes in, for example, the EC, often were interrelated. W. Wallace makes the point well: "Theories of political integration thus developed alongside political strategies of integration, feeding on one another as they grew."[7]

In addition, it has been all too clear in the last five decades that the idealists of federalism were not the major motivating force in the EC and the EU, although as Burgess and Wallace have both pointed out, the federalist ideal has always been evident in the visions of the political actors and many governments over time.[8]

Indeed, it would be nothing short of naive to assume that the federalist idealists or federally minded institutions such as the European Parliament have been crucial to the relance of the EC in the 1980s, for example. The relance of the 1980s was not due to the activism of Spinelli or the EP, but rather primarily due to the hardheaded pragmatism of the member states governments in their desire for economic recovery and international competitiveness of the EC. Indeed, the EC experience of the early 1980s was of institutional lourdeur, economic productivity problems, the costs of the Common Agricultural Policy, and budget wrangles. It has been pointed out[9] that the provisions in the Single European Act for streamlined decisionmaking procedures was due to the decisions of the memberstates that this was necessary than to the "the enthusiastic pressures for European union from within the European parliament." Nevertheless, as the chapter on Spinelli illustrates, the European Parliament has long been the repository of political ideals of European unity and democracy at the European level of governance, with a program for a firm constitutional basis for the EU's federal aims. Burgess has borne out this point in his analysis of Spinelli's thinking, especially in the 1980s.[10]

While Monnet was more active than Spinelli in the process known as formal integration[11] defined as deliberate actions by policy-makers to create rules to establish common institutions and regulate or inhibit social and economic flows, as well as to pursue common policies, nevertheless Spinelli can be seen as being active in the process of informal integration[12] along with political parties in transnational political groups and federations especially over the last decade, and in the European Parliament. The national party structures were never committed above other motivations to the ideals of European unity. The domestic factor was always paramount. The parties of western Europe are therefore best analysed through their platforms and programmes than through their mass support for European unity as such support simply did not exist. The ideal of European unity remained largely an elitist one in party organisations and did not gain support among the middle level party activists or among the voters, to date.

In some respects a neofunctionalism of a sort did occur in the course of the 1980s as the members of the EC agreed on the Single European Act in 1986, the Social Charter in 1989 and finally the Treaty on European Union at the end of 1991 establishing a European Union. The very effort of doing this, though, revealed the limits of neofunctionalism as a theory to explain closer European unification. Maastricht signified the end of an era centred on the Cold War and superpower domination of the European continent. It pointed to the fact that there is likely to be growing political opposition to further attempts to create a United Europe from the top down by elitist methods, without consideration to the attitudes of the various national electorates. The continued popular attachment to notions of national sovereignty in the various EU states has shown nationalism to be a more tenacious doctrine than Europeanism.

Nevertheless the fact that the Treaty on European Union was signed at all indicates that the European ideal has considerable durability. This book serves as a background to understand the ideals that led to the creation of the EU and also the ideals behind the framing of the Maastricht Treaty on European Union. That Treaty is itself not without its flaws—one critic Emanuele Gazzo, longtime federalist and editor of *Agence Europe*, referred to it thus,

> . . . the text of this treaty is largely incomplete, very ambiguous, deficient in relation to the hopes of Europeans and written in terms which have made it possible for adversaries of European integration to exploit it to create doubt and even rejection in a large part of public opinion.[13]

For federalists the Treaty did not go far enough in creating a United Europe. Nevertheless, the entire notion of Europe, and its boundaries, is now under scrutiny in the aftermath of the end of the Cold War. This volume thus reassesses the notions of what constituted the Europe of the post-World War era, in order to illuminate the present debate over the future of Europe. The analysis of the ideas behind European unity has been surprisingly thin in the extensive academic literature on the EU. Political scientists have tended to focus on the institutions of the EU, policymaking and the economic and political implications of unification rather than its intellectual and ideological dimensions. The idea of European unification constitutes an important body of geopolitical thought about a continent's common identity and future destiny. It carries echoes of nationalist ideology to the supranational level, though it also represents an attempt to overcome the problems of a continent dominated by rival national states that have periodically resorted to war and territorial aggrandisement at each other's expense.

Europe's Geographical and Political Diversity

The idealists of European unification come from a variety of traditions of European political thought. They recognised many of the traditional geographical and political patterns of national diversity in European history, while at the same time attempting to overcome their more negative aspects. At the heart of much of the thinking of such visionaries as Dante, Sully, Leibniz and Rousseau, lay the idea of Europe as a united republican order of Christian peoples—a republique Chretienne—which could galvanise a new continental-wide sense of common cultural and religious identity in the face of hostile enemies such as the Muslim Turks, who were seen as the quintessential "other."[14]

This ideological appeal was rather undermined by technological developments which, if anything, reinforced the trend towards political and regional diversity. The steady revolution in armaments reinforced Europe's competing political entities, which were able to purchase sufficient weaponry to ensure their continuing independence. Europe did not as a result come under the sway of a single imperial dynasty as in China or India, though a number of bids were made to this end such as those of the Hapsburg emperor Charles V in the sixteenth century and Napoleon in the early nineteenth. Hitler's bid in the twentieth century was only prevented by external intervention by the United States and the Soviet Union, ending centuries of European domination of global politics.[15]

The European continent after the Peace of Westphalia in 1648 remained characterised by continuing power rivalries among national states. Until the end of the Middle Ages, political discourse in Europe had been pivoted around the idea of a *unitas reipublicae christianae* being secured in the face of external threats from non-Christian enemies such as the Turks. The term "Europe" did not really enter into political parlance until the late seventeenth century when the Turkish threat was finally removed after the lifting of the siege of Vienna in 1680. Thereafter, it increasingly entered into popular discourse and replaced older notions such as "Christendom" even though it continued to remain a contested concept that did not easily command universal agreement.[16]

The notion of "Europe" also emerged during the first phase of European imperial expansion, a period characterised by a reckless pursuit of adventure as well as commercial profit.[17] In the course of the following two centuries the term "Europe" took on an increasingly imperial overtone of economic and cultural superiority. "European" came to be associated with the idea of being "civilised" and "cultured" in contrast to the "backward" societies outside Europe which were seen as economically and culturally dependent upon imperial metropoles such as Britain, France, Spain, Portugal and, by the late nineteenth century, Italy and Germany.[18] This cultural definition of European identity ensured that it remained the preserve of a relatively tiny elite and it is by no means clear that this problem has been overcome even now, as the continent remains dogged by the absence of any really cohesive cultural unity at the popular level beyond the more obvious common participation in a consumer society and mass sports and tourism. In the event of a major crisis it remains doubtful if these appeals would prove stronger than more conventional notions of national affiliation.[19]

The phase of European imperial expansion in the eighteenth and nineteenth centuries ended up sharpening nationalist sentiments and great power rivalries within Europe. The investment in empire-building diverted interest away from the idea of trying to forge a closer European unity. Imperialist ideologues emphasised the identity and superiority of the imperial ruling race and stressed the importance of maintaining links with colonies of European settlement overseas. It was only in the twentieth century that the idea of European unification really entered into mainstream political debate.

The Development of the Idea of European Union

The idea of European unification thus only came to the fore after the disaster of World War I. As Chapter 2 indicates, some form of United

Europe began to be debated in various elite circles in France and Britain and was even proposed by the French Foreign Minister Aristide Briand at the League of Nations in Geneva in 1929. However, it was far from being a popular ideal and was soon overtaken by the rise of fascism and extreme nationalism in the 1930s.

It was World War II and the virtual destruction of many European states as a result of Nazi occupation which decisively gave a fillip to the idea of some form of united European superstate. Smith has pointed to the "newness of the Vision" of the postwar definition of a stable Europe and that the instrument of stability would not be drawn from the past after the defeat of Fascism.[20] By 1945 it began to be espoused by various groups of politicians, intellectuals and bureaucrats, who sought some form of closer political and economic relationship of European states in order to prevent another war engulfing the continent. It was these intellectuals and politicians who initially seized the initiative for building a united Europe.

These original idealistic visions have been more recently superseded by constitutional and institutional debate on the future of Europe. The often conflicting role of the intergovernmental and supranational institutions which now constitute the EU also feature prominently since they are closely linked with economic and fiscal issues such as the creation of economic and monetary union in Europe and a common European currency and banking system. Some basic issues which confronted the original visionaries earlier this century still remain, particularly that of sovereignty. What does it mean for the nation state that the sovereignty of the member states of the EU is being pooled into a new supranational entity which could even act as a fully sovereign body in its own right in global affairs? The nation state has created the EU and it has also in some respects been altered by it, though how much remains a matter of considerable contention among scholars. Some have argued that the increasing interdependence of the EU's member states renders the traditional notions of the nation state questionable since the European Union now features forms of pooled sovereignty in decisionmaking on the Single Market or the Common Agricultural Policy. Others have remained sceptical of the degree to which the traditional sovereignty of the nation state in Europe has been transcended and point to the continuing need for the hegemony of a great power or powers to guarantee the continent's continuing security.

The Parallel with the United States

One of the most attractive models for some architects of European unity has been the United States; indeed, the US parallel inspired the very idea in the nineteenth century of a "United States of Europe," as a relatively young system with states which retained some power while being committed to federation. The European continent's diversity has rendered unity a difficult task, perhaps one that might be harder to accomplish than the vision that inspired the original founding fathers of the United States. The states attending the constitutional convention at Philadelphia had the advantage of having fought together in a revolutionary war with the former imperial power of Britain. Many of those who drafted the new constitution shared a political idealism stressing the essential innocence of man and his possible perfectibility under the right kind of government.

The US founding fathers had a number of advantages which the contemporary European states do not. There was a close relationship between politicians and intellectuals and some—such as James Madison—were both. They were unhampered by mass politics, large bureaucracies and a large enfranchised electorate. They came from a similar class and ethnic background and all spoke the same language. Unlike the governments involved in the EU, none of the states represented at Philadelphia had enjoyed a long period as sovereign nation states with proud national histories. All faced a similar set of goals of building up new societies, encouraging immigration from Europe and opening up a huge continent to their west, whereas Europe's unifiers had to deal with existing societies and political and economic models already well in place.

In Europe, the imperatives to political union are considerably different. Many of the early visionaries of European unity were impelled by a desperate effort to avert another major European war and to achieve Franco-German reconciliation. From the early nineteenth century until the 1920s and 1930s, visionaries of a "United States of Europe" were often considered utopian idealists who failed to understand the realities of international power politics. It was really only the catastrophe of World War II which made the whole idea of building a new supranational European entity in any way politically feasible. Even then, there were major differences between those who wanted to achieve a completely new European federal "superstate," such as Altiero Spinelli and the European Federalist Movement, and more cautious functionalists and neofunctionalists, such as Haas, wanting to see this evolve more gradually. Much depended too on the external support of the United States following the European Recovery Programme. Alan Milward has argued for instance that the real significance of this period is the resurrection of the nation state in Europe rather than its transcendence by a new supranational political entity.[21]

The Ideas Behind Postwar European Unity

In the years after 1945 the federalist grand design of a type of government above the nation state would probably only have been possible if there had been a popular revolution in Europe after World War II. This would have confirmed that the state structures that many believed to have been shattered by the Nazis had finally collapsed. Such a popular revolution might also have given concrete embodiment to the notion of a "European people" and a common "European culture" behind a European federal state structure. As the history of federal systems so often shows, it is important to have some form of common values behind such systems for them to work in the longer term and the idea of a People's Europe was an attempt by the EU institutions to give a voice and representation to this form of European "culture," however that might be defined.

World War II however displaced Europe from its pre-eminent position in global politics and led it to come under the domination of two new rival super powers. The onset of the Cold War had the effect of reviving European national sovereignties (also due to the success of economic reconstruction) as they contemporaneously merged into the common defence alliances of NATO and the Warsaw Pact. The creation of the European Coal and Steel Community (ECSC) in 1951 was both a functionalist and a federalist initiative in its pooling of sectoral interests and its creation of federalist-style institutions like the High Authority (later the Commission) and the Assembly (later the European Parliament). The failure of the initiative to create a European Defence Community in 1954 reinforced the gradualist functionalist perspective of step-by-step sectoral integration, which coincided with the revival of the nation state in Western Europe. Functionalism, as it was spelt out by Jean Monnet and Robert Schuman, became embodied in the Treaty of Rome in 1957 establishing the European Economic Community (EEC) and marginalised the more ambitious federalist project upheld by figures such as Altiero Spinelli.

The political project of European unification was to result in the creation of the European Community, consisting of the European Coal and Steel Community, the European Atomic Energy Community (Euratom) and the European Economic Community. This EC was remarkable in at least three ways. Firstly, it is the result of very specific political and historical circumstances which saw a temporary denigration of the nation state. As writers such as Alan Milward have shown, the nation state can be regarded as having been bolstered and even rescued or strengthened by the EC.[22]

Secondly, the EC constituted, like the EU, a remarkable international organisation, which is also more than an international organisation as it involved a transfer of some measure of sovereignty to the EC institutions, within which the member governments participate as the primary actors. This international organisation is defined by the fact that European law takes precedence over national law and is directly applicable in national law. Some of the implications of this are explored in the chapter by Meehan on the impact of EC/EU law and the issue of rights and citizenship. Thirdly, the EC, while radical in some of its components, was not the result of a radical popularism or of a revolutionary desire for change on a mass level. The EC was an elitist creation and this elitism was to be most strongly subjected to criticism in the aftermath of the Maastricht Treaty on European Union in the early 1990s. Indeed, for Wallace[23] the intellectuals' desire for a new order had only limited appeal to politicians and economic planners and "nor did they have much resonance for mass publics." Having said that, it is important to recall that these elitist attempts were to gain a certain legitimacy over the decades after World War II. Wallace refers to appeals to common traditions of Christian democracy and of European socialism and liberalism as well as the revulsion against nationalism on the part of many supporters of the European unity ideal, however that may have been defined, or ill-defined.[24] Despite the hopes of both federalists and neofunctionalists for a network of European groups committed to increased integration at multiple levels of loyalty, the task of integration continues to lie with national governments, some of whom have been proven over time to be positive towards the ideals of the intellectuals and visionaries of the time.

From the 1980s, federalism began to play a growing role in the debate on European Union, especially with the European Parliament's 1984 draft Treaty on European Union, the 1986 Single European Act providing for a single internal market, the 1990 Colombo and Martin initiatives on European Union in the European Parliament, and, more recently, the Intergovernmental Conference on Economic and Monetary Union (EMU) and European Union of 1991. This latter Intergovernmental Conference resulted in the Treaty on European Union of December 1991, signed in its final form in February 1992.

The progressive demise of the Cold War gave an impetus towards creating some form of Western European federalism, though it is highly debateable whether this can endure in the longer term as the EU increases in membership. One incentive for this federalist impulse was the prospect of the unification of Germany, which reinforced the desire to keep Germany integrated in Europe, especially within the European Political Cooperation framework of harmonisation of foreign policies. The need to extend the EU's scope also became evident after the demise of the Eastern bloc. The collapse of the former command economies in Eastern Europe made the provision of aid increasingly essential and raises the longer-term question of whether these economies, once they have been reconstructed, should enter into some form of association with the EU. The accession of new members, Sweden, Austria and Finland since 1 January 1995 and the applications for membership from a variety of states such as the Czech Republic, Poland, Hungary and Malta indicates that the shape of the EU has begun to change. The collapse of the Eastern bloc also led to intensive involvement by the EU in aid and reconstruction programmes with the countries of Eastern Europe and the "Europe" agreements of cooperation concluded with them by the EU has led many to believe that these agreements were precursors to full membership of a larger European Union.

What Is European Union?

The issue of what European Union constitutes has been itself a difficult one as European Union is not clearly defined according to a commonly accepted set of norms. The concept of European Union as expressed in the theoretical literature is one which differed according to means and ends. The ideal of European Union expressed by the Commission, and particularly the European Parliament, has been a federalist one, often in the Spinelli mould, for example the Martin and Colombo reports on the strategy to achieve European Union at the Intergovernmental Conferences of 1990-1991 and on the long-term strategy to achieve European Union.[25]

Within the Community, before 1990-1991, the European Union debate of analysts and actors themselves often examined the European Community as a potential polity, that is a formed political system at the supranational level. This idea of the EU as a polity in the making is not new.[26] The issue of whether the EU is actually a political entity is contentious and one about which there is little agreement among academics, politicians or European officials. In the tradition of Etzioni, a polity, in order to function needs to satisfy three basic integrative criteria: namely i) effective control over the means of violence; ii) a centre of political decisionmaking that can significantly affect the allocation of resources; and iii) act as the main focus of political identification for "politically aware citizens."[27] The means to achieve these three ultimate goals, or even agreement on these goals, may remain a matter of dispute among Europeanists, involving debates over issues like the comparative advantage of federal as opposed to looser political arrangements.

Some may argue that, for European union to succeed, it has to satisfy these basic criteria Etzioni has outlined leading to the creation of a common European economic, foreign and defence policy and increasingly close harmonisation of social and welfare policies. This of course implies that these in turn would have to command the loyalty of the majority of informed European political opinion and win significant electoral consent. For this to succeed, it may be essential to construct institutions such as a presidency and parliamentary system of government and more common European Union symbols in addition to the European flag that can command widespread political loyalty. This is a huge task that could take a considerable time to achieve.

In contradistinction to these criteria, it can be argued that the EU need not take on all the trappings of the modern nation state. We may be witnessing a new type of citizenship, based on different notions of how identities coexist, for example, multiple identities with loyalty to the nation, the state, the EU and even a region. Many of the visionaries of European unity had difficulty believing that the nation state was completely defunct. Many too did seek to create a superstate qua state though for some this remained the ultimate goal. They tended to emphasise that Europe was not to be a melting pot of identities. This was to be the enduring vision of Europe—of multiple identity and European citizenship and regional loyalties.

It may be possible too that the EU is moving gradually towards some form of "Europe of the Regions" as many of the powers of the nation state are either devolved downward to the regional level or upwards to the level of the EU. The establishment of a Committee of the Regions under the Treaty on European Union indicates that this is becoming an increasingly important issue as many regional authorities of EU members are developing as powerful lobbies in Brussels. The Committee represents more than 200 regional and local authorities ranging from powerful French regional authorities such as Rhone-Alps and Languedoc to smaller bodies that are still in the process of emerging such as those in Portugal and the Nordic countries. The powers of the regions are at the heart of the debate over the concept of "subsidiarity" in the Treaty on European Union. If they manage to gain increasing powers, then the EU may well be moving, after the 1996 review of the Treaty, towards a quasi-federal state, though some countries like Britain are likely to fight fiercely to retain what is left of their national sovereignty.[28]

Jacques Delors has referred to the strategy of small steps (often referred to as neofunctionalism) of European construction in suggesting in 1993 that "we have reached the limits of this so-called strategy of small steps and successive sequences, one measure calling for another. Today we must proclaim the kind of political Europe we want." and he called for the extension of the European Parliament's legislative powers, and increased importance to be accorded to subsidiarity.[29]

This subsidiarity principle, that decisions be made and implemented at the most appropriate level of government and administration is part of the new face of 1990s federalism and has been regarded as both a means of combating federalism by the British government and a means of making federalism and regionalism complementary and feasible by most federalists. The debate on subsidiarity, like that on citizenship will be carried on in the next few decades of the EU's development.

The issue of democracy and federalism have long been areas of intense debate among intellectuals and political parties in the debate on Europe's future political structure. This will no doubt continue to be the case particularly in the wake of the 1996 Intergovernmental Conference concerning the future of the EU and the evaluation of the Maastricht Treaty on European Union. In addition, there is an acceptance of interdependence in many of the contemporary debate on the EU. For example, the Belmont Centre is quoted as saying that "only integration and shared sovereignty—when and wherever it is necessary—will allow Europe to face its challenges."[30]

The debate surrounding the Treaty on European Union and its review in 1996 represented the latest phase of the struggle between the two opposing trends of intergovernmentalism and supranationalism regarding the future direction of the EC/EU. The EU is not yet a federation, as majority vote is essential to a federation while this is not the rule in the EU, due to the unanimity requirement since the Luxembourg Agreement.[31] On important issues, decisions have to be made by unanimity. The Maastricht treaty did introduce majority voting on several new policy areas and these may be extended after the 1996 review. Within the Union, federalist characteristics are also evident in the direct effect of EU law and the fact of the superiority of EU law over the law of the EU member states.

The major debate under the microscope in the 1991 Intergovernmental Conference (IGC) on European Union revolved around the need to define and establish a common foreign and security policy. Some intergovernmentalists, like the UK, envisaged this could carry on from the common EU action on drugs and terrorism. For federalists, defence and security would be pooled in the European Union to form a common EU policy. This raises major problems such as whether the EU needs to create a European army, an initiative which may be seen in embryonic form in the Franco-German creation of the Franco-German Army corps, dubbed the Eurocorps, which Belgium decided to join in July 1993.

The development of a common defence force will be essential if the EU is to play a fuller role in world affairs, as implied at Maastricht.[32]

At present, the Union is widely perceived to be insular in orientation with its main focus being on closer economic links among mainly western European states. If the EU fails to develop its external political role, especially in dealing with the Yugoslav war, it may end up confirming Stanley Hoffman's argument that European integration has ultimately failed to supersede the nation state.[33]

The Outline of This Volume

This volume explores these themes from a variety of different perspectives. The book illustrates two distinct yet interrelated approaches to the intellectual discussion of the ideal of European unity—the British and the continental European. It is hoped in the following chapters to illustrate that while the debates and the paths chosen may have differed, at times markedly, the ideals often had much in common, even if the British experience of war was unlike the continental West European experience of vulnerability of national boundaries and the common experience of the resistance against the common enemy of fascism. Chapter 2 by Paul Rich discusses the development of the European ideal in the inter-war period, focusing in particular on the debate on federalism. The chapter shows that liberal ideas of federalism in Britain from figures such as Philip Kerr (Lord Lothian) had some impact on the European resistance movement in Europe in the early 1940s, particularly in Italy, though they should also be seen alongside an indigenous tradition of continental federalism derived from figures such as Pierre Joseph Proudhon.

This sets the scene for a more detailed examination in Chapter 3 by Peter Wilson of the debate on the "new Europe" in Britain in the 1940s. This is a period when Britain is generally perceived to have excluded itself from the debate on European unification, though individual analysts of International Relations such as E. H. Carr considered that the nation state was in a crisis and began looking towards the creation of larger political entities in world politics. Wilson shows that there was also an important debate between federalists and functionalists in Britain at this time which got rather lost when Britain failed to join the European Community in the 1950s.

Next, in Chapter 4, Cornelia Navari explores the intellectual construction of the federalist and functionalist approaches to the debate on European unification. Navari examines the relationship between developments in social science thinking in this area and political developments in Europe, in particular, the evolution in Altiero Spinelli's thought. Navari is cautious in her assessment of the long-run chances of federalism succeeding in Europe and argues that the apparent federalist "victory" at Maastricht may yet turn out to be a pyrrhic one.

This analysis of federalism and functionalism in postwar Europe is followed in Chapter 5 by a discussion of the functionalist ideas of Jean Monnet by Martin Holland. The role of Spinelli and Monnet are scrutinised in this book, as two of the personalities who most influenced the movement towards European unity. The Brussels-based European news agency Agence Europe refers to these two men as "undoubtedly the two 'inspirers' most committed to the adventure of the construction of European unity."[34]

The editorial of the Agence Europe news agency pointed out the contemporary topical nature of Jean Monnet's words as being all the more striking "as the return of certain exasperated nationalism, moving towards tribalism, encourages those who have never believed in the need or the possibility even of building a united and integrated Europe to seize it as a pretext to move backward and destroy what has been built over the last forty years."[35]

Monnet was a major influence on the 1950 Schuman Plan and the creation of the European Coal and Steel Community. Holland argues that Monnet's influence lay less in his influence as a bureaucrat than as an intellectual exponent of a cautious functionalist strategy through his Action Committee for a United States of Europe. However, by the 1960s, this functionalism seemed inadequate to explain European integration and became increasingly superseded by the "neofunctionalism" of Ernst Haas who argued for a "spillover" from one integration process to others. This still depends upon successful intergovernmental bargaining and, as Navari also showed in the previous chapter, Haas' approach became increasingly less credible by the 1980s, leading to the resurgence of federalism.

In Chapter 6, Philomena Murray looks at the federalist ideas of Spinelli, particularly in the period of the 1970s and 1980s. Spinelli's ideas went through a number of phases. There was a period of some retreat in the 1950s and 1960s when the EU became largely characterised by functionalist ideas of progressive integration. By the late 1970s, Spinelli re-emerged in the European Federalist Movement, in a final creative phase, as a federalist activist, in which he acted as a major catalyst to a younger generation of European federalists eager to secure the fulfilment of some of the original visions of the 1940s. Spinelli's role is particularly important for indicating the centrality of Italy in European federalism right through the postwar period.

In Chapter 7, Richard Dunphy surveys Christian Democratic thought in Europe and compares it to the more free market-orientated philosophy of the British Conservative Party under Mrs. Thatcher. Dunphy shows that the organic dimension of European Christian Democracy led it to accept closer European union at a relatively early stage; indeed, many leading Christian Democrats such as Alcide de Gasperi played a major role in the creation of the EU.

This was not always the case with European socialist parties. In Chapter 8, Philomena Murray examines the responses of European socialists to European unification. While many of the parties from Southern Europe such as those from Spain, Portugal and Greece found it relatively easy to accept the EU, this was not true of all the northern parties. The British Labour Party remained generally insular and suspicious of European unification. This pattern began to change in the 1980s, as many British socialists saw the EU as a mechanism to resist or at least soften some of the policies being introduced by the Thatcher government in Britain, as they recognised the advantages which the EU offered to the workers of the UK. Ideologically, European social democrats had very disparate visions of European unification, seeing it as a series of pragmatic problems, often of a foreign policy dimension, rather than a coherent set of political goals.

At a pragmatic level, the EC/EU has been able to secure a slow and incremental seepage of citizenship rights at the supranational level. Chapter 9, by Paul Rich, looks at the longer term prospects of European integration. The pattern of postwar debate suggests two major "architectural" periods of European unification, the late 1940s/early 1950s and from the middle 1980s to the present. Neither of these has been able to override national sovereignty as it is presently understood. It is an open question whether it will be politically possible, or even necessary, to build up Europe as another superpower in the post-Cold War era. In one sense, the first real test for an independent European diplomacy came with the Yugoslav crisis and here it has been found singularly wanting, depending in the end on extra-European parties such as the UN and US. It is possible too that the European ideal will be captured by a much narrower vision of "fortress Europe," concerned mainly with excluding unwanted immigrants from Eastern Europe, the former Soviet Union and North Africa in an increasingly tight job market. This would represent a major denial of the hopes of the 1940s, which are becoming an increasingly distant memory for the present political generation in Europe.

In Chapter 10, Elizabeth Meehan examines the role of the European Court of Justice in securing greater citizenship rights for men and especially women outside those of their individual home countries. Meehan's chapter is important for revealing that one of the essential dimensions of the European vision is one concerning citizenship and gender equality. Drawing on the important work of scholars such as Derek Heater, Meehan shows that this is an expandable notion that can be embedded in European Union law that may increasingly override that of individual nation states. This trend qualifies Stanley Hoffmann's thesis on the resurgence of the European nation state.

The European vision may be superseded by a resurgence of a more realist assessment based on the centrality of dominant nation state interest such as those of France and Germany. The most that can be hoped for in this context is that these major powers will act as a more conventional concert in the maintenance of European security. While, on the one hand, the advocates of European federalism may find the post-Cold War world an increasingly tough time in which to disseminate their ideas, on the other hand, the post-Cold War era is a time of great flux. The very fact that so much change is a feature of contemporary European politics could still make federalism as valid a model for the post-Cold War era as it was for the post-World War II era of reconstruction.

The visions of European federalism and neofunctionalism could be valid models for a larger EU, now that the forty-year stability and security of the Cold War is no more in existence. The time is ripe now to examine the past and current visions of European Unity, and to learn from them in order understand a changing Europe, in political, geographical, economic and social terms, and changing expectations of that entity known as Europe.

Notes

1. S. Serfaty, *Understanding Europe: the Politics of European Unity* (London: Pinter, 1992), p. 59.

2. See the interesting discussion by R. Riemenschneider, "The Two Souls of Marianne: National Sovereignty Versus Supranationality in Europe" in M. Maclean et al., eds., *Europeans on Europe: Transnational Visions of a New Continent* (Basingstoke: The Macmillan Press, 1992), pp. 141-159.

3. D. Mitrany, *The Functional Theory of Politics* (London: Martin Robertson, 1975).

4. A point acknowledged even by federalists like Spinelli: "Functionalism, born in the minds of high public officials, seemed to be a much more practical approach than that of political federalism. It did not attack directly the problem of national sovereignty. It was based on experiences known to European politicians," A. Spinelli, "The Growth of the European Movement since World War II" in C. Grove Haines, ed., *European Integration* (Baltimore: Johns Hopkins University Press, 1957), p. 51.

5. M. Burgess and A. Gagnon, eds., *Comparative Federalism and Federation* (New York: Harvester Wheatsheaf, 1993). J. Pinder, *The European Community:*

The Building of a Union (Oxford: Oxford University Press, 1991). See also F. Duchene, "More or Less Than Europe? European Union in Retrospect" in C. Crouch and D. Marquand, eds., *The Politics of 1992* (Basil Blackwell, 1990). S. Hix, "The Study of the European Community: The Challenge to Comparative Politics," *West European Politics*, vol. 17, no. 1, Jan 1994.

6. E. B. Haas, *The Uniting of Europe* (Stanford: Stanford University Press, 1958). See also R. J. Harrison, *Europe in Question* (London: Allen and Unwin, 1974), esp. Chapter 4.

7. W. Wallace, *The Transformation of Western Europe* (London: Routledge, 1990), p. 61.

8. M. Burgess, ed., *Federalism and Federation in Western Europe* (London: Croom Helm, 1986). W. Wallace, *The Transformation of Western Europe* (London: Pinter, 1990).

9. Ibid., 1990, p. 86

10. Ibid., 1990.

11. Defined by Wallace, ibid., p. 54

12. Defined by Wallace, ibid., as "a matter of flows and exchanges, of the gradual growth of networks of interaction."

13. *Agence Europe*, 2/3 Nov 1993

14. G. Barraclough, *European Unity in Thought and Action* (Oxford: Basil Blackwell, 1963), p. 21.

15. For a useful discussion of the political significance of this geographical diversity see E. L. Jones, *The European Miracle* (Cambridge: Cambridge University Press, 1981).

16. H. D. Schmidt, "The Establishment of 'Europe' as a Political Expression," *The Historical Journal*, IX, 2, 1986, pp. 172-178.

17. T. K. Raab, "The Expansion of Europe and the Spirit of Capitalism," *The Historical Journal*, XV11, 4, 1974, pp. 675-689.

18. V. G. Kiernan, *The Lords of Human Kind* (Harmondsworth: Penguin Books, 1969).

19. H. Meuves, "German Unification, Nationalism and Democracy," *Telos*, 89, (Fall 1991), p. 83.

20. M. Smith, *Introduction: European Unity and the Second World War*, in M. L. Smith and P. R. Stirk, eds., *Making the New Europe: European Unity and the Second World War* (London: Pinter, 1990), p. 5.

21. A. S. Milward, *The European Rescue of the Nation State* (London: Routledge, 1993).

22. Milward, ibid.

23. Wallace, op. cit., p. 59.

24. Wallace, ibid., p. 75.

25. See, for example, "Resolution on the Intergovernmental Conference in the context of Parliament's strategy for European Union," *Official Journal of the European Communities*, C 96/114, 17 April, 1990, and "Report of the Committee on Institutional Affairs on the results of the intergovernmental conferences," Rapporteur: D. Martin, Document A3-0123/92, European Parliament.

26. See, for example, L. N. Lindberg and S. A. Scheingold, *Europe's Would-Be Polity: Patterns of Change in the European Community* (New Jersey: Prentice Hall, 1970).

27. A. Etzioni, *Political Unification: A Comparative Study of Leaders and Forces* (New York: Holt, Rinehart and Winston, 1965), p. 4.

28. "A share of autonomous power for the united peoples," *The Guardian*, 21 January 1995.

29. J. Delors, *Our Europe in the Global Village: Between Survival and Decline*, speech to Club Temoin, L'Orient, France, 28 August 1993, quoted in *Agence Europe*, 3 September 1993.

30. *Agence Europe*, 22 October, 1993.

31. The Luxembourg Agreement, or Luxembourg Compromise, was an agreement by the six founding members of the EC, in 1966, to allow for the exercise of the national veto over EC decisions on issues concerning "vital national interest."

32. Article J.4 of the Treaty on European Union states: "The common foreign and security policy shall include all questions related to the security of the Union, including the eventual framing of a common defence policy, which might in time lead to a common defence."

33. S. Hoffmann, "Reflections on the Nation State in Western Europe Today," *Journal of Common Market Studies*, 21, 3, 1982, pp. 21-37.

34. *Agence Europe*, Agence Internationale d'information pour la presse, 10-11 January 1994.

35. *Agence Europe*, 14 January 1994.

2

Visionary Ideals of European Unity After World War I

Paul Rich

European identity has always been a matter of contest. The very idea of "Europe" is a politically constructed notion that has had a relatively brief history. Before the eighteenth century the region now known as Europe was generally called "Christendon," "Rome" or "Hellas."[1] It was only with the end of threats of invasion from the Ottoman empire that "Europe" really developed as a political expression. The idea of Europe then became part of a wider struggle for modernity and progress, reaching its high point in the century of imperial expansion between 1815 and 1914.[2]

The ideal of united Europe was espoused by small groups of political idealists in the course of the nineteenth century, though it never became a popular movement. In France writers such as the novelist Victor Hugo were attracted to the concept of a "United States of Europe" on lines similar to the USA. This envisaged a united republican Europe transcending the sovereignty of the nation state and forming a large political union that would prevent the recurrence of war.[3] Such an ideal though flew in the face of the rising nationalism in nineteenth century Europe and seemed hopelessly utopian in an era when popular sentiments were increasingly focused around the symbols of national identity.

The proponents of European unity were strongly attracted to the idea of some form of federal Europe eventually emerging from the rivalries of individual nation states. By the late nineteenth century, federalism had ceased to be a constitutional mechanism for limiting the power of sovereign states but had become something of an ideological dogma and an ideal rather than simply a governmental structure. As a result of the writings of such theorists as Alexis de Tocqueville, James Bryce, Edward A. Freeman, John Calhoun and Pierre Joseph Proudhon federalism was increasingly seen as the embodiment of institutional liberty which could apply in virtually all circumstances. Federalism became in effect another variant of pluralism rather than a specific form of government depending on a balance between central and local forces and leading towards either closer political integration or the disintegration of the state altogether.[4]

The enormous faith placed in federalism by European intellectuals partly derived from the fact that in the second half of the nineteenth century a number of federal systems had been successfully constructed in areas under European imperial control such as Canada (1867) and Australia (1901). By the early years of the twentieth century, federalism had not as yet been really tested by the stresses of modern ethnic nationalism. It would not really be until the period of decolonisation after World War II that some of the problems associated with implementing federal systems among groups characterised by a high degree of ethnic rivalry really became evident when federal experiments in places such as East and Central Africa and the Caribbean collapsed.

If European liberals were strongly attracted intellectually to the appeals of federalism in the latter half of the nineteenth century, European radicals were drawn to defending the rights of independent nationalities. Despite growing evidence to the contrary in places such as the Balkans, many liberals and radicals envisaged in the years before World War I independent nationalities proliferating on generally peaceful lines.[5] This outlook tended to marginalise the federalist cause in a Europe of emerging nation states. When doubts did arise over whether smaller nation states would be able to defend themselves against larger ones in this emerging international order, the remedy usually took the form of proposals, like that of the British liberal J. A. Hobson, for an international government that could act as a tribunal with powers of intervention. Such an international tribunal would regulate a system based upon nation states rather than supersede it with a new supranational political order.[6]

World War I and the Emergence of Pan Europeanism

The link between radicalism and nationalism in Europe was undermined by the impact of World War I. The carnage in the trenches forced intellectuals all over Europe to reconsider their attitude towards claims for national self-determination. The issue became particularly pressing after 1918 as the collapse of four European empires—the German, Russian, Austro-Hungarian and Ottoman—produced an upsurge of nationalist movements in East and Central Europe.

The Peace of Versailles in 1919 and the establishment of the League of Nations succeeded for a period in allaying many of these anxieties. Over the next decade until the Manchurian Crisis of 1931 and Hitler's rise to power two years later, it seemed as though the League would provide the basis for a new system of collective security among nation states. In Britain the League of Nations Union acted as an important forum for this strand of liberal internationalism and looked towards some form of confederal solution as a means of preventing a future war between states.[7] For those further to the left, the Third International became an alternative model for outlawing war based upon the spread of socialism throughout Europe and the overthrow of capitalism and imperialism.

Given these two major appeals, it was not altogether surprising that in the 1920s only a minority strand of liberal and radical opinion became attracted to resurrecting the idea of European unity. This managed, however, to make a brief impact on European politics in 1929-1930 in the form of the French Briand Plan for European unity before it was overtaken by the Depression in the early 1930s and the Nazi revolution in Germany in 1933.

One of the most prominent advocates of the postwar vision of European unity was the Austrian aristocrat Count Coudenhove Kalergi. Of half-Japanese descent, he had been brought up in a cosmopolitan atmosphere in the last phases of the Austro-Hungarian empire before World War I. He was anxious to try and return Europe to some form of political unity that he felt had been shattered by the rise of nationalism.

Coudenhove Kalergi was a philosophical idealist who revolted against the materialism of Marxism. He was part of a group of patrician European intellectuals in the inter-war years who looked to European unification being a means to contain and control the entry of "the masses" into political involvement. He hoped an intellectual and moral aristocracy would eventually replace the numerical majority of democratic systems and shared many of the sentiments of the Spanish philosopher Ortega y Gasset expressed in his famous book *The Revolt of the Masses* (1930).[8] The ideal of Pan Europa was largely formulated in response to this ethical vacuum by reviving the *esprit de corps* of the traditional European ruling aristocracies at the continental level. There was a strong crusading spirit at the heart of the venture and when Coudenhove Kalergi formed a Pan Europa movement in 1923 to promote the goal of a federal Europe it had a flag with the cross of the medieval crusaders. The movement's aristocratic and nostalgic overtone led many liberals and democrats to refuse to take it very seriously though for a brief period in the late 1920s it looked as though it might make a major political breakthrough.

Coudenhove Kalergi considered that the leaders of Versailles had been short-sighted in excluding the new Soviet regime in Russia on the grounds that it would only survive a short time. He tried over the next few years to alert middle class political opinion in Europe to what he saw as an imminent threat from Soviet communism. He saw it as a means for uniting a European intelligentsia badly split between the rival ideological creeds of Wilsonian democracy and Soviet communism.[9] In 1926 he outlined his political vision in a book *Pan Europe* where he envisaged the creation of a European great power which could establish its own Monroe doctrine like that of the USA in the western hemisphere. Such a grand design was essential, he argued, in order to contain the threat from Soviet communism and he tried to appeal to European democratic parties to overcome their national differences and unite in pursuit of what he termed "world-historical necessities."[10] In a memorandum to the League of Nations he also suggested a reform of the League structure that would allow for regional power blocs including one for Europe. This proposal though met a cool response from the League's Irish Secretary General, Sir Henry Drummond.[11]

Many European political leaders and officials were hugely sceptical of Coudenhove Kalergi's ideas. In Britain the Under Secretary at the Foreign Office, Sir William Tyrrell, considered him "a thoroughly impracticable theorist."[12] However, the signing of the Locarno Treaty in 1925[13] enabled Coudenhove Kalergi to capitalise upon rival interpretations of what became known in popular parlance as the "spirit of Locarno." The Pan European ideal accorded with the desire of the French Foreign Minister, Aristide Briand, for Locarno to be a means for establishing an equilibrium in European power politics on the basis of the Versailles Treaty. Briand came out in support of Coudenhove Kalergi's scheme as a means of isolating his German rival Gustav Stresemann, who hoped the Versailles treaty would eventually be revised in order to re-establish Germany's claim to be treated as a major European power.[14]

Briand initially tried in 1927 to gain a guarantee from the United States to the Versailles Treaty, but had in the end to be content with the Kellogg-Briand Pact which declared itself against the use of war rather than specifically guaranteeing the Versailles boundaries in Europe. The following year he approached the Soviet Union to help organise a multilateral pact in Eastern Europe—an "Eastern Locarno"—that would bind together Germany, Poland, the Baltic states, the USSR and Romania. This failed too and Briand was still left without a political framework that would guarantee French security whilst at the same time allowing Germany to reconstruct its economy.[15]

In the autumn of 1928 Briand finally announced that he intended to raise the Pan European issue at the next assembly of the League. These plans were linked to attempts to get the Germans to agree to a final settlement of the reparations issue, which would prevent Stresemann from trying to trade off his support for Pan Europe with cancellation of reparations. Briand invoked the spectre of American economic domination of Europe as a result of the election of the protectionist Herbert Hoover as president the previous November. For Stresemann, though, American investment was needed for German industrial recovery and he did not share the same French concerns over American economic competition.[16]

Briand's raising of the Pan European issue on 5 September 1929 in the League Assembly in Geneva had many of the hallmarks of a gamble prompted by French weakness when confronted by Germany's growing economic and political power.[17] His decision to proceed was taken without any serious consultation with Britain and there was no real evidence that there was a sufficiently strong degree of anti-American feeling among the major European powers to ensure the cause's success. Considerable sections of British industry were favourable to the idea of closer European economic cooperation and some industrialists such as Alfred Mond began to champion proposals of this kind during the 1920s. They had failed, however, by the late 1920s to have much impact on leading political opinion either in government or parliamentary circles, which preferred to concentrate on maintaining and developing existing economic links with imperial markets.[18]

British political opinion was overwhelmingly against any form of closer European political union. The newly-elected Labour government of Ramsay MacDonald was suspicious of the anti-American nature of Briand's proposal. It was strongly guided in this outlook by the Foreign Office, which did not as yet have an economic section and was generally unaware of the impact of Britain on European cooperation. It did not even have any of Coudenhove Kalergi's publications in its library.[19] In fact the Briand Plan found few supporters in British political life, though the journalist Andre Siegfried warned in an article in *Foreign Affairs* that there would be considerable dangers in Britain cutting herself off from such a scheme and concentrating upon the Dominions since these in time might well drift out of her orbit.[20]

The Briand Plan looked increasingly less like getting off the ground following the death of Stresemann in October 1929 and the collapse of Wall Street the same month. Briand was himself removed from the French government in 1930 and the upsurge of nationalism in Germany led to growing loss of interest in Europe in the venture. In Britain the deterioration of European security strengthened Coudenhove Kalergi's links with imperial groups who began to fear that Britain's imperial role would be seriously disrupted by another war in Europe. To Winston Churchill, writing in The Saturday Evening Post in 1930, the attraction of Coudenhove Kalergi's ideas lay in the way they redefined Europe as a single imperial bloc with colonial possessions in Asia and Africa whilst at the same time letting the Soviet Union "slide back" into Asia.[21] For Leo Amery, too, (a former Conservative Colonial Secretary), the importance of Coudenhove Kalergi's ideas lay in the way they would enable Britain to sure up its rear in Europe while at the same time proceeding with plans for developing closer integration with her imperial and colonial possessions in some form of economic Zollverein.[22] The Pan Europa movement became increasingly influenced by these imperial ties over the following decade as the democratic impulse in European politics was thrown onto the defensive by the rising tide of fascism.

Pan Europeanism in Crisis

Right from the start of the Pan Europa movement in the early 1920s Coudenhove Kalergi had conceived of European unification entailing some form of bargain between rival imperial powers. In the late 1920s he proposed a re-arrangement of imperial control on a global scale, with Britain and France selling off their possessions in the Pacific and Guiana to the United States to help pay off their war debts and receiving as compensation the former German colonies held as mandates under the League.[23] The rise of Hitler led him to shift his focus away from trying to promote a German-French axis in Europe towards a Franco-British axis designed to contain an expansionist Germany. The destruction of the Pan Europa movement, first in Germany in 1933, and then its central headquarters in Vienna after Austrian Anschluss with Germany in 1936, made this more or less inevitable.

The diplomatic effort to pursue this revised conception of European unity in the early 1930s proved to be half-baked and was one of the reasons why the Pan Europa movement became increasingly marginalised by the upsurge of newer federalist thinking in Britain in the late 1930s surrounding the Federal Union movement. Coudenhove Kalergi forged only a limited series of contacts among the political and professional elite in Britain based upon the Round Table movement and the Royal Institute of International Affairs at Chatham House. His main political link was through Leo Amery and he did not actually meet Winston Churchill until February 1938.[24]

Coudenhove Kalergi appeal to keep these groups in Britain to adapt the model of the British Commonwealth on a global scale. In a Chatham House lecture in 1931 he outlined a plan whereby the League of Nations could become a federation of federations like the Commonwealth consisting of the Commonwealth itself, Pan Europe, Pan America, Eastern Asia and the Soviet Union. On this basis he hoped that it would eventually be possible to make national boundaries become effectively "invisible."[25]

The campaign failed to make much headway among the British political establishment and remained largely supported by a few enthusiasts such as Churchill and Amery. It did not even manage to win extensive support among the Round Table school of imperialists led by such figures as Philip Kerr, Lionel Curtis, F. S. Oliver, Arnold Toynbee and Geoffrey Dawson. This group had been important in the period after World War I in giving the British imperial drive a new ethical gloss by spelling out its goals in terms of the notion of a Commonwealth of Nations.[26] The movement's journal *The Round Table* proved to be cautious in its response to the Briand Plan in 1929 and suggested that an economic *Zollverein* could only be achieved through a common political authority which it considered unimaginable in the near future. It proposed an alternative scheme of phased tariff reductions in Europe with Britain allying itself to the lowest tariff countries whilst trying at the same time to maintain her own system of imperial preferences.[27] This kind of balancing act became unnecessary once the Depression ended any hopes of the Briand Plan becoming a success. In 1932 Britain went ahead and initiated with the Dominions a system of imperial preference under the Ottawa Agreement. Enthusiasm for European federalism progressively declined over the next few years.

The Round Table school has been seen as at least keeping alive the federal idealism that had been forged in the late nineteenth century, particularly through the work of one of its most prominent intellectual leaders, Philip Kerr. Unlike his rather more mystical colleague Lionel Curtis—whom he called "the prophet"—Lothian tried to define in precise terms the meaning of federalism in the British imperial context. In 1922 he delivered a series of lectures at Williamstown Massachusetts on *The Prevention of War*. Here Lothian sought to transcend national patriotism, which he saw as the source of war, by building a state at the super national level which would have the ultimate sanction of enforcing international law. "War between states will continue," he argued, "until we apply to the world as a whole the same ideas as are universally applied within the state."[28] The conception of the state in the lectures was strongly idealist, reflecting Lothian's intellectual background in late nineteenth century liberal Hegelianism. He still had a rather poor grasp of the role of force in binding communities together and preferred to see this as a result of Anglican ideals of duty and service.

This relatively optimistic starting point enabled Lothian to envisage a federally-based international system that would make war between nation states impossible. Lothian considered that national identities and boundaries would still exist in such a future international society and he resisted the idea that they could become completely invisible as Coudenhove Kalergi imagined. Lothian saw these national identities though as increasingly integrated into a comprehensive system of international political control and regulation.

By the early 1930s, Lothian's thinking, like that of the Round Table movement generally, increasingly moved in the direction of a federation of the Atlantic democracies rather than a united Europe. Relations between Britain and the United States had started to become rather closer after Hoover's election in 1928 and by the early 1930s social alignments were starting to take place which would later underpin the Anglo-American cooperation during World War II.[29] Lothian had been a strong Atlanticist since World War I and his conception of federalism was shaped by the model of the United States constitution. He saw federalism as a means of bolstering up a faltering British imperial power by integrating it into a wider Anglo Saxon Union which could in turn act as a force for world peace.

Lothian's ideas were not treated particularly seriously by the British political establishment in the 1930s. As late as 1929 he remained a supporter of the Briand Kellogg Pact and only moved during the course of the 1930s to a more realist recognition of the continuing importance of state interests in international relations.[30] The prime minister Stanley Baldwin considered him a "rum cove" who would be "thoroughly useless in the cabinet but useful outside."[31] It was in the latter capacity that he met Hitler in 1935 in the hope of securing a pact between Britain and Germany for the following ten years which would be accepted by the rest of the empire.[32] Until Munich in 1938, Lothian, like a number of other British appeasers tended to believe that Hitler could be taken at his word. He thought it would be possible to cobble together an agreement with Germany which would prevent Britain being involved in another European war. The main danger, he considered, lay in entering into an agreement under League of Nations auspices. "If Great Britain tries to prevent war in Europe by entering into commitments in the name of the League of Nations," he wrote to General Smuts in April 1936:

> she will be doomed and with her that association for freedom known as the British Commonwealth. If that is likely to be the real outcome of the

forthcoming negotiations, it is far better that we should limit our commitments in Europe *now* and leave Europe to make its own arrangements
with any intermediary help we can give her without commitment, and
get back to organised peace and liberty in the rest of the world.[33]

It was this outlook which shaped Lothian's approach to the question of federalism in his Burge lecture in May 1935 entitled *Pacifism is
Not Enough, nor Patriotism Either*. The lecture has been seen by some
scholars as a major re-statement of the European federalist ideal which
had a considerable impact on advocates of European integration over
the following years.[34] Lothian's lecture was not really a plea for a European federation; indeed, he doubted if one was possible in the foreseeable future. His main aim was to try and convince pacifist groups
in Britain that they could no longer hope for the League of Nations to
be capable of preventing wars so long as it rested upon an anarchical
international order based on sovereign nation states. There were, he
considered, only really two alternatives to this state of affairs: political
unity achieved by empires or by the creation of a federation. Lothian's
preference, despite his imperialist past, was for the latter and there were
signs that the ideal of a world federation had an almost mystical significance for it was the "predestined method by which alone the Fa-
therhood of God and the brotherhood of man can come into visible
expression on earth."[35] Much depended on the mobilisation of political
will to achieve the federal goal for Lothian did not doubt that the increased use of communications made such an ideal on a global scale
now possible:

> The United States discovered the federal principle and made possible com-
> monwealths of a continental size. Some equivalent discovery will have to
> be made whereby a government controlling those matters which lie be-
> yond the national domain can enact and enforce law and command the
> obedience of all citizens in its own sphere of power and be responsible
> to them. In this case, as before, when the will is there the way will be
> found. The main obstacles are only tradition and opinion.[36]

There were utopian aspects to this argument despite Lothian's attack
on the pacifists for failing to recognise the realities of state sovereignty
in international politics. By 1938 he began urging a return to a concert
of great powers as a means of enforcing peace. The anarchy of the nation state system simply reinforced the totalitarian challenge to democratic states and the only means left to ward this off was an alliance
centred upon Britain and the USA but also possibly including the Scandinavian states and the South American republics. If this was achieved

the "oceanic zone" might become the "one part of the world in which it is possible today to realise the ideals of the League of Nation$^{s.\prime 37}$

Right up to the start of the World War II there was little to suggest that Lothian considered a European federation a feasible political solution to the crisis that was facing the continent. He looked towards the continuation of some form of Anglo-American imperial role with a faint hope that the League might in some form be revived. To this extent, he had a considerably different outlook to newer groups that were starting to assert themselves in Britain in the late 1930s favouring a more Europeanist political focus in international affairs.

The Resurgence of European Federalism

After World War I some sections of liberal opinion in Britain had never entirely given up hope in the idea of closer European political integration or union. The individuals and groups who championed this tended to be eclipsed by a more general upsurge of enthusiasm for the League of Nations. The energies of many liberals tended as a result to be diverted into work for the League of Nations Union.

Some liberals were prompted to respond to the federal scheme of Coudenhove Kalergi. In 1929, J. A. Hobson wrote that the Pan Europa campaign represented only a partial fulfilment of the European ideal. As a long-standing anti imperialist (his book *Imperialism* (1902) had a major impact on European liberal and radical thought), Hobson objected to the way that Coudenhove Kalergi's scheme excluded two of the major European powers, Russia and Britain, whilst at the same time menacing the work of the League of Nations. He favoured the progressive lowering of tariff barriers and supported the general principles of the Briand Plan. He strongly doubted whether there was any "body of common sentiment or interest based upon local proximity and membership of the same continent" that would make a federal scheme anything more than a "chimera."[38]

These doubts continued to pervade liberal thinking until it became increasingly clear in the late 1930s that the League of Nations would be incapable of preventing another European war. The loss of faith in the League was accompanied by growing interest among British intellectuals in the idea of a federal scheme of some kind in Europe to enforce peace. This upsurge of Europeanist thinking was exemplified by the work of the economist Lionel Robbins who urged the establishment of a European federation in two important books *Economic Planning and International Order* (1937) and *The Economic Causes of War* (1939). Robbins was then teaching at the London School of Economics and argued against a series of academic orthodoxies on the left that warfare was due to a crisis of capitalist consumption or to the exigencies of imperialist expansion. He placed its root cause, like Lothian and the mainstream liberal tradition, in an international system anchored in sovereign nation states. He urged the establishment of a "United States of Europe" since this seemed far less utopian than more grandiose schemes for world federation. It also appeared that European history was following an evolutionary pattern based on the relationship between ruling elites and the capacity of armaments to project power:

> The system has reached breaking point; and, with the development of modern military techniques, it no longer has survival value. As gunpowder rendered obsolete the feudal system, so the aeroplane renders obsolete the system of independent sovereignties in Europe. A more comprehensive type of organisation is inevitable.[39]

Robbins supported the Federal Union movement after it was founded in 1939 by Charles Kimber, Derek Rawnsley and Patrick Ransome. There was a certain desperation to the way that the federal cause began to be spelt out in British politics, reflecting the disillusion of those who had earlier placed so much hope in the League of Nations.[40] Robbins argued the case for federation in terms of historical necessity rather than the political possibilities of a federal state being achieved in the European context.

As Peter Wilson points out in the next chapter, federalism began to be seen by some sections of liberal opinion in Britain as a political and moral panacea to the European diplomatic crisis. It failed to connect with more realist arguments that recognised that international relations were still centred in many respects on the pursuit of state interests. This view was well articulated by E. H. Carr in his book *The Twenty Years Crisis* in 1939, though Carr presented a more idealistic vision for the future of European politics in a later book *Conditions of Peace*, published in 1942. Here he outlined the revolutionary implications of World War II on European society. It would be impossible for Britain to stay aloof from European political developments, though he advocated a "tentative and empirical approach" rather than any pre-set formula like federalism.[41] He suggested a European Planning Authority which would be supported by existing great powers such as the USA, Russia and Britain in order to maintain international military control over the continent's affairs.[42] This sort of proposal represented a radical version of the functionalist ideas later promoted by Jean Monnet in the postwar period. Carr hoped that out of these new planning structures new loyalties would eventually arise which would eventually transcend the nation state.[43]

Carr's ideas reflected a more realistic assessment of the prospects of controlling sovereign nation states than those of the federal idealists. They tended to be taken seriously in British official circles as it became clear that the war was leading to a closer military and political relationship between Britain and the United States. By contrast the Federal Union movement began to run out of steam by 1943, even though its membership had now reached 3564. The death of Derek Rawnsley in North Africa that year proved a major blow, while the movement became split over whether to have a mainly political or educational focus.[44]

As the war widened into a global conflict, it seemed likely that Europe would fall under the hegemony of the emerging superpowers of the USA and USSR. Contrary to the conventional wisdom of the federalists of the 1930s, it would still be possible for the "anarchy" of the system of sovereign nation states to survive without necessarily leading to war since it would now be regulated by a new bipolar domination of the international system. Some former federalist enthusiasts such as Lionel Robbins began to recognise this, particularly as the new lease of life granted to the sovereign states under this system would provide the basic political terrain for Keynesian demand management of the postwar European economies.

In 1942 Robbins started work on questions of postwar reconstruction in the Central Economic Information Service in London. Though not so closely involved as Keynes in the proposals for a postwar system of international payments, he was associated with the general Anglo-American discussions on international monetary and commercial policy. His enthusiasm for federal and regional solutions as a consequence declined. Attending a conference at Hot Springs, Virginia, in May 1943 on food and agriculture he reflected how "acutely" and "lamentably" Europeans had failed to solve their problems:

> But perhaps a complication and a problem which we may turn to some use if it does not lure us too far in the direction of regionalism. Pan Europa? No, that dream, splendid though it was, recedes; it was always difficult to reconcile with the Commonwealth. But calling the old world back into existence to redress the balance of the new—that, in the context of Pan-America, has an attraction that is well worth considering further.[45]

The shift in Robbins' thinking reflected the continuing reluctance of British governing circles to engage with schemes for continental European unity during World War II.[46] Here the resistance to Nazi occupation led to a major upsurge in political idealism centred upon some form of federalised European super-state. As Andrea Bosco has pointed out, it is really not possible to understand the continental resistance without including the federalist perspective, though not all resistance groups were necessarily federalist.[47] The Italian resistance was a nucleus of this new federalism. The *Ventotene Manifesto*, drawn up in prison by Altiero Spinelli and Ernesto Rosso on the island of Ventotene was a major statement of faith in a new federal Europe which would replace a nation state system that was increasingly being seen as obsolete. The manifesto gave rise to the establishment of the European Federalist Movement (MFE) which became the central nucleus of the Italian federalist movement after the war.

Bosco and Pinder have seen the *Ventotene Manifesto* embodying much of the Anglo Saxon federalist tradition, particularly as it was reflected in the writings of Lothian and Robbins, whose works the prisoners were able to read.[48] Lothian though, as this chapter has shown, did not believe a European federal state was really possible and had mainly looked to an alliance of the Atlantic democracies. The main attraction of his federalist ideas to figures such as Spinelli and Rossi was that they seemed to be of a less dogmatic kind than that of their own compatriots stretching back to Garibaldi and Mazzini. They were also untainted by links with Italian fascism, which had done much to undermine Coudenhove Kalergi's Pan Europa movement following appeals for Mussolini's support for the campaign during the 1930s.[49]

Lothian urged the mobilisation of a political will behind the federalist cause. The MFE stressed this too in January 1946 when it outlined its aims as being not those of the "utopian federalists" in the creating a European federation but rather the fostering of a "federalist European mentality."[50] By this time the Italian federalist tradition had begun reasserting itself within the MFE based on the Christian Democrats and a small group of liberals, centred on the free trade economist Luigi Einaudi, who became in 1948 president of the postwar Italian republic. It was Einaudi who urged his colleagues to vote for the Marshall Plan in July 1947 and helped move the MFE towards a more pragmatic acceptance of postwar political realities in Europe.[51]

The liberal conception of Pan European federalism that had been articulated by figures such as Coudenhove Kalergi and Lothian in the inter-war years was mainly concerned with leadership and education rather than participation and democratic rights. It indicated that there was not quite such an unbroken tradition in European liberal thought from the nineteenth century as has sometimes been supposed, for ideas that were "liberal" in the nineteenth century ended up being elitist and antidemocratic in the twentieth.[52] These distinctions tended to be blurred by the upsurge of European idealism in the years after World War II, which saw the states of Western Europe as the repositories of a western civilisation threatened by a communist bloc in the east. In the process the essential unity of European civilisation tended to get lost as a line was drawn down the centre of the continent and Eastern and Central Europe to all intents and purposes disappeared for the purposes of political debate as part of "Europe."[53] As Chapter 9 shows, this anomaly has now been exposed in the post-Cold War era as the liberal model of European unification centred upon the creation of an enlightened federalist elite comes under growing political challenge.

Notes

1. H. S. Watson, "Thoughts on the Concept of West and East in Europe," *Government and Opposition*, vol. 20, no. 2, 1985, pp. 156-165; H. D. Schmidt, "The Establishment of 'Europe' as a Political Expression," *The Historical Journal*, vol. 9, no. 2, 1986, pp. 172-178.

2. A. Heller, "Europe: An Epilogue?" in Brian Nelson, David Roberts and Walter Veit, eds., *The Idea of Europe* (New York/Oxford: Berg, 1992), pp. 12-25.

3. P. Renouvin, *L'Idee de Federation Europeene dans la Pensee du X1Xe Siecle* (Oxford: Clarendon Press, 1949).

4. P. King, "Against Federalism" in Robert Benewick, R. N. Berki and Bhikhu Parekh, eds., *Knowledge and Belief in Modern Politics* (London: Allen and Unwin, 1973), pp. 151-176.

5. H. Weinroth, "Radicalism and Nationalism: An Increasingly Unstable Equilibrium" in A. J. A. Morris, ed., *Edwardian Radicalism, 1900-1914* (London and Boston: Routledge, 1974), pp. 218-233.

6. See for example J. A. Hobson, "Proposed Remedies for Existing Grievances" in *Nationalities and Subject Races: Report of Conference held in Caxton Hall, Westminster, June 28-30 1910* (Westminster: P.S. King and Son, 1910), p. 125.

7. M. Creadel, "Supranationalism in the British Peace Movement During the Early Twentieth Century" Andrea Bosco, *The Federal Idea, vol. 1* (London/New York: Lothian Foundation Press, 1991), pp. 169-191.

8. Ortega saw Europe as lacking any clear moral code and so depriving the "mass man" of a sense of submission and subservience. Ortega y Gasset, *The Revolt of the Masses* (London: Unwin Books, 1969), pp. 143-44. R. Coudenhove Kalergi, *An Idea Conquers the World* (London: Hutchinson, 1953), p. 137. Another intellectual who shared a similar view on European unity to contain a mass upsurge is H. Rauschnigg, *The Revolution of Nihilism: Warning to the West* (New York: Alliance Books, 1933). For more discussion of this theme see M. Biddiss, *The Age of the Masses* (Harmondsworth: Penguin Books, 1977).

9. R. Coudenhove Kalergi, *An Idea Conquers The World*, pp. 70-71.

10. R. Coudenhove Kalergi, *Pan Europe* (New York: Alfred A, Knopf, 1926), p. 185.

11. R. Coundenhove Kalergi, *An Idea Conquers the World*, pp. 113-114.

12. PRO FO371/11246 W. Tyrell minute 2 October 1926 cited in R. W. D. Boyce, "Britain's First 'No' to Europe: Britain and the Briand Plan, 1929-30," *European Studies Review*, vol. 10, 1985, p. 43, n 40.

13. The Locarno Treaty signed by Belgium, Britain, France, Germany and Italy guaranteed existing state frontiers and renounced war amongst themselves. See D. Urwin, *The Community of Europe* (London: Longman, 1991).

14. Ibid., p. 123. See also W. A. McDougall, "Political Economy Versus National Sovereignty: French Structures for German Economic Integration After Versailles," *Journal of Modern History*, vol. 51, 1979, pp. 4-23. For details of these rival views see A. Thimme, "Stresemann and Locarno" H. W. Gatzke, ed., *European Diplomacy between the Wars* (Chicago: Quadrangle Books, 1972), pp. 73-93; J. F. Freymond, "Gustav Stresemann et l'idee d'une 'Europe economique,'" *Relations internationales*, 1976, no. 8, pp. 343-360. See also H. L. Bretton, *Stresemann and the Revision of Versailles*, (Stanford: Stanford University Press, 1953).

15. C. Navari, "The Origins of the Briand Plan" in Bosco, *The Federal Idea*, vol. 1, p. 215.

16. It was pointed out at the time that Hoover was not in any case an extreme protectionist as he stood for "adequate" agricultural protection and some revision in manufacturing tariffs—a far cry from the demand of the Manufacturers Association for a large tariff on almost all manufactured imports. S.K. Ratcliffe, "President Hoover and Europe," *The Contemporary Review*, vol. 1, August 1929, p. 138.

17. Navari, "The Origins of the Briand Plan," p. 232; McDougall, "Political Economy Versus National Sovereignty: French Structures for German Economic Integration After Versailles."

18. R. Boyce, "British Capitalism and the Idea of European Unity Between the Wars" in Stirk, *European Unity in Context: The Interwar Period*, pp. 65-83.

19. R. Boyce, "Britain's First 'No' to Europe: Britain and the Briand Plan, 1929-30," *European Studies Review*, 10, 1980, pp. 25-26.

20. A. Siegfried, "European Reactions to American Tariff Proposals," *Foreign Affairs*, 8, 1, October 1929, p. 19.

21. W. Churchill, "The United States of Europe," *Saturday Evening Post*, 15 February 1930.

22. L. Amery, "The British Empire and the Pan European Idea," *Journal of the Royal Institute of International Affairs*, 14 January 1930, pp. 5-11.

23. R. Coundenhove Kalergi, *An Idea Conquers the World*, p. 145.

24. Ibid., p. 213.

25. R. Coudenhove Kalergi, "The Pan European Outlook," *International Affairs*, 10, September 1931, pp. 638-651.

26. For an assessment of the Round Table see J. E. Kendle, *The Round Table Movement and Imperial Union* (Toronto and Buffalo: The University of Toronto Press, 1975); R. Symonds, *Oxford and Empire* (London and Basingstoke: The Macmillan Press, 1986), esp. pp. 62-79.

27. "The United States of Europe," *The Round Table*, vol. 20, December 1929, pp. 79-99.

28. Lord Lothian, *The Prevention of War* (New Haven: Yale University Press, 1923), p. 5.

29. D. C. Watt, "America and the British Foreign Policy-Making Elite from Joseph Chamberlain to Anthony Eden, 1895-1956" *Personalities and Policies* (London: Longmans, 1965), pp. 39-40.

30. P. Kerr, "Navies and Armies," *Foreign Affairs*, 81, October 1929, pp. 20-29.

31. For details see R. Griffiths, *Fellow Travellers of the Right* (London: Oxford University Press, 1983), pp. 152-155. See also M. Cowling, *The Impact of Hitler* (Chicago and London: University of Chicago Press, 1975), pp. 133-134.

32. *J. C. Smuts Papers*, Archives of the South African Institute of International Affairs, Johannesburg, Lord Lothian to J.C. Smuts, 8 April 1935.

33. Ibid., Lord Lothian to J.C. Smuts, 8 April 1936.

34. A. Bosco, "National Sovereignty and Peace: Lord Lothian's Federalist Thought" in J. Turner, ed., *The Larger Idea: Lord Lothian and the Problem of National Sovereignty* (London: The Historians Press, 1988), pp. 108-123.

35. Lord Lothian, *Pacifism Is Not Enough, nor Patriotism Either* in J. Pinder and A. Bosco, eds., *Pacifism is Not Enough: Collected Lectures and Speeches of Lord Lothian (Philip Kerr)* (London and New York: Lothian Fioudnation Press, 1990), p. 259.

36. Ibid., p. 261.

37. Lord Lothian, "The Commonwealth and Dictatorships," *The Round Table* XXV111, June 1938, p. 447; "The Grand Alliance Against Aggression," *The Round Table*, XX1X (June 1939), pp. 441-456.

38. J. A. Hobson, "The United States of Europe," *The Contemporary Review*, CXXXV1 (November 1929), pp. 537-552

39. L. Robbins, *The Economic Causes of War* (London: Jonathan Cape, 1939), p. 107.

40. See Chapter 3.

41. E. H.Carr, *Conditions of Peace* (London: Macmillan, 1942), p. 208.

42. Ibid., p. 270.

43. Ibid., p. 273.

44. J. Baratta, "Henry Usborne and the Creation of the World Movement for Federal Government" in Andrea Bosco, ed., *The Federal Idea: vol. 11* (London: The Lothian Foundation, 1992), p. 82.

45. Diary entry for 5-7 June 1943 in S. Howson and D. Moggridge, eds., *The Wartime Diaries of Lionel Robbins and James Meade, 1943-45* (Houndmills: Macmillan Academic and Professional, 1990), p. 55

46. See H. Butterfield Ryan, *The Vision of Anglo-America: The US-UK Alliance and the Emerging Cold War, 1943-1946* (Cambridge: Cambridge University Press, 1987).

47. A. Bosco, "The Federalist Project and Resistance in Continental Europe" in *The Federal Idea*, vol. 11, pp. 64-65.

48. Bosco op. cit.; Pinder op. cit.

49. C. F. Delzell, "The European Federalist Movement in Italy: First Phase 1918-1947," *Journal of Modern History*, XXX11, 1960, pp. 241-242.

50. Movimento Federalista Europeo: "Essential Aspects," January 1946 reprinted in W. Lipgens and W. Loth, eds., *Documents on the History of European Integration, vol. 3*, (Berlin and New York: European University Institute, 1988), p. 153.

51. Delzell, "The European Federalist Movement in Italy: First Phase 1918-1947," pp. 249-250.

52. For a general discussion of this problem see M. Francis, "A Case of Mistaken Paternity: the relationship between Nineteenth Century Liberals and Twentieth Century Democrats," *The Australian Journal of Politics and History*, vol. 31, no. 2, 1985, pp. 282-299.

53. G. Barraclough, "The Continuity of European Tradition" in *History in a Changing World* (Oxford: Basil Blackwell, 1957), pp. 31-45.

3

The New Europe Debate
in Wartime Britain

Peter Wilson

This chapter gives an account of the debate on the future of Europe which took place in wartime Britain especially during the years 1941-1944. This debate was called by a number of political writers of the time the "New Europe" debate. Particular attention will be given to the contributions of E. H. Carr and David Mitrany. Carr's *The Conditions of Peace* (the longest chapter of which is entitled "The New Europe") and Mitrany's *A Working Peace System*, published in 1942 and 1943 respectively, were in their range, depth, and originality the two most important contributions to wartime British thought about postwar European and, indeed, world reconstruction. They also had an influence on postwar British attitudes towards European unity that has been underestimated in conventional accounts of the formative years of European integration.

The Nature of the Debate

The International Context

The nature of the European crisis and how it might be confronted and resolved had, of course, been debated from the very onset of the Nazi-Fascist challenge in the early 1930s. There was, however, something qualitatively different about the New Europe debate of the 1940s which set it apart from earlier debates, such as the one initiated by the formation of the Federal Union Movement in 1938, or the one sparked off by Churchill's famous proposal of Anglo-French Union in June 1940.[1]

The earlier debates, both in substance and tone, were characterised by their intensity and sense of urgency. The overwhelming purpose was to find a way of averting another catastrophic war. Thinking about Europe was not so much an attempt to build a new Europe as to shore up the rapidly disintegrating structure of the old one. In this respect it is significant that by late 1938 the newly formed Federal Union was beginning to take a place in British politics similar to the one previously occupied by the League of Nations Union. With its origins in the early years of World War I, the League of Nations Union became, by the early 1920s, a kind of umbrella group for various, though not always complementary, shades of progressive opinion on international organization and the prevention of war. The Federal Union began to occupy a comparable place around the time of the Munich Agreement. Many concerned individuals embraced the idea of federal union even though there was plenty of disagreement on the shape such a union would take. Some, like Lionel Curtis and Lord Lothian, advocated Anglo-American Union. Others, like Sir William Beveridge, advocated a union of Western European democracies. Others still, like Clarence Streit in his well known *Union Now*, advocated a union of all the world's democracies. To a large extent federalism was embraced out of sheer desperation. The League had visibly failed and many people concluded that this failure had been because of its inability to restrict national sovereignty. Since the federal idea was predicated on the restriction of sovereignty it seemed to provide an instant answer to the problem and offer at least a ray of hope that war could be avoided.

By the end of 1940, of course, the situation had dramatically changed. Europe had been almost completely conquered by Nazi Germany. The British, however, had just managed to fend off the massive onslaught of the Luftwaffe, and the Americans were showing increasing willingness to intervene militarily on the allied side. This change in the course of the war accounts for the changed character of thought on Europe. The vestiges of the old European order had been demolished. Political thinkers could now give their full attention to providing the intellectual foundations for a new, more secure, and prosperous Europe. Sober reflection and detailed analysis took over from the extemporary style of political thought of the late 1930s.

Characteristic Features

Along with its comparative sobriety and depth of analysis it is important to note three further features of the 1940s New Europe debate. Firstly, it was by and large a Centre and Centre-Left debate.[2] Those occupying this part of the political spectrum were generally more optimistic about the extent to which the future shape of Europe could be consciously determined. By contrast more conservative-minded observers took the view that contingent factors were so intrinsic to international politics that even the most carefully laid plans could easily come to nought. Whilst not completely hostile to drawing up plans for a New Europe, they felt that the exercise was at best rather futile and at worst a dangerous distraction.

Secondly, the debate was not exclusively concerned with Europe. Thinking about Britain's future relationship with the rest of Europe automatically called into question the relationship with the Commonwealth and also America.[3] If Britain was to become primarily a European power, or more radically a part of a single United States of Europe, then this obviously had implications for the historical, cultural, economic and other ties with the Dominions and America. In a sense all the participants of the debate were involved in weighing up the relative merits of the three concentric circles of British foreign policy. There was also the question of building a new world order as well as a new European order. By 1942 a predominantly European war had become a world war. Therefore it was not only the political and economic structure of Europe that, at the end of hostilities, would need to be reconstructed. The relationship between the New Europe, or a European-wide international authority, and any new world authority, such as the United Nations, needed to be examined and, if possible, defined.

A third characteristic feature of the debate concerns the calibre of its participants. The contributions of Sir William Beveridge, E. H. Carr, Lionel Curtis, Lord Lothian, David Mitrany, Friedrich Hayek, Lionel Robbins, Sir Ivor Jennings, and C. A. W. Manning were contributions from thinkers of the highest rank in their respective fields of Economics, Law, and International Relations. The debate was further fortified by a number of well respected political thinkers of an older generation such as Lord (David) Davies, Count Coudenhove Kalergi, and Leonard Woolf.

Although the New Europe debate was wide-ranging it essentially revolved around two problems—national self determination and sovereignty—and two ideas put forward as solutions to these problems—federalism and functionalism.

E. H. Carr and the "Crisis" of National Self-Determination

In 1919 national self-determination was for many the answer to a set of problems—imperial domination, tyranny, and war—rather than a problem itself. President Wilson rode a tide of popular enthusiasm in

Europe with his belief that the dismantling of the mainland European empires, in the name of national self-determination, would usher in a new era of peace. Based on the dual liberal belief that nations were objective and that, given the choice, they would choose to determine themselves into separate independent states, Wilson promulgated the view that national self-determination would do away with the main source of conflict in Europe.

More than anyone else it was E. H. Carr who demonstrated the flaws in the Wilsonian faith and the problems that the principle of national self-determination gave rise to in practice. Carr was for many years an official in the British Foreign Office, and from 1936-1947 he was, perhaps ironically, Woodrow Wilson Professor of International Politics at the University College of Wales, Aberystwyth. He challenged three aspects of the liberal faith.

First of all he contended that it could not be assumed that nations, even if their identity and scope were clear, would invariably wish to determine themselves into separate sovereign states. This was a liberal illusion arising from the tendency to draw exclusively from the western European experience and not that of central, eastern or southern Europe. The French, or those who had all the hallmarks of being French, were happy to determine themselves into a political unit called France. Likewise Danes, Germans and Italians. However the same was not true of many Poles, Slovenes, Serbs, and Czechs. Secondly, self-determination expressed itself in terms of territory. This in itself, Carr argued, presented immense difficulties since the rather neat patchwork of nations in Western Europe was not replicated in other parts of Europe. Whilst national groups were generally concentrated in particular localities, exceptions to this rule were considerable. This gave rise to the problem of minorities which was compounded by the first point that it could not be concluded with any certainty which political units such minorities would wish to belong to. Thirdly, Carr emphasised a formal problem that had been long identified: given the fragmented and overlapping distribution of nations in many parts of Europe who would decide who constituted the "self" that was going to do the "determining"? This was not a question that could be answered objectively. Any answer would ultimately be a political one. However, as the experience of the Irish Question amply demonstrated, any political decision was bound to be highly controversial. Thus one problem might be solved but only at the cost of creating a number of others, perhaps no less intractable.[4]

These problems led Carr to reject the principle of national self-determination as a foundation on which the new European Order should be built. Indeed Carr contended that the War was partly a product of a "crisis" of national self-determination. Rather than a cure it was a cause of war. The principle had relevance in the nineteenth century when liberal democracy and laissez-faire reigned supreme. But since then a "social revolution" had occurred which gave rise to a radically different set of conditions. It was essentially a revolution of large-scale economic, social and political organization, and its most profound effect was to render liberal democracy and laissez-faire obsolete. These bulwarks of the nineteenth century liberal order were now superseded by mass democracy and central planning.

The radical nature of Carr's thesis is nowhere better illustrated than in his discussion of the future of the small state. According to Carr, the new conditions had made the small state economically unviable. The separation of economics from politics that had underpined the nineteenth century order was vital for the small state. But the social revolution had put an end to this separation. Economics and politics were visibly united in Soviet planning and in the Nazi New Order and it was clear that the small state could no longer survive economically without the patronage of these larger units.

In an era of relative free trade and laissez-faire state boundaries did not matter so much. But in an era of planning, state trading, currency manipulation, and the "closed door," boundaries became crucial. Carr's conclusion was that in these conditions the small state would inevitably be the economic victim of the larger grouping. Hence the proliferation of small states in eastern and southern Europe, which the principle of national self-determination implied, would result in either economic instability or the domination of these small nations by larger ones. The implication of the latter was that such small states would not be self-determining at all. Hence, national self-determination, along with the other principles of the nineteenth century order, had become hollow.

Carr concluded that the small state could survive "only as an anomaly and anachronism in a world which has moved on to other forms of organization."[5] Given this, nothing was more absurd than the Wilsonian creed of national self-determination:

> By treating the principle of national self-determination as an absolute and by carrying it further than it had ever been carried before, they [the makers of the 1919 peace] fostered the disintegration of existing political units, and favoured the creation of a multiplicity of smaller units, at a moment when strategic and economic factors were demanding increased integration and the grouping of the world into fewer and larger units of power.[6]

Carr did not, however, reject the idea of self-determination in its entirety: *national* self-determination may have lost its relevance but not self-determination *per se.* Carr, as some of his critics pointed out, was vague on this matter, especially with regard to the means by which this self-determining process was to be established.[7] However, in broad terms, it is clear Carr envisaged a pluralistic political order in which individuals would determine themselves into different groups for different purposes. In such an order the meaning of territorial boundaries would be transformed as individuals increasingly identified with one set of institutions for certain purposes, that is security, but other institutions for other purposes, such as production.[8]

In advocating that individuals would determine themselves into different groups for different purposes Carr was arguing very much along functionalist lines, except that, significantly, his specific proposals were all European in scope. It is important to note that Carr proposed the creation of a whole range of European institutions: for instance, a European Relief Commission, a European Transport Corporation, a European Reconstruction and Public Works Corporation, a "Bank of Europe," and, overseeing them all, a European Planning Authority. Each institution would have a different task to perform and, anticipating Mitrany, their constitutions would vary according to function.[9] Whilst some institutions would be set up immediately to deal with relief from hunger and preventing the spread of disease, others would be established only when these and other problems, the rebuilding of devastated cities for example, had been successfully dealt with. Similarly, some institutions would begin their life quite modestly but later on, if conditions were conducive, he felt that it would be possible to envisage creating the institution that he felt was "the master-key to the problem of postwar settlement"—the European Planning Authority. At first its job would be the coordination of the relief and reconstruction agencies. But in time it could "develop into the ultimate authority responsible for vital decisions on "European" economic policies."[10]

The evolution of what Carr with purposeful frugality called "The European Unit," would be gradual and cautious. He repeatedly emphasised that economic reconstruction would have to proceed a long way before the political institutions and structure of Europe could be formally established.[11] New institutions could be made effective only if they were underpinned by the emergence of new loyalties; and new loyalties would develop only as a product of experience in the performance of common tasks.[12]

So, despite his reputation as one of the main figures of postwar realism—a doctrine which emphasises the inevitable struggle for power between sovereign states—Carr was clearly a proponent of European unity, and it was unity based on functional organization of Europe because, like David Mitrany the high-priest of functionalism, he was of the firm opinion that nationalism had reached its apogee and would henceforth fall into decline. However his evidence for this was rather scanty. It consisted primarily of two observations. Firstly, that World War II was far more of an ideological war than the, primarily nationalist, World War I: the Allies were fighting Nazis whereas the Allied and Associated Powers fought Germans. Secondly, Carr was impressed by the success of the US and especially the Soviet Union in building the first multinational states where national particularisms had been neutralised through the pursuit of general well being.[13]

Interestingly, Carr's critics did not so much challenge his sanguine view of the fate of nationalism as the future he mapped out for the small state. C. A. W. Manning, at the London School of Economics, when reviewing *Conditions of Peace* asked with regard to his "dimly-adumbrated supranational groupings": "if the Nazi way with small sovereign states is indeed to become common form, what is the war about?"[14] Similarly in his general opposition to what he called the "New Europe School" A.A. Milne asked: "What are we fighting for, if not for the right of people and peoples to live as they wish to live, rather than as some conqueror thinks that they ought to live?"[15]

F. A. Hayek echoed this view and, in particular, felt that Carr's disregard of the individuality and rights of small nations was symptomatic of the implicit totalitarianism not only of Carr's thinking but also of the bulk of thinking about postwar reconstruction.[16] Nonetheless, Hayek agreed with Carr that international order and lasting peace could not be built on "unfettered sovereignty in the economic sphere." He cautioned, however, against the kind of international economic planning that Carr proposed. Powers that had not yet been intelligently used by *national* authorities, namely the central direction and control of economic activity, could not, and should not, be extended to an *international* authority. Planning should go no further than devising a set of rules to prohibit various kinds of restrictive measures.

In contrast, some writers agreed with Carr's strictures about the vulnerability of the small state but disliked the implication that the problem was not also one to do with the strength and irresponsibility of the great powers. This line of argument was expressed with great clarity by the Fabian, and long-standing advocate of international government, Leonard Woolf. Woolf agreed with Carr that the proliferation of small states in Europe had been a major source of tension during the inter-war years and that defining their future position in the postwar order was one of the most crucial tasks of the peace settlement. However, contrary to Carr, Woolf argued that the status and position of the great powers was also a matter of crucial importance. Whilst agreeing with Carr that the sovereignty and independence of small states would have to be curtailed, Woolf was critical of the idea, strongly implicit in

Carr's analysis, that small states would inevitably be reduced to the status of satellites. The wings of sovereignty of both the small and the great powers had to be clipped. Both needed to consent to submit themselves to some form of international government.[17]

Clipping the Wings of Sovereignty

While there was a diversity of opinion on the place of the principle of national self-determination in the New Europe there was general agreement on the related question of sovereignty. Though there were differences on how it might be done, all were agreed that the sovereignty of states needed to be limited in some way. This view found its most clear expression in the work of Leonard Woolf,[18] who considered sovereignty to mean "the claim that the government of that State can make up its mind to do anything or not to do anything without interference from the government of any other State."[19] More strongly, sovereignty entailed the "sacred right" of a state to do anything it chose to "without reference to anyone else or any other State or government."[20] The problem was that this claim to sovereignty—and for Woolf it is important to note that sovereignty was something "claimed" rather than an actual state of affairs such as "constitutional separateness"—was at odds with the actual pattern of international life. States were not, in fact, "independent" as the claim to sovereignty implied but were "inextricably dependent on one another" due *inter alia* to the highly developed internationalisation of industry, agriculture, trade and finance. Human society had become so internationalised "and the relations between States and peoples [had] become so many and complicated" that, for example, "what happens in a Balkan village may have a profound effect upon the livelihood of a South Wales miner or a Pittsburgh steel worker."[21] What one State did with a port or a tariff could be economic life or death to another. The claim to sovereignty implied that states had no responsibility for the welfare of other states and, according to Woolf, this had become patently untrue.

This view was also shared by Lord Lothian who saw sovereignty as meaning self-centredness without automatically implying the ability to control. Indeed this had been the American experience in the late eighteenth century, an experience which had direct relevance for war-torn Europe. Prior to 1789 the states of America were not sovereign because division prevented them from exercising any control over America's future. Only by uniting in order to pursue their common interests could such control be achieved. Though from 1781 independent from Britain they were "not free, for they could neither agree or act about anything."[22]

During the late 1930s and early 1940s the idea that the institution of national sovereignty was the main villain of the piece received a chorus of approval. Woolf was certainly not alone in asserting that sovereignty had become "incompatible with law, order, and peace."[23] Clarence Streit popularised the view that the League had failed, and Europe was consequently on the brink of another major war because it sought to safeguard national sovereignty rather than transcend it. Lionel Robbins was of a similar view though he was perhaps less willing to suggest that the institution of national sovereignty was purely a product of human folly. "How much misery might have been avoided," he asked, "how much poverty prevented, had the accident of history not divided the seat of sovereignty."[24] Not surprisingly, condemnation of sovereignty went hand in hand with support for federation. Robbins considered the right to make war as central to the concept of sovereignty, and it was this right more than any other that states had to give up. However, this did not mean that states should surrender all their rights of independent government. Nor did it mean that any international authority subsequently created would have unlimited powers. The solution for Robbins was clear: "There must be neither alliance nor complete unification, but Federation; neither *Staatenbund*, nor *Einheitstaat*, but *Bundesstaat*."[25] As one reviewer noted, "Federal Authority should supersede the bloodstained moloch of national sovereignty."[26]

Hayek, Robbins, and the Prerequisites of International Liberalism

The idea of restricting state sovereignty by creating a federal or some other kind of international authority became the dominant idea of the period. Even those who are nowadays customarily thought of as hostile to such international interventionism were, at the time, committed advocates of it. As well as opposing unfettered sovereignty in the economic sphere, Friedrich Hayek, for example, also opposed unfettered sovereignty in the political sphere. Indeed the latter was more important for Hayek than the former. What was needed was not an international economic authority with the power to direct states in the use of their economic resources, but rather an international political authority which would be able to "truly" hold powerful economic interests in check because it was not itself "a part of the economic game." Accordingly,

> The need is for an international political authority which, without the power to direct the different people what they must do, must be able to restrain them from action which will damage others. The powers which must devolve to an international authority are not the new powers as-

sumed by the states in recent times, but that minimum of powers without which it is impossible to preserve peaceful relationships, i.e. essentially the powers of the ultra liberal "laissez-faire" state.[27]

In calling for an international political authority Hayek was to a large
extent echoing the view of Lionel Robbins, who wrote two books in
the late 1930s arguing for the establishment on the international level
of a juridical and political framework.[28] Rather than being inconsistent
with the successful operation of a liberal economy, Robbins argued that
such a framework was a logical prerequisite. This was not something
which had gone unnoticed by the classical economists, though some
contemporary economists assumed that it had, but it was something
that they had perhaps not sufficiently emphasised.[29] Robbins, therefore,
was eager to point out that he was drawing on the classical economists
in his adumbration of the governmental underpinnings of liberalism.
According to Robbins a framework of institutions was needed to safeguard property rights and ensure the sanctity of contracts. Also, a wide
range of other things were needed that the market by itself could not
provide or could only provide inadequately eg. roads, sewers, water
supply, parks, provisions for public health, relief of destitution, and
"some instruction of the young." Above all else, however, the liberal
economy required an authority "armed with coercive power" to provide security. And for Robbins, as with Hayek, this applied to the international realm as much as it did to the domestic realm. International
liberalism required an international authority, and the type of authority
most conducive was federal in structure.[30]

Mitrany's Critique of Territorial Sovereignty

Perhaps the most sophisticated critic of state sovereignty during this
period was David Mitrany, whose starting point, like Woolf's, was that
of the interdependence of the modern world:

> We may go on splitting up the world into as many states as we like, but
> life, the inexorable product of our great scientific cunning, has by now
> made us all into one indivisible community, with inescapably one and
> the same fate—either to live or to vanish together.[31]

This indivisible economic and technological community had been a
product of the dynamic nineteenth century. However the nineteenth
century had also bequeathed the contradictory trend of nationalism.
While one served to unify the world the other served to divide it. Nationalism had led to the creation of more and more national units all

of whom claimed sovereign status. Such a claim, allied to international economic, political and military competition, severely held back natural integrative processes and diminished material efficiency. This frustration of the achievement of material welfare was the ultimate source of conflict.

The contradiction, Mitrany claimed, could not be resolved as long as sovereignty remained co-extensive with territory. Hence the central proposition of Mitrany's functional theory that sovereignty should be linked to a specific activity rather than territory. In other words sovereignty needed to be transferred from the territorial unit to the functional unit.

The Limitations of National Sovereignty and the Federal Solution

By the early 1940s, the concept of national sovereignty was besieged from all sides. The assailants differed in many ways, particularly regarding the underlying assumptions of their analyses. Hayek and Robbins wanted to overturn, or at least relocate, sovereignty in order to make capitalism work more effectively. Mitrany, and certainly Woolf, wanted sovereignty to be similarly overturned or relocated but as part of a broader non-capitalist reorganization of production and distribution. However, these differences notwithstanding, there was a sense in which all the critics of national sovereignty in the early 1940s were making the same basic point, though they perhaps failed to state it with the clarity it deserved. The point was that although Europe and the world remained wedded to the principle of national sovereignty the ability to reap its rewards—in terms of the societal goals of peace and prosperity—had never been so limited. National sovereignty, though not necessarily other types of sovereignty, had become outmoded and dangerous. They also shared the rationalist belief that if enough people could be convinced of the truth of the proposition its solution would not be far off. If only people realised the actual limitations of sovereignty, its popularity, as an idea and a value, would soon evaporate. The dissemination of information and the raising of public consciousness were, therefore, crucial. Indeed that was the main purpose of writing on the subject.

The idea of a federal solution to the European problem of peace and war is, or course, not a new one. As the last chapter showed, a Pan-European movement was founded in 1923, with Count Coudenhove Kalergi as its self-appointed head. The movement did not win mass support but it did attract a following among a number of continental diplomats, intellectuals, and politicians. Importantly it was embraced by both the French Prime Minister, Herriot, and by Gustav Stresemann. In

1929 Briand called for a "European Union" between all the European members of the League, though rather curiously he claimed that such a union would not impinge on the independence and national sovereignty of the state. A year later Briand called for a "United States of Europe."[32]

Britain was not immune from this trend in political thinking. The conventional view is that the British have always been hostile to the federal idea. Pragmatism rather than constitutionalism, it is widely held, is their natural political inclination.[33] Yet, in 1938 the Federal Union was founded in London and by 1940-41 had become the focal point for various bodies of opinion—pacifist, League internationalist, socialist internationalist—all of whom had seen their reformist hopes dashed by the tragic events of the previous few years. Through the Federal Union's activities—intellectual, organisational, and propagandist—federalism came to occupy a central place in thinking about European political organization. The Union attracted considerable support not only from scholars, journalists, civil servants, military men, and politicians, but also from the wider public.[34] By the Spring of 1940 it had over 8,000 members, in over 200 branches, including branches in France and Geneva. It organised frequent public meetings, attendance at which sometimes reached 2,500.[35]

Nor should it be assumed that the Federal Union lacked a British liberal tradition on which to build. On the contrary British liberalism provided a rich seam of federalist thought, from the proto-federalist and highly influential ideas of Locke, through to J. S. Mill, John Seeley, Lord Acton, Henry Sidgwick, James Bryce, and Ernest Barker. It was true that much federalist thought in the British liberal tradition was prompted by a need to find solutions to imperial problems and the Irish Question. However, attempts to apply the federal idea to Europe, and indeed the world as a whole, although rarer were not unknown.[36] It is noteworthy that one of the leading postwar pioneers of the European Community, Altiero Spinelli, considered federalism "a typically Anglo-Saxon conception."[37]

Along with Jennings and Beveridge one of the firmest and in many ways most interesting advocates of European federalism during the 1940s was Hayek. Rejecting all schemes for international economic planning Hayek nonetheless welcomed, as mentioned, the idea of creating a supranational political authority with the power and authority to hold the international ring in the classical liberal sense of what is now known as the nightwatchman state. Without saying how it was to be done Hayek's idea was to establish an authority with certain minimum powers, but not the power to control all aspects of life. Federation did not mean centralisation. Rather it was a way of forming an association of different peoples "which will create an international order without putting an undue strain on their legitimate desire for independence."[38] Indeed Hayek argued that federation would actually lead to a reversal of the process of centralisation that had to such a large extent epitomised the growth of the twentieth century state. One of the chief implications of such centralisation—economic and military competition between states (to be distinguished from economic competition between individuals and firms)—would be diminished and a trend towards the devolution of power to local authorities set in motion.

Nor did federation put an obstacle in the path of all planning. Hayek was not opposed, at least not in the 1940s, to the local planning of public goods and utilities such as the supply of water, gas, electricity, street lighting, and various other infrastructural goods. Federalism meant that this type of planning could happily take place at the level at which it worked best—the localities. Only at this level could agreements be reached between all the economic interests immediately concerned and among all those—not the least consumers—who would be affected. It also should be noted that along with other prominent federalists then working in Britain such as Beveridge, Sir Ivor Jennings, Lionel Robbins, Lord Lothian, and Count Coudenhove Kalergi, Hayek was sceptical of proposals for a world-wide federal union. Even less ambitious attempts at universality, such as the League, had not been successful. The reason for this was that the more ambitious the scope of the union the more cohesion had to be sacrificed in order to secure initial agreement. Catering for the least common denominator resulted in a loose, ineffective institution. A more tightly knit body was possible among states more similar in their civilisation, outlook, and standards:

> The comparatively close association which a Federal Union represents will not at first be practicable beyond perhaps even as narrow a region as part of Western Europe, though it may be possible gradually to extend it.[39]

The idea that a group of like-minded states should form a federation but hold out the possibility to other states of joining on the satisfaction of certain criteria goes back, of course, to Kant. In the 1940s most federalist writers supported this view and felt that such a possibility would constitute a source of inspiration, or a goal, for those nations currently excluded.[40]

However, there were several thinkers who remained unconvinced by the federal approach. Among whom were Carr and Mitrany. For Carr federalism was almost definitive of "utopianism." Visions of European federation were merely "elegant superstructures" which had no chance of succeeding "until some progress [had been] made in digging the foundations."[41] Peaceful change had to be bottom up rather than top down: substructural rather than superstructural. This is summed up in Carr's claim that,

> the fundamental problems of the world today express themselves in economic terms, and that a political settlement will have little chance of lasting unless it emerges as the crown and coping-stone of a successful economic reconstruction.[42]

Carr did not brand as "utopian" all proposals for change, even radical change. Rather, it was the large scale constitutional blue-print for change that was the particular target of Carr's venom. Indeed it might be argued that at root "utopianism" for Carr meant little more than "constitutionalism": that is, the idea that reform could be achieved merely by drawing up and signing a covenant or charter. The Briand-Kellogg Pact was the apogee of utopianism because it sought to rid the world of war via a written and verbal undertaking not to resort to it. Federalism was a method of doing the same by much the same means. Carr was not opposed to reform—his proposals for the establishment of various European agencies and authorities are testimony to this—but he argued that reform needed to be firmly predicated on substructural, economic and social, change. Hence the title *Conditions of Peace*: peace could not simply be subscribed to, the conditions had to be right.

Mitrany objected to federalism in general, and European union in particular, on several grounds. First, there was the question as to whether the federation should be composed of states or peoples. According to Mitrany federalists leaned towards the latter due to the perception that one of the principal flaws of the League of Nations was that it was composed of states. However, there was an immediate problem with a federation of peoples, namely, which peoples? Whole communities would have to be chosen, rather than parts of them on the basis of social class or political party. This would mean that those who were opposed to the federation would be included as well as those who supported it. Even if the former were a minority they could, given the democratic process, become a majority. And, Mitrany asked, "What will happen to the union of peoples if some of the new majorities begin to tug at the common bonds?"[43]

Secondly, there was the question of whether the union was to be founded on the basis of geography or ideology. Both had their drawbacks. With geography there was the danger of merely substituting continental rivalry for rivalry among powers and alliances. Also such a union would be capable of a good degree of autarchy which as well as potentially undermining the economic gains from a wider set of relationships would also make for division. With ideology, e.g. restricting membership to democratic states only, there was the problem of what to do if a member ceased to be democratic, or alternatively, if a non-member were to become democratic. Would the former be expelled and the latter invited to join? For Mitrany the question was a crucial one since,

> Federation under present conditions means a fairly close organization, political and economic; to revise the membership every few years would mean to disrupt periodically those very factors which are the lifeblood of any union.[44]

Thirdly when Mitrany referred to "present conditions" he had in mind the inability of laissez-faire to secure general well-being: "Security, economic and social development, all require under present conditions, whatever the unit of organization, centralized planning and control."[45] Such centralization and control of economic activity would inevitably sharpen divisions between a union and the outside world. Indeed, anticipating in some respects Carr's claim that "the socialization of the nation has as its natural corollary the nationalization of socialism,"[46] Mitrany summed up his objection to federations as follows:

> Close sectional unions would in effect represent merely a rationalised nationalism, with wider limits for the individual units but otherwise reproducing the working characteristics of the system of nation states.[47]

However, Mitrany did not rule out the possibility or efficacy of federation as long as it was a product of "organic growth" rather than a "green-table" creation. If this was the case Mitrany maintained that "functional arrangements might indeed be regarded as organic elements of a federation by instalments."[48] However, a European federation as such was not something that Mitrany found favour with.

A number of writers whilst taking on board many of the criticisms of Carr and Mitrany nonetheless supported the idea of a European or democratic federation as long as it was part of a broader plan for international reorganization. Leonard Woolf, for example, did not rule out the possibility of a European federation though he felt that conditions were not yet conducive. Like Carr and Mitrany he strongly advocated practical international cooperation and the setting up of functional agencies which would operate regardless of national boundaries. However, unlike both Carr and Mitrany, Woolf felt that a political organization would be needed both at the regional and the world level in order to

settle disputes which would inevitably rise and which would not always be amenable to technical resolution.[49]

The Functional Alternative

A functionalist future for Europe was embraced by all those who,
either in whole or in part, rejected federalism. The core idea of the
doctrine was that peace and prosperity could best be secured by bringing nations actively together rather than by seeking to keep them apart.
In essence functionalism was a doctrine of community building. The
idea was to build a shared identity, common values and sentiments, by
practical cooperation. Hence the idea of a *working* peace system as opposed to a protected peace system.

The problems of territorial sovereignty and self-determination could
be tackled by reducing the significance of national frontiers through the
forging of transnational bonds. Boundaries could eventually become
meaningless "through the continuous development of common activities and interests across them."[50] At the very least boundaries could be
rendered less important. After all this is what had happened in the
domestic sphere. To use Woolf's analogy the task was to make the
boundaries between Germany and France of no more significance than
those between British countries like Middlesex and Surrey.[51]

In the New Europe debate of the 1940s criticism of Mitrany's functional approach was relatively thin on the ground. It was certainly not
subjected to the kind of detailed scrutiny that Carr and Mitrany had
inflicted on *laissez-faire* liberalism and federalism. Indeed, by the early
1940s the functional approach had become highly fashionable.[52] The
main reason for this was that it seemed to hold out the prospect of
bringing countries closer together without at the same time requiring
them to face head on the question of surrendering their sovereignty.
Many people were convinced by Mitrany's argument that whilst national
sovereignty would not succumb to a frontal attack, there was a good
chance that it could be side-stepped through functional cooperation.

However, the functional approach was not completely free from criticism. The principal objection to it was that it failed to provide an adequate basis for international security, at least in the short term. Mitrany
initially claimed that there could be "no real transfer of sovereignty"
from the nation state to functional units "until defence is entrusted to
a common authority, because national means of defence are also means
of offence and also of possible resistance to that authority."[53] Mitrany
later felt that this "common authority" had found preliminary expression in the Security Council and the International Atomic Energy
Agency. However, if such bodies were to be separate from states, which

is in any case difficult to conceive, it still needed to be demonstrated how they differed from a world state—an outcome that Mitrany envisaged as the conclusion of the functional process rather its precondition.

Mitrany never satisfactorily resolved this problem. Indeed on the question of security, he engaged in much side-stepping of his own. In 1943 he argued that an international political authority was a prerequisite of functional organization. In 1944, on realising that the powers implied in the creation of such an authority would in effect make it into a world sovereign, he rejected this view. A world sovereign, Mitrany declared, was neither practicable or desirable. Then, in 1948, he accepted that functional organization necessitated a framework of law and order and announced, though without further elaboration, that this would be provided by the United Nations.[54]

But what about the federalists? How did they respond to Mitrany's, and indeed Carr's, scathing attack? After the fall of France, and with the ever closer alliance between Britain and the US, the federalist movement began to lose support in Britain (though the ideas it generated were later to have a profound impact on continental federalists).[55] It is true that the New Commonwealth Society founded by the Liberal peer Lord David Davies had elevated European federal union to a central place in their Programme. However, in common with a number of organisations the Society also strongly supported functional cooperation. Federalism and functionalism were not seen as being in any way contradictory. For example, *The New Commonwealth* devoted much space to the idea of a European Air Force to put down aggression. Despite the regional and "protective" nature of such a proposal it was not seen to be inconsistent with Mitrany's functional idea. The reason for this was that such a force, remarkably, was not to be controlled by politicians but, *à la* Mitrany, by "persons individually qualified in the technique of the undertaking."[56]

In a similar way many proponents of federalism welcomed functionalism and did not consider the two approaches to be inconsistent. Rather than digesting Mitrany's message as a whole they tended to give emphasis to his rather strange claim that functionalism could be seen as a kind of "federalism by instalments."[57] However, this failed to satisfy Lionel Curtis. More than anyone else Curtis realised that Mitrany's thesis was fundamentally antagonistic to federalism. After all, functionalism was essentially concerned with the detachment of sovereign authority from territory, whereas federalism sought to create larger and fewer territorially based sovereign units (and ultimately, for some, a single world-wide unit). Curtis, whose understanding of the federal idea had been sharpened by work on South African Union and for the Round Table, argued that the transfer of sovereignty would not occur unless the people of the separate states agreed that there was an overriding reason for doing so. For Curtis, this proposition was confirmed by the American experience. Although bankrupt and on the verge of civil war, the states of the confederation had no intention of abandoning their sovereignty. However, "Washington came forward . . . and got the congress of Philadelphia to tell the people what they must do if they wished to save themselves from another disaster; with the result that within twelve months the people, by popular vote, accepted the proposed [Federal] constitution."[58]

From his reading of the American case, Curtis drew the conclusion that state sovereignty could not be merged, transferred or transcended by functional cooperation alone. Prior political agreement was needed and, in particular, it was necessary to establish a "Union Government." Unless this was done, functional ties would inevitably fall victim to state rivalry and animosity. The experience of the German *Zollverein* demonstrated this: within a few years of its formation "one state after another began twisting it in its own interests."[59] Only by appealing to the whole people could the problem of sovereignty be dealt with and political union forged. The criticism presages later federalist attacks on neofunctionalist ideas of European unification in the 1970s.

Conclusion: Craftsmen or Visionaries?

By 1944, enthusiasm in Britain for European unity, while still strong in certain quarters, had generally subsided.[60] Increasingly, Britain's future was seen in terms of continuing to foster the "special relationship" with America, or in terms of strengthening the bonds of the Commonwealth. Yet the picture is not a clear one. Many on the Left were uneasy with the idea of Britain forging closer links with an inexorably capitalist America. With the onset of the Cold War a number of political observers began to express concerns of a different kind about too close an alliance with America. Neutrality and even isolationism, however, rather than European unification, were for the most part their preferred alternatives.[61] Those who did continue to advocate the idea of European union, encouraged by Churchill's "United States of Europe" speech in Switzerland in 1946, became ambiguous, as indeed Churchill was himself, as to whether any future European union would or would not include Britain.[62]

Several reasons can be put forward for this loss of enthusiasm. After the fall of France, many in Britain began to lose faith in their European allies who were increasingly held to be unreliable. This contrasted sharply with the highly dependable Americans. The "miracle of Dunkirk" and the rise of "English exceptionalism" compounded this loss of faith.[63] Successfully "standing alone" against Hitler restored confidence in the British state and British national sovereignty. Momentum gathered for the view that if the British state could triumph in wartime it could also triumph in building a prosperous and secure social order in peace time.[64] Hence there was no need to surrender sovereignty. Indeed, quite the reverse. To fulfil national objectives, British power and influence needed to be preserved and, if at all possible, enhanced. This marked a significant departure from the assault on national sovereignty which characterised much British political thought between 1938 and 1944.

These reasons are, of course, central to the conventional, and very cogent, explanation of Britain's scepticism towards the more ambitious visions of European unity. However, there is another reason which, although difficult to demonstrate empirically, has perhaps been overlooked. Of the many competent wartime books on the future of European order, and international order generally, the two works of Carr and Mitrany examined in this chapter were by far the most impressive. Importantly, they were generally regarded as such by contemporary political commentators. The works received much attention and were extensively, and usually positively, reviewed.

This is significant because both books were scathing about federalism. Furthermore, while Carr's *Conditions of Peace* did argue for a unified Europe of sorts, Mitrany's *A Working Peace System* did not. Although Mitrany was occasionally equivocal on this matter, the thrust of his thesis was entirely antipathetical to the creation of regional political unions. Moreover, while both books were highly critical of national sovereignty they did not seek to present a "vision" as such of what their preferred European or international order would look like. They were both opposed to such "visions" seeing them as fundamentally flawed since they put the constitutional cart before the economic and social horse. This is the nub of the matter: both Carr and Mitrany felt that economic and social forces were the true determinants of community, and it was a sense of community that underpined political union, not the other way around. The task was to harness and channel these forces in the light of growing social and technical knowledge. Whether such an approach may itself be said to constitute a "vision" is, in one sense, not important. At the time it was not seen as such.

The influence this approach had on British thinking about international cooperation can be seen in the pages of both *International Affairs*, to the right of centre, and *Political Quarterly*, to the left. From 1944 to 1950 there are numerous articles on such "practical," "functional," matters as food, refugees, population problems, the ILO (International Labour Organization), civil aviation, international monetary organization, health, education, social services, the financing of exports, and the like. However there are few articles on the idea of European union.[65] This in no small part is due to the influence of Carr and Mitrany. It did not take long before the functional approach completely superseded federalism as the principal paradigm for thinking about European reconstruction. The rich tradition of British federalist thought became something "remembered briefly then forgotten."[66] However it is important to note that although the functional approach was widely embraced, the radicalism of Carr's and Mitrany's initial proposals became heavily diluted. Gradually functionalism was stripped of much of its original content and by the end of the 1940s came to mean little more than pragmatic international cooperation on technical, economic and social matters.[67] The influence of Mitrany and Carr and the subsequent dilution of their ideas may go some way in explaining why, in the recent words of the British Foreign Secretary, the British tend to see themselves as the "craftsmen" of Europe rather than the "visionaries."[68]

Notes

This is a revised version of a paper presented at the British International Studies Association Annual Conference, Warwick, December 1991. I am grateful to those who commented on the paper and especially to Ken Booth, Spyros Economides, Paul Rich and Hidemi Suganami.

1. For accounts of these debates see R. A. Wilford, "The Federal Union Campaign," *European Studies Review*, vol. 10, no. 1, January 1980; and A. Bosco, *Federal Union and the Origins of the "Churchill Proposal"* (London: Lothian Foundation Press, 1992).

2. In the sense that the participants were for the most part anti-authoritarian, opposed to Empire and protectionism, and supportive of international organisation. There were, of course, disagreements over central planning between socialists (eg. E. H. Carr and Leonard Woolf) and liberals (eg. L. Robbins and F. Hayek).

3. It should be noted that in their references to the Commonwealth the participants in the New Europe debate invariably had in mind the Dominions. Britain's colonial empire was rarely referred to as something that could be problematic for the reorganization of Europe. In the various proposals for European federation, for example, it was assumed that British colonies would automatically become part of the wider set-up.

4. E. H. Carr, *Conditions of Peace* (London: Macmillan, 1942) pp. 37-66.

5. E. H. Carr, *Nationalism and After* (London: Macmillan, 1945), p. 37.

6. Carr, *Conditions of Peace*, p. 49; see also *Nationalism and After*, pp. 54-5.

7. See for example C. A. W. Manning, review of *Conditions of Peace* in *International Affairs*, vol. XIX, no. 8, June 1942, pp. 443-4.

8. Carr, *Conditions of Peace*, pp. 241, 274.

9. Carr, *Conditions of Peace*, p. 271.

10. Carr, *Conditions of Peace*, p. 254. It is perhaps significant that Carr never felt quite able to bring "Europe" consistently out of its inverted commas. This reflects his uncertainty over both the nature of the "European Unit" and its geographical scope. Carr gave little indication of the countries he felt would be part of the Unit though he did see it as one which would be gradually extended outward. See also *Conditions of Peace*, pp. 243-4.

11. Carr, *Conditions of Peace*, pp. 238, 241, 270, 273.

12. It should also be noted that, like Mitrany, Carr spoke of functional cooperation as a "psychological substitute for war." See Carr, *Conditions of Peace*, p. 252.

13. See Carr, *Nationalism and After*, pp. 34-37, and E. H. Carr, *The Soviet Impact on the Western World* (London: MacMillan, 1946), pp. 100-101.

14. Manning, Review of *Conditions of Peace*, *International Affairs*, p.443.

15. Milne, *War Aims Unlimited*, p. 20.

16. See *The Road to Serfdom* (London: Ark Publications, 1986, first published 1944), pp. 171-2. Hayek was perturbed by the prevalence of such attitudes towards small states evident even in such contrasting publications as *The Times* and *The New Statesman*. Hayek considered Carr to be one of the prime examples, along with various Fabian thinkers, of the unconscious drift in Britain towards totalitarianism.

17. L. S. Woolf, "The Future of the Small State," *Political Quarterly*, vol. XIV, no. 3, July-Sept 1943.

18. See especially *The War for Peace* (London: George Routledge, 1940); *The Future of International Government* (The Labour Party: Transport House, 1940); and, *The International Postwar Settlement* (London: Fabian Publications, 1944).

19. Woolf, *The Future of International Government*, p. 4.

20. Ibid.

21. Ibid., p. 11.

22. See A. Bosco, "Lord Lothian: A Critique of National Sovereignty," in D. Long and P. Wilson, eds., *Thinkers of the Twenty Years' Crisis* (Oxford: Oxford University Press, forthcoming).

23. He also described it as "a dead fossil which must give place to a living organism adapted to the new conditions." See *The International Postwar Settlement*, p. 6.

24. L. Robbins, *Economic Planning and International Order* (London: MacMillan, 1937), p. 240.

25. Ibid.

26. Millward, review of *A Federated Europe*, p. 42.

27. Hayek, *The Road to Serfdom*, p. 172.

28. *Economic Planning and International Order and The Economic Causes of War* (London: Cape, 1939). Hayek was much influenced by the former work. See Hayek, "The Economic Conditions of Inter-State Federalism," *New Commonwealth Quarterly*, vol. 5, 1939, pp. 146-9.

29. Robbins, in particular, criticised Keynes for suggesting that the importance of a governmental framework for the operation of a market economy was a new discovery. See *Economic Planning and International Order*, pp. 225-6. Hayek

completed the picture by pointing out that the nineteenth century heirs to classical liberalism (Cobden, Mill, etc.), by ignoring what Hume, Smith, and
Bentham had to say about the importance of government, were principally responsible for the conventional assumption that liberalism was a doctrine of
absolute laissez-faire which denied government virtually any role at all. Hayek,
"Economic Conditions of Inter-State Federalism," p. 147.

30. Robbins, *Economic Planning and International Order*, Chapter IX, pp. 221-
68. See also J. Pinder's excellent, "The Federal Idea and the British Liberal Tradition," in A. Bosco, ed., *The Federal Idea: The History of Federalism from the
Enlightenment to 1945* (London: Lothian Foundation Press, 1991), pp. 105-6.

31. D. Mitrany, *A Working Peace System* (Chicago: Quadrangle Books, 1966,
first published 1943), p. 13.

32. This adds credence to Spinelli's claim that twentieth century continental
thought on federalism lacked coherence until it came into contact with the ideas
of the Federal Union. See A. Spinelli, "The Growth of the European Movement
since World War II" in M. Hodge, ed., *European Integration* (Harmondsworth:
Penguin, 1972), pp. 43-7.

33. For an excellent account of the pragmatic style of British foreign policy
see J. Frankel, *British Foreign Policy, 1945-1973* (Oxford: Oxford University Press,
1975), pp. 112-150. See also F.S. Northedge, "British Foreign Policy," in F. S.
Northedge, ed., *The Foreign Policy of the Powers* (London: Faber, 1968), pp. 150-
186.

34. See Thomson et al., *Patterns of Peacemaking*, pp. 163-72; John Pinder, "The
Federal Idea and the British Liberal Tradition," pp. 113-115; Martin Ceadel,
"Supranationalism in the British Peace Movement During the Early Twentieth
Century," in A. Bosco, *The Federal Idea*, pp. 188-9.

35. See Bosco, *Federal Union*, pp. 67-8.

36. Pinder, "Federalism and the British Liberal Tradition," pp. 99-112.

37. Spinelli, "The Growth of the European Movement," p. 45. In this context
it should be remembered that the British drew up federal constitutions of both
Canada and Australia and set the constitutional process in motion which later
led to the formation of the federal constitution of India.

38. Hayek, *The Road to Serfdom*, p. 173.

39. Ibid., p. 176.

40. See for example Beveridge, *Peace by Federation?*, pp. 11-12, 18-20; Woolf,
The Future of International Government, pp. 9-10. For the opposing view that fed-
eration should be based on geography rather than ideology see Count R. N.
Coudenhove Kalergi, "Europe Tomorrow," *International Affairs*, vol. XVIII, no.
5, Sept-Oct 1939, esp. p. 63. Also see Dr. Milan Hodza's plan for a "Central
European Federation," and war-time plans for a "Balkan Union" and a "Polish-
Czechoslovak Confederation," summarised in Thomson et al., *Patterns of Peace-
making*, pp. 165-70.

41. E. H. Carr, *The Twenty Years' Crisis*, 2nd ed. (London: Macmillan, 1981,
first published 1946), p. 239.

42. Carr, *Conditions of Peace*, p. 241.

43. Mitrany, *A Working Peace System*, pp. 43-44.

44. Mitrany, *A Working Peace System*, p. 47.

45. Mitrany, *A Working Peace System*, p. 52.

46. Carr, *Nationalism and After*, p. 19.

47. Mitrany, *A Working Peace System*, p. 54.

48. Mitrany, *A Working Peace System*, p. 83.

49. Woolf, *The Future of International Government*, p. 9.

50. Mitrany, *A Working Peace System*, p. 62.

51. Woolf, *The War for Peace*, pp. 79-80. For a discussion of the difficulties involved in such an exercise see H. Suganami, *The Domestic Analogy and World Order Proposals* (Cambridge: Cambridge University Press, 1989), esp. pp. 165-96.

52. See Curtis's response to Mitrany's "The Functional Approach to World Organization," *International Affairs*, vol. XXIV, no. 3, July 1948, pp. 362-3.

53. Mitrany, *A Working Peace System*, p. 54.

54. See Mitrany, *A Working Peace System*, pp. 30-31; Mitrany, *The Road to Security* (London: National Peace Council, 1944), p. 14; Mitrany "The Functional Approach to World Organization," pp. 17-33.

55. For the ebbs and flows in the fortunes of the Federal Union see R. Mayne, J. Pinder, and J. C. de V. Roberts, *Federal Union: The Pioneers* (London: Macmillan, 1990), especially Chapter 2, pp. 17-33.

56. E. Abraham, "A Working Peace System" : A Comment on Professor David Mitrany's Pamphlet, *The New Commonwealth*, November 1944, pp. 304-5. See also T. A. Williams, "The Organisation and Functions of a European Air Police—I," *The New Commonwealth*, November 1938 (and the second part of the article which appeared in the December issue). See also H.G.Wells, *The Common Sense of War and Peace*, pp. 50-79. Wells opposed the schemes of the Federal Union but not federalism in the sense of the devolution of certain tasks, including "control of the air," to a world directorate.

57. See for example, R. H. S. Crossman, "Britain and Western Europe," *Political Quarterly*, vol. XVII, no. 1, January-March, 1946, p. 11.

58. Curtis's response to Mitrany, "The Functional Approach to World Organization," p. 362.

59. Ibid.

60. See Mayne et al., *Federal Union*, pp. 80-108.

61. See Woolf's controversial Fabian pamphlet, *Foreign Policy: The Labour Party's Dilemma* (London: Fabian Publications and Victor Gollancz, 1947). The dilemma was whether to side with America or Russia. Woolf advocated neutrality with the principal objective of staying out of any conflict between them. European unity, something that Woolf previously supported, is not mentioned. See also Crossman's case for a "great neutrality union" of Western European states and "their overseas possessions" ("Britain and Western Europe," p. 9).

62. See, "United States of Europe?" *The New Commonwealth*, November 1946, pp. 365-6.

63. See C. Coker, *Who Only England Know: Conservatives and Foreign Policy* (London: Alliance Publishers for The Institute For European Defence and Strategic Studies, 1990), pp. 25-34.

64. This view was particularly pronounced among the Labour leadership. See M. Newman, "British Socialists and the Question of European Unity, 1939-45," *European Studies Review*, vol. 10, no. 1, January 1980.

65. And these tended to be less than enthusiastic about the idea of European union. See D. Warriner, "The Real Issues in Europe," *Political Quarterly*, vol. XVIII, no. 1, January-March, 1947; W. Pickles, "The Strasbourg Illusion," *Political Quarterly*, vol. XXI, no. 1, January-March, 1950.

66. J. Pinder, "Federalism and the British Liberal Tradition," p. 113.

67. One acute observer recognised this as early as 1950. See Pickles, "The Strasbourg Illusion," pp. 56-57.

68. Douglas Hurd, interview, *Today*, BBC Radio 4, 21 September 1992.

4

Functionalism Versus Federalism: Alternative Visions of European Unity

Cornelia Navari

Of all the ideas represented in the New Europe Movement, it was the doctrines of functionalism and federalism that dominated the process of integration. It was their advocates who brought elites and governments to the Hague and to Strasbourg, and who drafted the Paris and Rome Treaties. It was their vision, sometimes the one and sometimes the other, which established the general guidelines by which governments carried forward the European construction. Indeed, the history of integration is often written in terms of federalists and functional "phases," as each at various times established the framework within which the European construction proceeded.[1]

During the respective phases, the doctrine in dominance did more than set the general architecture of Europe; it also established a realm of opportunism for the doctrine in the wings. During the late 1940s and early 1950s the adherents of the functional programme tried, in the event successfully, to insert their programme for functional organisation onto the agenda of the growing European federal movement; while from the early 1950s, and again in the 1980s, the advocates of federalism would direct their efforts to building federalism onto the emerging functional organisations.

The importance of the two doctrines, and the degree to which each drew from the enthusiasms of the other, has created a myth of historical complimentarity. Luciano Levi has assigned world historical roles to Monnet "in starting the unifying process, Spinelli in seeking to conclude it."[2] But this rather benign view of the relations of functionalism and federalism would distort the historical record. The fact is that the

European experience represented a battle ground between their respective proponents. Each entered that ground with a distinctive vision of Europe's future. Each opposed the other's vision and sought to demonstrate its theoretical and political inadequacy. Each sought to shift the union movement towards its own views and to turn it from adherence to the other. Since Europe went through different doctrinal phases, it is also the case that each respective victory in the European construction was viewed by the other side as a danger for the European prospect. Each tended to view various episodes in the European construction as a victory for their view or for the view of the other side, with appropriate responses in their evaluations of the prospects for European unity as a whole. At the same time, their respective successes and failures reflected on the doctrines of the other, and both successes and failures forced each to confront the other's programme and doctrine. Nor did this involve merely tactics: some of their most basic theoretical innovations were derived from their grappling with the positions of the other.

The Origin of Quarrels

Federalism and functionalism emerged as opposed doctrines in the context of interwar critiques of the League of Nations, whose failure represented the most serious challenge to twentieth century liberal thought. They may be located more precisely in two critical documents: the lectures of Philip Kerr (Lord Lothian) at Williamstown, Massachusetts, published as *The Prevention of War* in 1922; and David Mitrany's *International Sanctions* prepared for James Shotwell's Committee of Inquiry in 1925 to suggest how the United States might become more closely associated with the League's security functions.

Lothian's analysis turned on a distinction between the "mechanical" cause of war—what today we would call the sufficient cause—and its social features or impulses. By the latter he meant factors such as race, religion, nationality, commerce or despotic rivalries. He assigned as sufficient cause the division of mankind into sovereign states, to social impulses he assigned the mere occasions of conflict. Sovereignty, particularly absolute sovereignty, assured that each state was a law unto itself and also assured that each state must rely on itself.[3] Accordingly, good intention or good will, the broad social impulses he detected in the peace movement, could never of themselves produce peace.[4]

Within the context of these causal imputations, the problem with the League was clear: it rested on such "sentiments of good will." People had believed that good thinking or the rational organisation of cooperative impulses was enough to secure orderly conduct among nations. The further problem was that they might go on thinking so. Unless the public was educated in the direction of right thinking, "unless people see clearly what is the ultimate goal and recognize that these methods are just steps towards that goal . . . they send the world to sleep; they make it think that it is dealing with the real causes of war, whereas it is not, so that eventually it finds itself suddenly awakened, as in 1914, to the horrible reality by the shriek of bullet and the roar of the guns."[5]

Mitrany's diagnosis pointed in quite another direction. He maintained that the obstacles to American commitment to the League did not lie in any generalised concern with sovereignty, but in the plural nature of American social attitudes and commitments which led them to wish to disassociate themselves from one or other specific articles of the League, such as its mandatory functions. On this basis, he began to develop an argument concerning the "holistic" ambitions of the League. Mitrany saw the League as embodying, even if this had not yet realised, the idea of single legal order in which all states should participate. This idea, reflected in the idea of a single sanctioning order, was an obstacle to state commitment, because of the diverse and pluralistic nature of social and political orders and the different sorts of interests and commitments those orders produced. Security arrangements, he argued, should be diverse and "facultative."[6]

These diagnoses opposed the "too little" to the "too much." For Mitrany, the League had failed because it tried to compose a multiplicity of states into a large single order which did not respect the diversity of their social and geographical situations, the diversity of the problems they faced or the different levels at which such problems appeared. For Lothian, on the contrary, the chief failure of the League was that it had not been ambitious enough, that it had relied on general good will and rational solutions to social and economic problems without addressing the central problem of political order. They also posed the centralising to the diversifying: for Lothian, powers had to be handed upwards, to a new level of authority; for Mitrany, they had to be dispersed laterally, to a variety of diverse institutional bodies. Behind these lay distinct, and opposed, theories of the political. For Lothian, political impulses were created by political structures—the political was an autonomous sphere which had its own demands and determinants. For Mitrany, the political order was but a reflection of an underlying social and economic order—it was precisely not autonomous and what was required was a correct aggregation of social impulses.[7]

The Battle Joined

The historical evolution of these positions, and the battle between them, began in earnest in the spring of 1939 with the publication in

America of Clarence Streit's *Union Now,* a call for liberal democratic states to unite in order to preserve themselves from fascism, and the launching in Britain of Federal Union, which aimed to establish not a league but a federation of nations, and which had by the middle of 1940 some 225 branches around the country and some 15,000 members. A recent account tells us that between the fall of 1939 and the spring of 1940, articles and letters appeared weekly in the British press analysing the European situation in federal terms.[8] That same year, Mitrany had come from Princeton to serve in the Foreign Office's information section from which position he hoped to influence construction of the post war international order. The growing federalist challenge posed a threat to these hopes, and forced him to define both the precise selection of functional tasks and the institutional shape of functional authority. He also had to deal with the issue of sovereignty, a point never directly confronted in his earlier writings.

According to federalist doctrine, cooperation had to be instituted by "constitution," a point seen as essential by Spinelli. To counter this claim, Mitrany devised the contrary doctrine of allocation by shared need, praising its superiority to the more rigid delimitation by legal ordinance: areas would be identified for common action on the basis of their shared communality and would shift accordingly.[9] It was in this document that the oft-quoted functional "principle" first appeared.[10] He also framed his organisational philosophy in opposition to the constitutional approach: "The functional dimensions as we have seen, determine themselves. In a like manner the function determines its appropriate organs." Not only was there "no obvious need for constitutional division of authority and power, but any except the most general formal rules would embarrass the working of the system."[11]

The argument on sovereignty was more complex, and Mitrany's sensitive handling of it indicated the degree to which the federalist view was persuasive. He treated it in the introduction to the fourth public edition of his tract, arguing that sovereignty could not be "transferred effectively through a formula, only through a function."[12] He maintained that to entrust an international administration with a common task, in effect transferred a "slice of sovereignty from the old authority to the new," and that the accumulation of such partial transfers "brings about a translation of the true seat of authority." But the real innovation was in the concept of "shared" or "pooled" sovereignty, the first use of these terms, and which he devised to get around the accusation that functional arrangements made no real inroads on national sovereignty: "when ten or twenty national authorities, each of which had performed a certain task for itself, can be induced to perform that task jointly, they will to that end quite naturally pool their sovereign authority insofar as the good performance of the task demands it."[13]

In Britain, meanwhile, several important federalist schemes were drafted during the course of 1940, but they were rather undefined as to the areas in which the federation would operate, their institutional recommendations were rudimentary and they tended to confuse social with political cooperation. Above all, they had no strategy by which to accomplish their respective aims. The gauntlet thrown down by Lord Lothian was not in fact taken up in England; it was taken up on the Italian island of Ventotene by two men of the Italian left, Altiero Spinelli and Ernesto Rossi, political prisoners who had both left the Communist Party in the thirties. Spinelli saw himself as a theoretical and political innovator. In his memoirs he records that "No political formation was waiting for me . . . It was up to me to start a new and different movement for a new and different battle from scratch."[14] He had, however, a background that was a "muddled, tortuous and rather incoherent ideological federalism of the Proudhon and Massini type found in France and Italy."[15]

Often called integral federalism and akin to the "federalists" of the English organic school of Hobhouse and Woolf, this school was heavily influenced by organicist theory, from which school Mitrany himself derived. According to this theory, society constituted a whole, with however, separate parts which integrated naturally and organically as society developed; its adherents opposed the monolithic aspects of the centralized "Jacobin" state.[16] Many within the English federalist movement were integralists and "localists," as Peter Wilson notes above, and many were rather sympathetic to functionalist views (rather, perhaps, they did not see any difference). Adherents of this school believed in broad social reform and personalist development, and opposed centralising legal reform entirely. Spinelli called this movement "federalism as an ideology," and it was the movement he had briefly associated himself with when he left the Communist Party in the 1930s. For Spinelli on Ventotene, the new programme was to be above all an analysis of the failure of integral federalism and a correction of its mistakes. This movement, he later recorded, confused the issue between state and society and presented no clear programme of a political nature. It also sought to build on national power and national institutions which, however, it had no theory to transcend. Moreover, its federalism was ancillary to the liberal and socialist agendas which were inspiring it. Much of it was not in fact inspired by the federalist dream at all, but by other objectives. Finally, it placed federalism in an indefinite future, "whereas for me, federalism was an immediate programme."[17]

The programme of Ventotene derived accordingly; it was clear and precise in its objectives, which was "the definitive abolition of the division into sovereign states."[18] Nor were these objectives to be realised in some vague and indefinite future as a natural outcome of social reform or other organic development. According to the authors, the "foundation must be built now for a movement that knows how to mobilize all forces for the birth of the new organism . . ."[19] This was to be a specific political formation whose sole aim was the establishment of a federation. Spinelli's criticism of integral federalism took him to what some would see as the crucial features of postwar federalism: on the one hand, the establishment of a political movement, a movement which would engage in a direct political struggle, not merely a social or spiritual movement; and on the other, a movement with a specified political agenda—the immediate establishment of a federal constitution.

The Federalist Confrontation with Functionalism

In Britain, Mitrany's tract had undergone four reprints and his conception of functionalism became promoted in a series of important speeches and conferences during the course of 1945 and 1946. Functionalism become, in consequence, quite well known, if its theoretical basis remained somewhat obscure. It also penetrated the British European Movement's leadership, providing virtually the "official" formula to describe their objectives: Churchill at the preliminary session at the Hague would employ Mitrany's concept of "merging sovereignty" in specific areas; and Sandys, his son-in-law who actually founded the movement, used the term to comprise what was clearly interest in widened intergovernmentalism with the federal enthusiasm on the continent.

On the continent, the federalist groups establishing themselves tended to mix federal, functional and integralist ideas indiscriminately. The International Committee for a European Customs Union and federalists like Paul van Zeeland wanted genuine delegations of sovereignty in specific and delimited areas of the economy—that is, "genuine" functionalism. On the other hand, the French movement fell under the influence of integralist ideas and this, in turn, influenced the overall profile of the united federalist organisation, the European Union of Federalists, producing a split at its first Congress at Montreux, in August 1947, between its Italian constitutionalist and French integralist wings.[20]

These splits structured the Hague Conference. Its three working parties on political, economic and cultural cooperation, in fact, reflected the three different "federalist" approaches. They also structured its debates. Some integralists tended to join "unionists," as the British intergovernmentalists were called, in supporting partial organisations with specific purposes while others joined them in objecting to any federal construction whatsoever. Functionalism at first tended to imply ambiguously both intergovermentalism and sectoral organisations of shared sovereignty, as well as social front cooperation.[21] More importantly, it also provided the basis for a series of complex (and crosscutting) alliances among the various tendencies. Thus Henri Brugmans, federalist but with strong integral tendencies, found himself in sympathy with the idea of functional organisations and with those "rationalists" like Paul van Zeeland primarily interested in economic unions and the problems of modern economies. On the other hand, the British "unionists"— essentially intergovernmentalists (and centralists) but strongly attracted by Mitrany's functionalist ideas, found themselves supported by integralists generally opposed to the centralised state altogether and also functionalists who wished for a genuine pooling of sovereignty in specific areas.[22]

The developing alliance between functionalism, unionism, and integralism, all under a functionalist banner, together with the anodyne outcome of the Hague conference, alerted Spinelli to the dangers of functionalism for the federal programme; in his memoirs for December of 1948, he records his determination to deal with the functionalist "sofism." The result was a major position paper presented to the third Congress of the MFL at Florence in April 1949, whose aim was to discredit functionalist ideas and demonstrate their dangers for the union movement.

In this attack, Spinelli drew on his early Marxist training and deployed the concepts of false consciousness and ideology as an aspect of retrograde system maintenance. He analysed the relation of functionalism to unionism (and anti-federalism) as relations of ideology to political formation or impulse, presenting functionalism as the official ideology of a unionist tendency which was responding to and reflecting entrenched national sectoral interests, interests which a European federation would disadvantage. Unionism, he declared, was "the last stronghold and refuge of camouflaged European nationalism"; and functionalism was the ideology of "interests linked with the maintenance of national sovereignty."[23] From this time, and for more than a decade to come, functionalism would appear in Spinelli's writings as a nationalist (and especially British) ideology which had to be unmasked.

This argument had implications for federalist strategy. Originally, the European Federalist Movement (MFE/EFM) had aimed at popular organised pressure on the allies to immediately transfer sovereignty to a new body.[24] After the confusions of the Hague, however, this strategy appeared grossly inadequate (besides partially discrediting the integralists). In preparation for the EUF's November conference in Rome, Spinelli, Rossi and Piero Calamandrei, one of the drafters of the Italian

state constitution, had drafted a paper proposing that the coming Strasbourg Assembly should be seen as a form of "constitutive assembly"
which would directly draft the new constitution for Europe, a strategy
formalised in Spinelli's April paper. At Florence, stressing the importance of continuous agitation for federalism against the specious
functionalism-disguising-nationalism, Spinelli urged the movement to
shift from direct pressure on states to pressure for a democratic assembly (in the first instance Strasbourg) which would institute federalism
from below, to bypass entrenched national interests and, above all, British obstruction. In the event, the first meeting of the Strasbourg Assembly in August and September 1949 only saw a repetition of the quarrels.[25]
In consequence, both Spinelli and Henri Frenay, then Chairman of the
EUF, began to agitate in earnest over the winter of 1949 for a properly
constituted constituent assembly, now possibly bypassing the Strasbourg
Assembly, to which was added however a new element, that of a full
federal pact to be concluded immediately between those countries so
willing and which was aimed to isolate the anti-federal and "unionist"
British.[26]

Fearful that the emerging split in the movement would endanger his
evolutionary strategy, Duncan Sandys moved immediately to try to comprise the two sides. He proposed the establishment of an "Ad Hoc Political Authority Committee" to agree a common approach. At its first
meeting in December of 1949, the division between a federalist and
contractual approach and a functional and evolutionary approach first
came clearly into the open and was debated in those terms, with the
functionalist Boothby arguing that the federalists should accept functional organisation while reserving their right to go further. Since, however, Spinelli had identified functionalism as a disguised form of
nationalism, the federalists were unwilling to allow any such thing; and
Spinelli and Frenay continued to press for the immediate conclusion of
a federal pact among those government so willing, splitting the Council if necessary. Under Sandys's influence, they agreed, however, to a
temporary truce. The Council of Europe should remain the principle instrument through which the union of Europe would be achieved, provided, however, that it should increase its influence and extend its
organs.[27]

But the second session did neither, primarily because of the Schuman
Plan, announced in May 1950 between the "Ad Hoc" meeting and the
second session at Strasbourg. On the one hand, the Schuman Plan, and
its fair prospects for success, appeared to vindicate the integralists and
gradualists; and they led the Assembly down the road to proposing
numerous other functional organisations, vitiating its own institutional
development.[28] On the other hand, it gave Spinelli the idea for yet a

new strategy of attack from without, one building on his idea of a constituent assembly, but on quite a different basis.

The new plan was laid out in a report to the EUF's third session at Strasbourg in November of 1950, entitled "The Proposal for a European Assembly to draft a Pact of Federal Union."[29] It centred on a comparison of the Strasbourg Assembly and the modalities of the Schuman Plan. With his usual acuteness, Spinelli noted that the Assembly had no authority to draft a federal pact, that it mixed delegates of movements with delegates of countries, but above all that it was under the tutelage of the Council of Europe. Hence, it was essentially a diplomatic conference, with the consequence that it embedded state interests. The Schuman road was quite different; the French foreign minister had begun with a direct invitation by a state to other states to determine the form and powers of the new community, "but he stipulated that there must be first agreement on the basic issue." In this could be seen the indicative of the way forward: the federalists must ask some countries to take the initiative in concluding a regular treaty in which they would convene a European Assembly. That Assembly would determine which functions should be transferred to a European Political Authority and how they would be governed. That constitutional document would in turn be submitted to national parliaments for approval or rejection.

In this argument, and deriving from his reflections on the Schuman Plan, Spinelli began to developed the two-step strategy: a constituent assembly along the American model in which states began the process and yet could be bypassed when it came to agreeing the outcome. In this plan, the federalists must not try to take everyone with them, but work with governments with federalist inclinations and take the issue directly to "the people" in the form of parliaments where "states as such are not represented" and where members are "free to vote according to conscience." This model, which sought to build a federal nucleus from the intergovernmental initiatives of parliamentary states (and in which can be viewed the germs of the Maastricht procedure), would inform Spinelli's strategy over the next two years and beyond.[30]

Functionalists and Federalism

While federalists were learning from functionalists, functionalism itself was evolving. During the late 1940s, the functionalist with the foremost experience in functional organisation was Jean Monnet who had served on the joint war boards during both world wars, from which Mitrany had drawn his model of functional organisation.[31] Convinced of the value of functional organisation, Monnet had declined to become involved in the union movement, and because of its dominance by integralists and federalists, both of whose programmes he rejected.[32] Equally, however, he was impressed by the federal enthusiasm and wished to harness it to practical institutionalised sectoral cooperation. The problem was how to link, conceptually, small scale particular organisation to the federal vision.[33] His far-reaching innovation, and the basic idea behind the Schuman Plan, was that Europe could be built by experiments. The functional experiment would demonstrate to the peoples of Europe and of course to their elites (Monnet's elitism is notorious) that problems, apparently intractable, could be solved by a simple expedient of concrete cooperation of a technical and administrative nature. This would then have a demonstration effect, inducing further experiments.

Less than five months after the drafting of Schuman's speech, Monnet would carry the strategy forward into the area of defense. In the autumn of 1950, when the French defense minister was seeking a formula by which to forestall or limit German rearmament, Monnet and his team quickly drew up a scheme, which formed the basic elements of the Pleven Plan, for an integrated force whose organisation they modelled closely on the emerging coal and steel community; that is, a Council which would instruct a High Authority which would "command" an integrated army.[34] It was Monnet's role to link functionalism to a federal future. Schuman's Declaration on Europe, drafted by Monnet, declared that Europe "will be built by concrete achievement which first creates de facto solidarity." The European Coal and Steel Community was to be understood as the first step in a broader process. In his memoirs, he records that "I was sure that the lessons we were learning day after day from our difficulties and our success would spread far beyond the circle of the ECSC which itself was growing ever wider."[35]

This federalisation of functionalism would eventually lose Monnet Mitrany's support; a firm advocate of the Coal and Steel pool at its inception, he would in the late fifties dissociate himself from its founder's wider enthusiasms. Nor did it endear all the federalists to Monnet. For the constitutional federalists who had remained faithful to Strasbourg, the Council represented the natural home of the European construction. Separate efforts threatened that locus; they also threatened the very prospect of a single community. Moreover, Monnet was never a federalist in the constitutional sense implied by Spinelli and the federalist movement. He had no great regard for a division of powers and was known to be hostile to the Assembly with which the European Coal Steel Community (ECSC) had been saddled, preferring to deal directly with producer and consumer associations.[36] Avoiding this meant associating the Council of Europe with the ECSC as closely as possible, perhaps even taking it over. Robertson is cautious on this period of the

Council's history, but he is clear enough. It was a general consensus that the emerging organisations should be linked, but Strasbourg federalists saw that link as one of necessary subordination. Resolutions from this wing at the 1950 session pointed to the necessity for the "political control" of sector organisations, and called upon member states to maintain the Council of Europe as "the organisation best qualified to supply the general framework." Recommendation 6 called for the ECSC's assembly to be to be chosen among members of the Strasbourg Assembly.[37]

These ambitions were to grow when, in March 1952, Eden put forward what became known as "the Eden Plan," a proposal to the other council members that the Council of Europe take over the emerging ECSC, remodelling itself so as to "serve as the institutions of the European Coal and Steel Community, the European Defence Community and any future organisations of the same structure and membership."[38] The proposal was greeted with enthusiasm by the Assembly which resolved on immediate concrete implementation in the form of shared assemblies, secretariats, ministers and even "high authority."[39]

The independence of the coal-steel pool was vital to Monnet's strategy of achieving "de facto solidarity." The whole point of the new community was that it should be shielded from "benevolent sentiments" and federalising strategies. He moved immediately to block the Assembly's efforts, calling upon the secretaries general of the six national parliaments to organise the first meeting of the new assembly and demanded that the Council of Ministers clarify the issue, which in the event endorsed separate organisations.[40]

While the Strasbourg federalists were trying to secure federalism via the Council, Spinelli had seized upon Pleven's announcement as an unrivalled opportunity for the deployment of his new strategy. Over the winter and spring of 1950 and 1951, in a movement designed to outflank the Assembly as well as Monnet, and which would achieve considerably more success, he initiated an astonishing circuit of meetings and exhortations, directed first at the French People's Assembly, a federalist group of constitutional persuasions, then at the UEF, whose conference at Lugano in April 1951 endorsed what were essentially Spinelli's guidelines for the drafting of a federal constitution. He thereupon carried both endorsement and the guidelines to the Italian Chamber of Deputies and the Senate, gaining the support of their members. By the following October, the latter were calling upon the Italian government to promote the creation of a European political authority through a European constitutive assembly; the People's Assembly had approved a draft treaty which the UEF was promoting; and de Gasperi, largely under Spinelli's influence, had agreed to support the creation of a genuine political authority in the treaty negotiations for a defence community.[41]

The crucial issue was the role of the constituent assembly, the pivot of the Spinelli strategy. De Gasperi prevailed upon Spinelli not to press for the convocation of a special assembly to draft the "future constitution of Europe" but to be satisfied with the involvement of the ECSC Assembly. He and Schuman worked out a modified proposal and, at the intergovernmental conference in April 1952, prevailed upon Adenauer and the other state leaders to agree. An article, Article 38, was added to the draft treaty calling upon the Common Assembly to study the constitution of a permanent Assembly, elected on a democratic basis, "so conceived as to constitute one of the elements of a subsequent federal or confederal structure."

Neither side was to be satisfied with the formula. According to Spinelli, Article 38 created ambiguity as to who exactly was responsible for drafting Europe's constitution and who was to act as the spur forward. Monnet, for his part, was even more doubtful, particularly when he saw the eventual result, an odd combination of coordinated national foreign policies with a bicameral federal structure.[42] His defence of his own inactivity, for which he was reproached, was the "risk of compromising the growth of the ECSC . . . the success of the ECSC was my first duty, and my only duty if a choice had to be made."[43]

Given such doubts, it might be supposed that Monnet would have welcomed the French failure to ratify the EDC treaty. In fact, he regarded the death of the European Defence Community, and the proto-federal Europe structured around it, as a near-disaster. It "put the clock back four years" and created a coalition between "opponents of the very principle of integration and advocates of a neutrality who found it hard to evolve a positive policy." Above all, it threatened to return France to "political resistance," as Monnet termed it: the immobilism which French governments had displayed during 1948-1949, and which Monnet considered some of France's darkest days.[44] At the same time, it confirmed his doubts about the frontal approach; in November following the failure to ratify, he announced his intention of resigning his post with the High Authority, freeing him to lead a direct battle against both popular opposition and French policy stagnation. Monnet's aim in convening the Action Committee was to restart Europe at once, moving sideways into the areas of transport and, especially, atomic energy. The scheme was to mobilise elite endorsement in areas central to French governmental concern, and absorb those areas into the competences of the Coal and Steel Community. Governments would simply be asked to persuade their Parliaments to extend the range of the High Authority's mandate.[45]

Barely eight months after Monnet's resignation, however, Beyen had put forward his proposal for a complete common market, the six had agreed to meet at Messina and negotiations for a more general Economic Union were in the process of being undertaken, all of which threatened to strand Monnet's efforts. Such evidence of the lack of obstacles to further progress deprived the Action Committee of its rationale; it also called into question the necessity, and wisdom, of his resignation from the High Authority. Above all, however, was the fact that the negotiations on the Euratom and the Common Market were taking a different shape than he had hoped: they were being established as autonomous organisations, separate from the Coal and Steel Community. The problem was that a plethora of "functional" organisations might be founded with no connection between them. Monnet began to fear that disparate functional experiments would proceed without producing a single *point d'appui*, a single European centre or a single community. He attempted to withdraw his resignation, which was not taken up.[46] Thereafter, he redirected the work of the Action Committee: its first task would now be to ensure that the new treaties did not become prey to the same confusions and alliances from which the EDC treaty had suffered; that task completed, it would then undertake a campaign of pressure for a union of the various European executives, a further federalisation of functionalism.[47]

For the mainstream federal continental movement, the Beyen initiative and the conferences as Messina and Rome were no less perplexing developments. On the one hand, Europe had taken a great leap forward to a much wider union than the Coal and Steel Community. On the other hand, Europe was even further from a federation; in the Rome Treaty establishing the EEC and Euratom, the Council of Ministers had been given the main legislative initiative, and subsequent analyses showed it to be, at best, a confederation. It was, moreover, upside down from the federal perspective, being largely concerned with the realm of the economic and leaving political matters largely untouched. The 1958 conference's final reports noted the limitation to the economic union (between 1958 and 1960, the EUF and other federalist circles would constantly refer to the EEC as "an economic union"), and pressed for full political union. Their views were expressed most fully in the important "22 Theses," agreed by the 1961 conference.[48] More pertinent, however, was the question of how to move from the one to the other.

At the time, leadership of the EUF was in the hands of Henri Brugmans. Brugmans was by instinct an integral federalist, a point well demonstrated by his efforts to establish a College of Europe, in which he served as its first rector; he liked to term the College a "European microcosm." He favoured evolutionary integration, that is building on the emergent functional structures which implied also "using the existing national power structure."[49] But following the failure of the EDC, Spinelli had lost faith with national power structures altogether and had begun to support a truly revolutionary approach of convening direct plebiscitory assemblies which would demonstrate federal support from below. At the Luxembourg conference of the UEF in 1956, a fundamental dissension had become apparent between the advocates of evolutionary integration and those who favoured the pursuit of Spinelli's strategy of a direct plebiscitory initiative or "nuovo corso," a confrontation from which the Spinellists had temporarily emerged victorious. With a Common Market now in evidence, however, the battle was rejoined with increased intensity.[50] For the next three years, arguments between the two approaches would dominate what was also a dwindling membership.

Not satisfied with what was to be, in any event, an incomplete victory, the Italian federalists struck out on their own. From 1958, there began to develop an outright campaign against the institutions of the EEC, led by a second generation of Italian federalists inspired by Spinelli. For almost two decades, Italian federalist writing would see as its historic task the demonstration of the limitations of "Monnet's Europe."

From Spinelli, the Beyen proposals and the Messina agreement grew the vitriolic "The Mockery of the Common Market."[51] They also produced what the author felt had to be a basic statement of political values in endorsing a continuation of federalist faith. In *Pourquoi je suis europeen* (*Why I am European*), Spinelli presented the Europeanist faith as a political orientation on its own, one which absorbed liberalism and socialism and "surpassed" them, and whose aims could not, accordingly, be gained though the limited instrumentalities of the Rome Treaty.[52] Thus began that evolution in Italian federalist thinking which later commentators were to term, somewhat confusingly given Spinelli's terminological preferences, "federalism as ideology."[53] Its central concept emerged as a crisis of the nation state, a concept familiar from Spinelli's earlier works but in which the nation state was now presented not merely as an obstacle to other social goods but whose federalist reform in itself constituted a social programme.

Developments in Functionalist Theory

The early success of the Commission in meeting the targets laid down in the Rome Treaty establishing the EEC, coincided with a remarkable spate of development in functionalist theory.[54] Two works in particular were to have enormous influence in a growing body of functionalist writing: *The Uniting of Europe* by Ernst Haas, which appeared in 1958, and Leon Lindberg's *The Political Dynamics of European Integration*, published in 1963.[55] Drawing upon the insights of Mitrany, and incorporating into functional theory the work of the American political scientist, Karl Deutsch, Haas and Lindberg made the European experiment the subject of a scientific predictive theory which purported not merely to recommend or to provide a strategy for, but also to explain, the uniting of Europe. This combination of practical success and scientific theory gave European integration the appearance of ineluctability. It also gave functionalism the role of preeminent theory, casting the divided federalists into the shade.

Ernst Haas shared Deutsch's "sociological" approach: he viewed the ECSC as a testing ground for Deutschian ideas of growing international linkages, emerging international interest formation and (resultant) communal development. Lindberg, a student of Haas', carried the investigation forward into the first Hallstein Commission, to refine the theory. Both theorists worked closely with the emergent European organisations in question, evolving their ideas through observation of the work of the various "supranational" European bodies.

Haas' work produced several important theoretical innovations. The first was "consensus formation." According to Haas, a natural attraction towards problem solving characterised the lower order elites upon which, in the view of Deutsch's theory, the integration movement depended. Common problem-solving involved elites in a mutual process of consultations, out of which "transnational" consensus tended to develop, a thesis he developed in a later study of the Council of Europe. The second innovation of *The Uniting of Europe* was the important concept of "spillover," the theory of natural linkages of issue areas such that integration in one area would set up pressure for integration in allied areas.

Lindberg's work added to this social and technological determinism a political dynamic. His thesis proposed a naturally developing self-perception among the European bureaucrats who, in seeing themselves as problem solvers, would naturally seek to spread their views to the sub-national elites and to convert them. As they found successful solutions to the problems with which those elites were concerned, they would simultaneously invoke their confidence, inspiring in his language a gradual "transfer of loyalties" from the national to the supranational bureaucrats.

The status of the concepts and processes identified by the neofunctionalists was that of self-standing autonomous and objective entities. Integration below the level of the nation state, spillover, even transfer of loyalties, were all presented as independent of the wills of the actors. But this was scarcely the case. Monnet had deliberately involved groups below the level of the state in the work of the ECSC, a strategy he had derived from his experience with the joint war boards which had worked directly with producers and consumers. He was, moreover, one of the drafters of the Paris Treaty establishing the ECSC, and the role of producer and consumer associations was given deliberate prominence in the Treaty at his behest. Hallstein, who had been Monnet's deputy, had consciously carried forward the practice into the Common Market, adding the proviso that he would not deal with sector organisations unless they were "euro-organised." "Engrenage," or the involvement of local civil servants in the Commission's work was also a deliberate Hallstein strategy, as was "resolution at the higher level."

This confluence of theory and practice, of academics and bureaucrats, presents a spectacle of what Max Weber had considered the paradigmatic role of the relationship between theory and practice, the notion of ideal typification of practical experience. The academicians "typified" (in Max Weber's sense) the work of the Brussels bureaucracy; they abstracted it and gave it an ideal form. This work, in turn, added to the bureaucrats' self-consciousness; it provided the Commission with what was in effect a rationalised political strategy for moving the Community forward.[56] The Brussels bureaucrats actually read Haas and Lindberg, with predictable consequences. Harmonisation would probably have never become the shibboleth it did during the first Hallstein Commission but for the notion, put forward by Haas, that common policies were the mark of an emerging community.

If functionalists and bureaucrats were engaged in an essentially reflexive process of thought-informing-action, this implies also a theoretical corollary. None of the claims of the functionalists represented a true positivist theory, in the sense of identifying a set of determinants apart from the understanding of the participants themselves. On the contrary, the processes the functionalists identified were self-conscious political strategies, and became more so as they typified them. Nor were the features they identified as essential to integration true "scientific determinants." They were nothing more than the features displayed by the advanced countries of Western Europe.

Nonetheless, the fact that the Community went from strength to strength in its first five years, and along lines suggested by the neo functionalists, gave an enormous prestige to the theory. Regional integration theory appeared to be one of the first successes of American political science. It also established functionalism as the model of the successful international organisation.[57]

Neofunctionalism Under Attack

Critiques of neofunctionalism followed soon on its heels. At the Stichting Grotius Semarium in 1961, Mitrany countered Haas' claim for the functional approach with the first version of his oft-reprinted *Federalism Versus Functionalism*, in which he distinguished true functionalism from the specious federal functionalism of the neo-functionalists.[58] He maintained that the federal goals of the neofunctionalists were taking them back into the federalist trap of trying to devise a single legal order for a diversity of social entities and problems, and that their hopes were bound, accordingly, to be disappointed. He also attacked the notion of spillover, maintaining that system change could not come from a simple enhancement of a functional body, which required in fact constitutional change, a position that took him uncommonly close to the federalist viewpoint. That same year, Spinelli produced *Europa Non Cade dal Cielo* (Europe will not fall from the sky), an historical account of the integration process which was intended to demonstrate that functional organisations did not displace national consciousness.

These attacks were generally launched by academics and theoreticians and aimed at other academics and theoreticians, and they remained therefore at a certain theoretical level. The Community's success also made them appear like cavelling. More telling, because it reflected on the political reality of the integration process itself, was the direct political attack mounted by President de Gaulle from the beginning of 1963 on the supranational elements of the Community institutions.

Gaullism challenged functional theory on several grounds. One problem was the "externality" of the French president's actions; de Gaulle had deliberately acted outside the institutional framework to adjourn negotiations on British entry. Neofunctionalist literature had treated the process of European integration as proceeding within a relatively closed and self-determining political system of European and indeed Community dimensions; de Gaulle's veto, as well as the responses to it, indicated that "Europe" was itself set within a wider political system.[59] The second problem was the freedom with which de Gaulle had acted. Neofunctionalist, as well as functionalist, theory had predicted a narrowing compass to the action of the high political actors in the system, but de Gaulle had acted with an apparent freedom greater than that which the major powers had enjoyed within the much looser framework of the League. This autonomy presented enormous problems of explanation within the terms of the theory. The third problem was the absence of any great popular protest against French action. That elites were distressed by it was obvious, but the "masses" seemed to feel little effect; in particular there was no rush to aid the Commission in its difficulties. This boded ill for a theory which declared the ascendancy of "low politics"; and in which bread and butter issues were supposed to induce a transfer of popular loyalties to Community institutions.

One of the first effects was to create interest in alternative analysis of the Community. The realist, Stanley Hoffmann, in a much quoted article which declared the nation state "obsolete but obstinate" pointed to the wide range of powers which the modern state held, and focused attention on the degree to which the European experience had in fact increased state capacity.[60] In 1966, Spinelli produced *The Eurocrats*, pointing out that the functionalist conception was essentially an updated version of a Europe of "offices"; these were administrations which worked well in periods of consensus among member states "when common choices were already made" but which had no base from which to fend off political storms or defend political choices.[61]

Perhaps the most serious theoretical innovations came from within the ranks of the neofunctionalists themselves. From 1966 they began to reconsider their own positions, with the result that much of the neofunctionalist corpus was watered down. Indeed, in the case of Haas, it would amount to virtual theoretical suicide.

The Internal Decline of Neofunctionalism

In 1966, Lindberg began to identify integration itself as a "source of strain" on the integration process. In an article of that title, Lindberg posited that the integration process was part of the political world of integration; and that it, itself, set up contrary tendencies from which de Gaulle had benefited, giving one explanation for his "autonomy."[62] Lindberg continued to hold by his forward dynamism, however, maintaining that de Gaulle had not destroyed the Community because he could not and that the internal links which bound states into integration must hold up.[63] In demonstration of this thesis, he and Stuart Scheingold began to prepare a more thorough-going piece which would demonstrate how such contrary tendencies emerged and how they were incorporated into "the system," a work which would appear in 1970 as *Europe's Would-be Polity*.[64]

In the meantime, the Community had definitely slowed down and the earlier predictions of "no going back" appeared over-optimistic. This was reflected in *Europe's Would-be Polity* whose authors cast doubt on the Commission's future capacity for what Lindberg had termed "forward linkage." They questioned the ability of the Commission to push integration forward through the deliberate linking of issue areas, noting that these had proved inadequate to "system transformation," the transformation from an economic to a political community, and which had been presented as an almost automatic progression in *The Political*

Dynamics.[65] The authors also introduced the concept of "permissive consensus," the first systematic incorporation into functionalist theory of what the federalist had always argued was vital—the importance of building Europe from below, and it introduced into functionalist thinking a popular, and federalist, element previously missing in functionalist ideas. That their predictive failures were also leading them to reconsider federalism's claims was further evinced by a new concern with lack of representation within the institutional bodies; indeed, it was in *Europe's Would-be Polity* that the two theorists began to entertain the desirability of direct elections to the European Parliament. The third new element was attention to the role that crisis played in the integration process, and the pursuit of outright political goals, elements which created a more politicised picture of the integration process than earlier works had drawn.

In this work, automaticity was questioned and a new scenario of the Community's future was envisaged. In this scenario, as more areas entered into the integrative process, far from this carrying Europe forward, strains would be encountered, offsetting the forward movement and bringing Europe into an equilibrium. This led them to conclude that "We see very little prospect of a federal or near-federal European political union."[66] The message was clear, simple problem solving did not, in itself, bring a real union closer. Instead, it was producing a *sui generis* type of political body which they described as a "curiously ambiguous pluralistic system," a body which apparently defied classification.[67]

This denial to the Community of the kind of political future implied by the federalists was damaging to the theory's ideological presence. Functionalism had been attractive, after all, not just because it solved the international problems of a set of advanced industrial states, by whatever *sui generis* means possible, but because it offered a clear and comprehensive road to a comprehensible and desirable end. Laudable as Lindberg's efforts were to be "honest" about the future prospects for the Community, his description of the integration process as possibly leading nowhere made integration theory much less attractive to those who desired such an end.

A second consequence derived from the large number of variables which began to appear in the work. Lindberg and Scheingold began to introduce popular consensus, differential interest group activism, external situations, varying elite goals, different national political structures, availability of leadership, which Lindberg attempted to systematise two years later. But the result which was little more than a list of things the analyst must take into account, a feature which did not endear it to political scientists.[68]

Most serious of all, however, was the 1975 piece by the "father of integration theory," Ernst Haas, on "The Obsolesence of Regional Integration Theory."[69] Here, Haas attacked the central proposition of integration theory—its, in his own words "anchor"—the notion of incrementalism. Haas argued that this notion only made sense if one assumed constancy of actor motives but that it could not apply when "the actors decide to alter the objectives." He also maintained that it was quite possible for them to do so and that such a change "may herald a new commitment to dramatic institutional change" or the reversal of the process. But incrementalism could not itself explain such choices. The argument saw both federalism and incrementalism as political strategies, not reflections of objective determinants, and demolished functionalism's remaining pretensions to scientific predictor. In 1992, a panel on integration theory at the inaugural meeting of the European International Studies Association at Heidelberg would be told that there had been no real development of functionalist theory since its publication.[70]

Federalism Re-emergent

In the functionalist scheme, there were essentially two criteria for testing the validity of the theory's dynamic elements. One was the growing inclusiveness of the Community itself and the breadth of its concerns. The second was the growing power and scope of the Commission. Hence it was a serious matter for functionalists if there were a number of executives or only one; equally serious was the question of the Commission's relative capacity and independence. The weakening of the Commission, accordingly, reflected badly on functional theory. For the federalists, on the other hand, this weakening had the benefit of proving their viewpoint—that a Community could only be built on a political will and had to represent it. Equally, however, the Commission's weakening offered a challenge. After the veto, federalists had to confront the question, hitherto left rather vague, of the precise locus of that political will.

In the early days, the federalists saw the European will as vested largely in, and expressing itself through, a popular movement. Even after the establishment of the various European assemblies, the populist idea continued; the refusal of the Spinellists to countenance the idea that either Strasbourg or Brussels could serve as the political frameworks for the new Europe, along with the rejection by the gradualists of the constituent assembly strategy tended between them to dislocate the idea that the extant assemblies could or should serve as that locus. Even during the construction of the European Political Assembly, the Assembly had been considered, briefly, only as a present incarnation of a popular will, a specific locus of its voice at that moment, not a body with general representative capacity; hence, the term Ad Hoc Assembly. Of course, federalists in general tended to be for the widening of Assembly powers, but only as part of a general federal programme. After the veto and the boycott, however, there began to emerge a quite different attitude on the part of the federalists, and not merely to the Parliament but to the Community institutions as a whole.

Spinelli's shift towards the institutional framework of the Community can be detected as early as 1963, when, following de Gaulle's veto, he laid out a series of recommendations for the Community's reform, at sufficient length and with sufficient care to evince that he saw its endangerment as no insignificant matter.[71] More significantly, in *The Eurocrats*, he was brought to admit that "the Europe of Offices is, with all its limitations, the only European connective tissue presently existing," an admission which must have cost him dearly.[72] The actual turn came however only in late 1969, with an invitation to join the Commission.

Affecting Spinelli's choice to join a body he had so long scorned was the collapse of the "new course," which he had pretty much abandoned in 1961. (When he abandoned hope altogether for a movement from below is unclear, but that he had done so by the time of drafting *The Eurocrats* is clear enough: he could not otherwise have described the EEC as Europe's "only connective tissue.") It is also clear from his memoirs that he was tired of being a critic on the outside.[73] More pertinent, however, was the prospect of the Community's widening and its advance to, in his words, "a full-blooded economic union," agreed at the Hague Summit in October 1969.

Spinelli's road to Canossa was *The European Adventure*. Hastily prepared over the summer of 1972 to lay out his strategy for European reconstruction from the office of Commissioner, its first chapter, presented in the guise of an analysis, is also an apologia. In it, Spinelli reconstructed the history of Europe as a movement between new and old tendencies. Governments required to be innovators when new problems that could not be solved within national frameworks confronted them, leading them to establish centres of common action which in turn "corroded and weakened national resistance." Governments might then fall back to old ways, reflecting national resistance, but the centres for common action had nonetheless been created. The Commission had proved the most effective of such common centres. It had survived Gaullism and "may be considered today as the original nucleus to be reinforced."[74]

The stress on the "nuclear role" of the Commission, the references to problems outreaching national frontiers and the declared end of common problem solving all pulled Spinelli uncommonly close to the functionalism which the functionalists were rapidly abandoning. His analysis also, and more importantly, accepted gradualism, the central element of the functionalist theory and the feature which the constitutional federalists had hitherto most consistently and strenuously opposed. Spinelli's new commitment to gradualism was always to have in sight an enhancement of the Community's federal features, but it was gradualism nonetheless. If the functionalists were losing faith in a forward-developing institutional incrementalism, the pre-eminent federalist had discovered it, in part through coming to terms with Monnet's Europe.

Suffice it to say that Spinelli's functionalist interlude proved a brief one. Fighting for his institutional reforms from within, he saw them fall prey to conservative tendencies within the Commission and to governmental caution. Neither the Tindemans report on European Union nor the Genscher-Colombo Declaration appeared to bring any of his agenda any closer, and he abandoned the effort, leaving the Commission to stand as a member of the European Parliament in 1979. Once in the Parliament, his imagination soared again, as seen in Chapter 6, and he began the campaign for the Union Treaty, constituting the European Parliament as his constituent assembly. Spinelli, at least, had finally determined the locus of the elusive European political will.

The final phase of emergent federalism concerns the conversion of the Commission to the idea of the Union Treaty and its acceptance by President Mitterrand who initiated the Single Market strategy within the framework of its institutional recommendations. Between 1986 and 1992, policy advances in creating the single market, in determining common immigration policies, in constituting a single monetary union would all fall within an expanded institutional framework which, if it did not absorb all of the provisions of the Spinelli Union treaty, nonetheless made a striking advance towards a federal future.

The Strains of Federal Europe

The association of advances in integration with a federal future was to have unhappy consequences for the coalitions which had supported European integration. It split the Conservative party in Britain, which had been its political party of Europe, and laid the foundation in France for a union of the far right and the left, both opposed to various aspects of the Maastricht Treaty. In Denmark, it dynamised concerns for loss of national identity. Moreover, those federalists who insisted that a monetary Europe must, at last, be a federal Europe found themselves confronted by those would prefer to reject a monetary union rather than lose political sovereignty. That is, the attachment of the term "federalism" to borders, monetary unions, drug policing and the like, politicised such issues and forced those who supported coordination in all these areas to ask whether a federal union was what they had in mind, or whether it had been, rather, better management of the internationalised problems of the contemporary nation state. In the process, governments would be driven to defending in national interest terms provisions that federalists insisted were the first steps to a federal future, with understandable confusions. In the course of such defenses, Europe's future would be painted in increasingly confederal terms, as governments sought to explain how desirable areas of coordination could be comprised with retention of state sovereignty.

Of course, constitutional federalists had always argued that the kinds of coordination needed by the modern political community demanded federation. Within the frame of this argument, Maastricht might therefore be seen as the moment of choice. This very crystallisation involved risks, however. It may be that the federalists were right and that a choice had to be made, but they had posed this argument at a time when popular sentiment for a form of federation was widespread. By the end of the 1980s, a new generation had emerged which had not witnessed the failure of the League nor confronted the prospect of war. The consequence would be, ironically, to promote widespread uncertainty about the proper goals of European union, and a lowering of sights.

Seen from this point of view, the victory of federalism over functionalism may prove to be of a phyrric sort. The ideological strength of functionalism was that it allowed a wonderful variety of institutional experiments without having to invoke a definitive decision on the question of Europe's future. It also evoked a potential federal future for those who wished to dream of one. When functionalism failed, it left only confederation as the alternative vision of Europe's future. And between federation at a time of recession and inflation, with its requirements for discipline and national sacrifice in crucial areas of national concern, and confederation with its links to heroic past struggles, national traditions and the promise of the protection of national interests, it is scarcely a subject of wonder that confederation has begun to evoke some sympathetic responses.

Notes

1. In such schemas, the early stage is generally denoted the federalist phase and the period from 1955-1965, the functionalist phase; Paul Taylor has nomi-

nated the 1970s Europe's "confederal phase"; Paul Taylor, "The Politics of the European Communities, The Confederal Phase" in *World Politics*, vol. 27, 1974-75. John Pinder has coined the term "neofederalism" to mark federalism's reemergence in the 1980s; John Pinder, "European Community and Nation State: a Case for Neo-Federalism" in *International Affairs*, vol. 62, no. 1, 1986, pp. 41-54.

2. L. Levi, *Altiero Spinelli and Federalism in Europe and the World* (Milan: Angeli, 1990), p. 12.

3. P. Kerr and L. Curtis, *The Prevention of War* (New Haven: Yale University, 1932), pp. 25-6. See also Andrea Bosco, "National Sovereignty and Peace, Lord Lothian's Federal Thought" in J. Turner, ed., *The Larger Idea* (London: The Historian's Press, 1988) pp. 108-23.

4. It was a point he would continually stress: his famous 1935 Burge Lecture "Pacifism is not Enough" was primarily intended to demonstrate that peace was not a mere outcome of social cooperation; see also his speech to the Herald Tribune Forum in 1939, "peace will not be achieved by sentiment or emotion, by mere negation, or by mere horror of warn"; *The American Speeches of Lord Lothian* (Oxford University: Oxford, 1941) p. 20.

5. P. Kerr and L. Curtis, *The Prevention of War*, pp. 5-6.

6. D. Mitrany, *The Problem of International Sanctions* (Oxford University: Oxford, 1925), pp. 16, 26 and 40; Mitrany's basic principle was "to seek the probability of the action itself and not of its effect," Ibid. pp. 40-1.

7. Mitrany criticised the Briand Plan precisely for its federalist and territorial conception, relating it to "a closed geographical state" and the "same brand of view as that which sees national security in self-sufficing armies and navies, rather than in international cooperation for the avoidance of problems"; that is, federalist enthusiasts had not surpassed the limitations of the nation-state, "they merely wish to stretch the conception"; D. Mitrany, "Pan-Europa - A Hope or a Danger" in *The Political Quarterly*, no. 1, 1930, pp. 460, 463.

8. A. Bosco, *Federal Union* (London: Lothian Foundation Press, 1992), pp. 84-132. There were also five major publications, all published during 1940, proposing federal unions: William Beveridge's *Peace by Federation*, W. Curry's *The Case for Federal Union*, I. Jennings' *A Federation for Western Europe* and R. W. G. MacKay's two works, *Federal Europe* and *Peace Aims and the New Order*.

9. "But as the line of separation is always shifting, under the pressure of fresh social needs and demands, it (the functional task) must be let free to move with them, and cannot be fixed through any constitutional redrafting"; "A War-Time Submission" (1941) reproduced in D. Mitrany, *The Functional Theory of Politics* (London: Martin Robertson, 1975), p. 115.

10. "The essential principle is that activities would be selected specifically and organised separately, each according to its nature, to the conditions under which it has to operate, and to the needs of the moment." Ibid., p. 116.

11. "The function, one might say, determines the political instrument suitable for its proper activity, and by the same means provides for its reform at every stage." Ibid. p. 118.

12. D. Mitrany, *A Working Peace System: An Argument for the Functional Development of International Organisation* London, National Peace Council, Pamphlet no. 40, 1946.

13. Ibid., pp. 128, 129.

14. A. Spinelli, *Come ho tentato di diventare saggio. Io Ulisse* (Bologna: Il Mulino, 1984), p. 343.

15. Ibid., p. 309; see also A. Spinelli "Pourquoi je suis europeen" *Preuves*, no. 81, 1957, p. 37.

16. A. Hick "The European Union of Federalists" in Walter Lipgens and Wilfred Loth eds., *Documents on the History of European Integration* (Berlin and New York: de Guyter, 1990, 4 Vols.), hereafter referred to as Lipgens, *Documents*, vol. IV, pp. 8-13.

17. "Storia e Prospettiva del MFE" in A. Spinelli ed. *L'europa nel mondo* (s.l., 1953), pp. 165-70; see also A. Spinelli, "Pourquoi je suis europeen."

18. A. Spinelli and E. Rossi *The Ventotene Manifesto* (Pavia: 1989), p. 35; see also Lipgens, Documents, vol. I no. 148.

19. Ibid.

20. Spinelli records that: "The Italian movement was anti-ideological, the French one was profoundly ideological. The Italian movement was fixed on creating European institutions with the view to developing a new European political framework which would profoundly revolutionize the whole of national and political life. The French movement regarded European institutions as being a simple element of coordination, incapable in itself of providing change, and for this reason supported a multiform programme of action which concern all the parts of existing society." Quoted in A. Hick "The European Union of Federalists," p. 11; see also A. Spinelli "Storia e Prospettiva del MFEH," pp. 156-60.

21. A characteristic to be repeated at the first meeting of the Council of Europe Assembly at Strasbourg; see A. Zurcher *The Struggle to Unite Europe* (Westport: Greenwood, 1975 [1958]), pp. 50-1. For a contemporary account of the confusions see C. C. Walton "The Fate of NeoFederalism in Western Europe" in *Western Political Quarterly*, vol. 5, no. 33, 1952, pp. 366-90.

22. Hague Conference: Political Debates 1-9 May 1948 in Lipgens, *Documents*, vol. IV, no. 75., pp. 340-41.

23. Lipgens, *Documents*, vol. III, pp. 237, 240.

24. In a 1943 paper on strategy, Ernesto Rossi had contrasted the integralist ideal of a gradual and "spontaneous emergence of federalism with the immediate transfer of powers by governmental agency," arguing that "in the latter case we must do all we can to help it on, encouraging intervention and supporting to the maximum extent the ruling class in carrying out the federal programme," in E. Rossi "Federalist Tendencies," L'Unita Europea, no. 2, August 1943, reproduced in Lipgens, *Documents*, vol. I, no. 158, pp. 510-11.

25. See H. Lange, "European Union: False Hopes and Realities," *Foreign Affairs*, vol. 28, no. 3, 1950.

26. See the Motion Adopted at the Third Conference of the EUF, Paris. 19. November 1950; Lipgens, *Documents*, vol. IV, no. 30, p. 98.

27. Minutes of the meeting of the Ad Hoc Committee held in Paris on 16 December 1949; Lipgens, *Documents*, vol. IV, no. 100, pp. 420-3.

28. A. H. Robertson concludes that "its sights had been lowered, by comparison with the first enthusiasm of 1949"; A. H. Robertson, *The Council of Europe* (London: Stevens and Son, 1956), pp. 90-1.

29. Lipgens, *Documents*, vol. IV, no. 29, pp. 95-7.

30. The strategy was first presented to the public in A. Spinelli, *Dagli Stati Sovrani agli Stati Uniti d'Europa* (Florence: La Nuova Italia, 1950), and further articulated and defended in "Il modello constituzionale americano e i tentativo di unita europea" in L. Bolis ed., *La Nascita degli Stati Unit1 d'America* (Milan: 1957).

31. See Mitrany's memoir in *The Functional Theory of Politics* (London: Martin Roberston, 1975), pp. 17-8.

32. He referred to integralism as "the doctrine of concerted good will and to federalism as "the frontal approach"; *Jean Monnet, Memoirs* (London: Collins, 1978), pp. 273-4.

33. Ibid. pp. 273-4.

34. Indeed, it would appear from Monnet's memoirs that he did not envisage a separate organisation; he notes that his team "managed to work out how to do so on the same model as our existing Plan, within the same institutional framework . . ."; Ibid. p. 394.

35. Ibid. p. 393.

36. "It was an open secret that Jean Monnet . . . looked forward to wielding powers within the executive more substantial than those granted by the Treaty, and that he would not suffer gladly the further restrictions imposed upon his work by the Council of Ministers and the Common Assembly." H. Schmitt, *European Union from Hitler to de Gaulle* (New York: Von Nostrand Reinhold, 1969), p. 124.

37. Council of Europe, Documents, 1950, Doc. 74. Note, also, the Mackay Protocol; put forward by the ardent British federalist, RWG Mackay, it called for the functions of the Council to be enlarged to include those of the two extant organisations, the Brussels Treaty Organisation and the OEEC, whose administration should be transferred to the Council, as a precedent for the continuous inclusion of other "functions"; A. H. Robertson, *The Council of Europe*. pp. 90, 93.

38. Council of Europe, Documents, 1952, Aide Memoire, Doc. 11; Robertson, The Council of Europe, pp. 99-100.

39. Ibid., p. 100. The effort was led by Camille Paris, then the organisation's secretary-general; *Jean Monnet Memoirs*. p. 380.

40. J. Monnet, *Memoirs*. pp. 381-1; Monnet made his satisfaction very evident: "With that," he notes, "the Eden Plan ceased to exist."

41. For the cruciality of Spinelli's role in widening Monnet's original conception, see D. Preda "From a Defence Community to a Political Community: The Role of De Gasperi and Spinelli" in A. Bosco ed. *The Federal Idea* (London: Lothian Foundation Press, 1991, 2 Vols.) vol. II, pp. 189-206.

42. Commenting on the eventual product of the Ad Hoc Assembly, as it came to be known, he records that "if the constitution-makers were perhaps too cau-

tious on these points [formulation of a common policy], they were insufficiently so when they imagined that European unity would begin with the establishment of a federal political system." The system recognised "the reality of the member States" but "it proposed to go too fast, without waiting for the force of necessity to make it seem natural in the eyes of Europeans." *Jean Monnet, Memoirs.* p. 396.

43. Ibid.

44. Ibid., pp. 398-9.

45. Ibid., p. 400.

46. Richard Mayne interprets Monnet's volte face, correctly in my view, in the light of the rapid development of events; according to Mayne, Monnet believed that returning to his position on the High Authority at a time of rapid institutional evolution would have placed him in a position to influence both the form and the content of the new initiatives; R. Mayne, "The Role of Jean Monnet" in G. Ionescu, ed., *The New Politics of European Integration* (London: Macmillan, 1972), pp. 49-50.

47. RIIA and PEP Action Committee for the United States of Europe, Statements and Declarations, 1955-67; see, esp. Resolution 25 of November 1957 and Press Communique of 13 October 1958. The Action Committee supported the European Parliament's Resolution of 17 May 1960 on direct elections but also resolved that "the discussions of the election of the Parliament by universal suffrage must not slow down the merger of the Executives," p. 53.

48. Reproduced in H. Brugmans' *Vingt Ans de L'Europe, Temoinages, 194666* (Bruges: De Tempel, 1966), pp. 203-13; the first thesis states: "There is no integration without political integration."

49. N. Kohlhase "Henri Brugmans: His Contribution to Federalism" in A. Bosco, ed., *The Federal Idea.* vol. II, pp. 206-20.

50. For Brugman's account, which tries to be fair, see *L'Idee Europeene, 1918-65* (Bruge: De Tempel, 1965), pp. 99-112, 175-81.

51. Written in 1957, Spinelli included it in *L'europa non cade dal cielo* (Bologna: 1960), pp. 282-7.

52. A. Spinelli, "Pourquoi je suis europeen," p. 37.

53. See, especially, L. Levi "Spinelli, Albertini and the Italian Federalist School" in A. Bosco ed. *The Federal Idea*, vol. II, pp. 220-33.

54. See C. Pentland *Integration Theory and European Integration* (London: Faber and Faber, 1973) pp. 10-46.

55. E. Haas' work was published by Stevens and Son; he summarised his theoretical postulates in *Beyond the Nation-State* (Princeton: 1964) chs. 1, 2. Lindberg's work was published by Stanford University.

56. "Academics moved easily in the corridors of Brussels, interviewing Eurocrats and absorbing the Community ethos. Eurocrats, in turn, read the resulting publications and found their behaviour described, rationalised and even prescribed in a persuasive manner . . . one neofunctionalist . . . remarked on 'the unnerving experience of hearing our special jargon spouted back at us by those whom we are studying.'" Charles Pentland "Functionalism and Theories of International Political Integration" in J. Groom and P. Taylor eds. *Functionalism* (University of London Press: 1975), p. 19.

57. At an international conference in 1961, Haas summarised the essence of the theory in a paper entitled "Integration, the European and Universal Experience," identifying that essence with the establishment of a supranational body with autonomous rights to propose community solutions, and defended the record of supranationality against any other approach to international cooperation. S. Grotius, *Seminarium Limits and Problems of European Integration*, 3 May-2 June 1962, intr. B. Landeer (Hague: Nijhoff, 1963).

58. Ibid.; Haas and Mitrany appeared on the same platform. The article has been reproduced as "The Prospect of European Integration, Federalism versus Functionalism" in, among others, *The Journal of Common Market Studies*, vol. IV, no. 2, 1965, pp. 119-49 and slightly revised, in J. Groom and P. Taylor eds. *Functionalism*.

59. First noted by J. Nye "Patterns and Catalysts in Regional Integration" *International Organization*, no. 19, 1965, pp. 870-84.

60. S. Hoffmann "The Fate of the Nation State" *Daedalus*, vol. 95, 1966, pp. 867-881.

61. In 1966, Spinelli retreated from immediate involvement with the federalist movement to found the Italian Institute of International Affairs whose journal, *Spettatore Internationale*, kept up a steady criticism of the institutional framework of the Community. In 1969, it published an important and thorough analysis of the Community since the veto, criticising the Marjolin Commission for its lack of political activism but also relating its difficulties to the bureaucratic philosophy with which the Common Market had been infused, identifying Hallstein and his misapplication of the experience of the Coal-Steel Community as the real culprit.

62. "Integration as a source of stress on the European Community system" *International Organization*, vol. 20, no. 2, 1966.

63. He maintained, for example, that the crisis had "confirmed the validity of spillover"; Ibid. pp. 234, 240.

64. L. Lindberg and S. Scheingold, *Europe's Would-be Polity* (Englewood Cliffs: Prentice Hall, 1970).

65. Ibid., p. 225 ff.

66. Ibid., p. 305.

67. Ibid., pp. 306-7.

68. "Political Integration as a Multidimensional Phenomenon Requiring Multivariate Measurement" *International Organization*, no. 24, 1970; Nina Heathcote would find "not much explanatory power in concepts of equilibrium and conservative dynamic," and charged the two theorists with "avoiding questions of substance and taking refuge in appeals to methodological complexity; N. Heathcote, "Neofunctional Theories of Regional Integration" in Groom and Taylor, *Functionalism*, (University of London Press: 1975) pp. 47 and 49-50. See also her "The Crisis of European Supranationality" *The Journal of Common Market Studies*, vol. 5, no. 2, 1966-7, p. 140.

69. *Monograph*, Institute of International Studies, University of California, Berkeley, 1975.

70. Paper by Morten Kelstrup, published as "European Integration and Political Theory" in M. Kelstrup ed., *European Integration and Denmark's Participation* (Copenhagen, Political Studies Press, 1993) pp. 13-4.

71. In A. Spinelli ed., *Che Fare per l' Europa?* (Milan, edizione de Communita, 1963), pp. 19-51.

72. A. Spinelli, *The Eurocrats.* p. 196.

73. Almost the last line of his *Diaro Europeao*, which covers the period from 1948 to 1969 and which was written on the 25th of October, reads, Uma chi ascolta piu le mie parole? Dico "ascolta," non "accoglie" (Bologna: Il Mulino, 1989), p. 558.

74. A. Spinelli, *The European Adventure* (London: Charles Knight and Co, 1972), p. 16.

5

Jean Monnet and the Federal Functionalist Approach to European Union

Martin Holland

Everything always takes longer than one expects—which is why one must never set time-limits for succeeding.

Jean Monnet, "Jean Monnet's Philosophy"
Proceedings of the Centenary Symposium

Monnet's cautious warning to avoid a rigid timetable for integration went unheeded at Maastricht where European Union, in particular Economic and Monetary Union, was specified in a Treaty format. His ideas continue to be relevant in the debate on European integration. In a period of massive change in both the international and European system, it is difficult to gain the correct focus on events, to detect underlying trends amid a mass of events which often appear volatile and seemingly contradictory. The distractions of contemporary affairs can lead to conclusions that are both disarming and specious. Monnet saw the Community as an experiment whose end could only be a matter for conjecture: clearly, being axiomatic or predictive about the shape or content of Europe in the 1990s would be foolhardy. As Duchene has observed, the development of the Community today is "subsumed, as in fact it always has been, in the fate of the international order around it."[1]

In such a period of international flux, it is instructive to return to first principles—particularly the ideas of Jean Monnet and the earlier federalist, functionalist and neofunctionalist theorists who for almost two decades were mistakenly seen as increasingly irrelevant to the European debate. A re-evaluation of Monnet's ideas in the light of the Community and Union experience and European integration is thus both appropriate and long overdue.

The Heritage of Jean Monnet

While Jean Monnet is best remembered for his vision of European unity through the European Community, the earlier part of his life is also instructive in understanding his deep-rooted philosophical approach to peace and cooperation. During the 1914-18 war he was responsible for the rationalization of the separate French and British Allied transport systems into a combined Allied Maritime Transport Committee. At an early stage of his career therefore he approached issues from a supranational rather than national perspective.

At the end of the World War I he was briefly appointed Deputy Secretary General of the new League of Nations. The League's inability however to cooperate persuaded Monnet in 1923 to leave public office for the commercial world. Perhaps ironically for a man of peace, it was the prospect of Europe's second war of the twentieth century that brought Monnet back into a public role. He was instrumental in France's pre-1939 military preparation; with the outbreak of war he continued to advocate Anglo-French cooperation and proposed the quite revolutionary Franco-British Union which would have merged the two nations under a single and indissoluble sovereignty. Although the fall of the French Government and the armistice agreed to by French Prime Minister Petain overtook this proposal, the 1939-1945 war confirmed rather than dissipated Monnet's belief in the necessity of cooperation that went beyond just intergovernmental agreements.[2]

After the war, de Gaulle appointed Monnet first as the head of the French Supply Council and then as head of the *Commissariat du Plan* responsible for French reconstruction and modernization. In this position of Planning Commissioner Monnet was instrumental in securing American aid through the Marshall Plan. While French reconstruction was the immediate priority, Monnet's perspective remained supranational. He saw that economic development could not be achieved by national measures but demanded cooperation across frontiers.

Monnet's approach to the idea of European Union has been a matter of some debate. His contribution was considerable although some critics would argue that this was to the detriment rather than to the advantage of the European integration. Schuman, Spaak and Spinelli can lay justifiable claim to being key contributors to Community development, but the role of catalyst and initiator lays properly with Jean Monnet. As one commentator has remarked, Monnet's role was vital in generating the font for ideas for such a "revolution" in international affairs.[2] His influence over the Community was remarkable given that he was not directly involved in the formal committee meetings that eventually produced a constitutional formula for European integration. Monnet's only public role within a European institution in the postwar period was as the first President of the High Authority of the European Coal and Steel Community (1952-1955) (ECSC). However, the principles behind the Messina conference of 1955 and the text of the 1957 Treaty of Rome owed much to Monnet's guiding influence.[4]

Monnet's Ideas on Western Unity

One of the main inspirations behind postwar European integration was the desire to secure a lasting peace. National sovereignty and competition over resources were seen by an increasing number of influential individuals to be counter to this objective. In his memoirs Monnet records that in 1950 the prevalent atmosphere was of an "increasing acceptance of a war that is thought to be inevitable."[5] Hindsight should not make us undervalue this preoccupation: East-West relations were confrontational; the status of Berlin remained precarious; Germany was formally divided; French economic recovery was stagnating; and the proliferation of atomic weapons had begun. Echoing Winston Churchill's famous call for "a kind of United States of Europe" built around a Franco-German axis, Monnet believed that the key to European peace was an alliance between France and Germany.[6]

The precise nature of such an agreement was less important than the realisation of this historical reconciliation. Even at this early stage Monnet had begun to experiment with federal principles for the new Europe. Reflecting on the establishment of the Organization of European Economic Cooperation (OEEC) in 1948, he remarked in his *Memoirs*:

> I could not help seeing the intrinsic weakness of a system that went no further than mere cooperation between Governments . . . The countries of Western Europe must turn their national efforts into a truly European effort. This will be possible only through a *federation of the West*. (emphasis added).[7]

Two successive European civil wars had illustrated the inherent dangers of unrestrained nationalism and an international movement towards federalism inspired many of the post-1945 generation of political leaders.[8]

In some respects the ECSC of 1952 can be regarded as modern Europe's first peace movement: former national control over these key products for the armaments industry were placed under joint or pooled authority thereby creating, according to Monnet, "the first concrete foundations of the European Federation which is indispensable to the maintenance of peace."[9] The importance of this objective evident in the preamble to 1952 Paris Treaty which began:

> Considering that world peace can be safeguarded only by creative efforts commensurate with the dangers that threaten it . . .

> Resolved to substitute for age-old rivalries the merging of their [the Six] essential interests; to create, by establishing an economic community, the basis for a broader and deeper community among the peoples long divided by bloody conflicts . . .

It is myopic to regard the past four decades of European integration as a technocratic economic exercise principally devoted to capital expansion. The success of the ECSC and latterly the European Community can disguise the original purpose of creating a European organization that would prohibit the outbreak of Europe's third civil war of the twentieth century. While Europe was a political and economic concept, Monnet also considered it to be "a moral idea."[10]

The reorganization of Europe in a way that sublimated national rivalries was regarded by Monnet as a incremental process. This approach has opened him up to attack from more ideologically-committed academics and politicians. Burgess, for instance, has argued that despite his periodic usage of federalist language, Monnet cannot be regarded as "a champion of the federal cause in Europe" since he was primarily an economic functionalist and only secondly an incremental federalist.[11] There is considerable evidence in Monnet's *Memoirs* to support this view, although uncharacteristically for Monnet this issue lacks clarity and the case that he did not hold federalist principles is far from conclusive. Monnet placed a strong emphasis on "concrete achievements" and was cautious in pushing Europe too quickly along an ill-defined road. He was reticent for example over establishing a European Defence Community in 1954.[12]

Monnet remained both a pragmatist and a political opportunist who valued incrementalism over the purity of federalist principles and regarded an ad hoc approach as the more effective strategy for uniting Europe. Ends, rather than means, characterize Monnet's political style. If the route towards European integration involved a temporary detour into intergovernmental territory, if it meant forgoing logically the most direct path to federation in order to safeguard current gains,

these were the costs that Monnet was prepared to pay in order to secure the deepening and solidifying of European union. As Monnet wrote:

> Little by little the work of the Community will be felt . . . Then the eve-
> ryday realities themselves will make it possible to form the political un-
> ion which is the goal of our Community and to establish the United States
> of Europe . . . the idea is clear: political Europe will be created by hu-
> man effort, when the time comes, on the basis of reality . . . [13]

Quite what the specifics of European union might look like were left
intentionally vague. However, the broad plan was consistent, indicating that Monnet was in a general sense a European federalist a well as
a functionalist. Functionalism for Monnet meant the creation of a supranational regime or organization that was based on the principle of
international authority.

Monnet's contribution as a bureaucrat to the creation of Europe
lacked the same impact as some of his political contemporaries. This
should not disguise his pervasive influence in the Community debate
for more than three decades. He can take credit for the "idea" of the
1950 Schuman Plan and served as the first President of the High Authority of the European Coal and Steel Community (1952-1955). The success of this first attempt at a supranationalism lay the foundations for
the wider Community as set out in the 1957 Treaty of Rome. His resignation from the High Authority and reluctance to be a candidate for
the newly established Commission in 1957 did not indicate a loss of
commitment to the European cause, but reflected his pragmatic approach on how the development of the Community might best be influenced. He exchanged the direct responsibility of public office for a
more informal role as an independent counsellor and source of ideas.
In 1955 he formed the *Action Committee for the United States of Europe*
and served as its inspiration and President until his resignation on 9
May 1975.

Monnet's role as the President of the *Action Committee for the United
States of Europe* provided him and his organization with the advantage
of being able to influence political elites directly without having to face
the disadvantage of public scrutiny. Europe was being constructed by
a cohesive and remarkably small elite; while public support was welcomed, it was never a prerequisite for Monnet's Europe. Freed from
institutional constraints, Monnet through the *Action* was able to shape
the debate Committee on the emerging form of the new European Economic Community structures.

Monnet was not always successful in his lobbying for a progressively
federal-functional arrangement for Europe. For most of the 1960s the

supremacy of the nationstates of the Community stood in stark contrast to the ambitions of both the *Action Committee* and the *Spaak Committee* ,[14] and to the expectations developed from the ECSC experience. The inability of the Community to agree upon a single European 'District' to house the institutions was a prescient omen underlining the resilience of national self-interest. Successive failures at enlargement, the constraints imposed on extending Community-level competences and (most notoriously) the inappropriately named Luxembourg Compromise all combined to stifle the development of Community political integration.

Perhaps the attractiveness of Monnet's Europe was the breadth of its conception. Uncluttered with precise institutional relations, or even a clearly described destination, the "idea" of European integration could be sufficiently flexible to appeal to a broad political spectrum, from cautious intergovernmentalists to unabashed federalists. This ubiquity has been challenged as both a strength and a weakness. It allowed successful if pragmatic integration to a substantial degree, while it simultaneously facilitated the opportunity for intergovernmentalism due to the very absence of precise institutional and policy objectives.

Monnet equated nationalism with a "spirit of domination" based on the inequality between states that had been responsible for the previous centuries of European wars. He was opposed to the substitution of nationalism at the state-level by a new nationalism at the European level. The Treaty of Rome reflected this desire to ameliorate the fervour of nationalism by establishing the principle of the "protection of the minorities" within the Community's institutional balance. What had to be realised was a Community in which domination by one power (Germany) or an alliance (Franco-German) was impossible.

He also considered that institutions were the key to successful integration as "only institutions grow wiser; they accumulate collective experience."[15] Once established, institutions have a tangible impact that far outweighs the metaphysical influence of ideas or theories. Duroselle maintains that this emphasis on concrete institutions is Monnet's most enduring legacy for the Community. Competing ideas concerning integration or Political Union have come and gone during the Community's turbulent history, yet what has remained largely untouched since the Schuman Declaration of 1950 has been the institutional structure and relationships of the European Community. After four decades of supranational experience the need has urgently resurfaced to reform the institutional balance and decisionmaking process. The 1991 Intergovernmental Conference on European Union leading to the Maastricht Treaty reform process and the resultant Treaty on European Union should not be regarded as invalidating Monnet's approach. The success of the Community has resulted in its enlargement to the point where the structures developed to accommodate the integration of six economically similar western European states of the 1950s, are now in need of adaptation to the new political geometry of contemporary Europe.

The doubling in the number of Community member states in the three decades that spanned 1957-1986, and further enlargement by the year 2000 is evidence that Monnet's belief in an "open" Europe has become ingrained within the Community idea. The conditions of membership set down in the Treaty of Rome were intentionally expansive: the preamble encourages "other peoples of Europe who share their (the Community) ideal to join in their efforts," whereas Article 237 simply states that "Any European State may apply to become a member of the Community" with accession determined by the unanimous approval of the Council of Ministers and, since the Single European Act, majority support in the European Parliament. In practice, informal criteria (such as democratic legitimacy, compatibility of economic structures and, increasingly, a common approach to foreign and security issues) have been used to evaluate potential applicants. This general principle of "openness" has not gone unchallenged: the aborted enlargements of the 1960s and the transitional problems experienced by applicant states have all periodically marred "openness." During the ECSC negotiations Monnet sought to express this principle by courting British participation. This ended up being thwarted on two separate occasions by de Gaulle. However Monnet never deserted his assessment of the importance of a Franco-British union within the context of the Community.

Despite periodic trade disputes, the United States has fully supported the development of the Community and the European-American partnership advocated by Monnet has been influential in the Community's history. The complexity of the linkages as well as the necessity for an Atlantic consensus, have become increasing clear in the 1990s. The possibility of the EU gaining an extended competence in the sphere of security and defence has placed the question of NATO and American involvement in Europe back onto the agenda of European political integration (particularly in the context of the Bosnia crisis).

Some writers have challenged the assumption that Monnet was principally a "technocrat" or economic expert and emphasized his importance as an *original thinker*. Monnet's contemporaries and colleagues have stressed that without Monnet's "mercurial personality" it is doubtful whether the EC would have happened at all.[16] It was not just that his ideas were remarkable. He displayed a strong dedication to collective action at the expense of individual power: it was this personal philosophy that was translated, albeit imperfectly, to the principles of the European Communities. Throughout his career in public office (which

spanned some forty years), a commitment to problem-solving by collective action rather than by single and independent national policies
is evident. Perhaps his most direct influence was in drafting the
Schuman Declaration and acting as the president of the French delegation that, together with the other five national delegations, produced
the basic articles that shaped the ECSC. The full significance of this
event may not have been apparent to many of Europe's political elite
at the time.

Monnet's principle of collective action was recognized by the creation of the ECSC High Authority, a "method" that has shaped the development of the European Communities into the 1990s. Monnet's
absence from public office after May 1955 should not be taken as a sign
of declining influence. The intergovernmental Spaak Committee, charged
with the responsibility of drafting the terms of the new Community,
included a number of Monnet's closest former aides and associates from
the High Authority. As Mayne has noted, the "resultant Rome Treaties
establishing the European Economic Community and Euratom, were
thus very clearly the offspring of Monnet and his friends."[17]

Through his *Action Committee for the United States of Europe*, Monnet
continued to exert considerable influence on the debate on European
integration. He succeeded in embodying his essential ideas both formally within the constitutional provisions, and informally within the
practices of the new European Communities. A substantial number of
its members subsequently served in both Community and national political office, thereby extending the influence of Action Committee directly. For almost a decade de Gaulle's conception of "L'Europe des
patries" seemed to be ascendant, though paradoxically, the role of
Monnet and the Action Committee was perhaps at no other time more
important. It remained loyal to the principle of collective action and
continued to argue for integration within the European debate. It is not
coincidental that the relaunch of the Community in 1969 drew heavily
from Monnet's approach to European Union.

Monnet considered the popular support for an integrated Europe was
of secondary importance and would develop only after the creation of
institutions. Though essentially elitist, this strategy proved to be the
more practical in the early 1950s.[18] The support of national elites across
the political spectrum was essential if some form of supranational authority was to begin to be established. Possibly Monnet's greatest
achievement was in helping to engineer this elite consensus.

Some critics consider that Monnet contributed to the confusing diversity of principles that underpin the Community. Burgess has found
these principles are "often incompatible and sometimes contradictory"
producing a "conceptual enigma" that "defies simple categorisation."[19]

While federal ideas were instrumental, they did not form the exclusive ideological base on which the Community was to be founded. Monnet's incremental strategy precluded this single-mindedness and sought to balance, for pragmatic reasons, federalism, functionalism as well as intergovernmentalism. Burgess has also argued that the initial success of Monnet's elite bargaining functional strategy disguised a fundamental flaw in his approach as it "did not provide Europe with the effective means to go beyond what existed."[20] National governments retained their pivotal role: the opportunity to create a new central federal level of authority was surrendered as political authority was not fundamentally transformed. This was because, Burgess points out, Monnet's ideas lacked a clear ideological base and depicts him not as "a champion of the federal cause in Europe" but, somewhat disparagingly in comparison with Spinelli's consistent federalist principles, as a "functionalist" or "incremental federalist." Monnet's view of human nature stressed rationality and benevolence derived from mutual interest and he sought through the Community to transform the context and eradicate the historical reasons that lead to conflict and human rivalry.[21]

Whether Monnet qualifies for the accolade of a Community federalist, or the designation as practical visionary, his imprint on the structure of the Community is incontestable. It is perhaps a fitting testimony to Monnet's ideas that almost half a century later his basic principles should still be relevant to the current debate about the development of the European Union. He is unquestionably the EUs most original and important thinker, and his enduring legacy is the belief in the central role of institutions in determining the future shape of Europe integration. However, as Monnet concludes towards the end of his *Memoirs*,

> the Community we have created is not an end in itself. It is a process of change . . . It is impossible to foresee today the decisions that could be taken in a new context of tomorrow. The essential thing is to hold fast to the few fixed principles that have guided us since the beginning: gradually to create among Europeans the broadest common interest, served by common democratic institutions to which the necessary sovereignty has been delegated.[22]

It is perhaps too grand to talk of Monnet's "theory" of integration, as well as being an unfair responsibility to place on him. He exhibited "an existential style that was rather intellectual by the standards of most politicians, yet owed little to theory and books."[23] Consequently, it is the Monnet "method" that is more instructive as a guide to European integration. The essence of this method was that for Monnet Europe was the focus of all his activities and achievements.

It was his single-mindedness and dedication to this idea that differentiated Monnet from his contemporaries. Imagination combined with a realism that appreciated pragmatism and incrementalism as necessary strategies epitomized the Monnet method. The eventual goal was never in question, but the choice of route always open to debate. Concrete institutional achievements remained paramount, however, for without any such formal structure ideas and idealism could have no practical expression.

Monnet's "Method" and Theories of Integration

As William Wallace notes, integration theory flourished during the 1950s and early 1960s, but since then the record has generally been disappointing. The inability to predict or explain the development of the Community adequately—either in practice or in theory—led to "the collapse both of the political commitment to European integration and of the conceptual framework that had supported it."[24]

The Community's history has been chequered, with periods of significant progress towards integration, and other periods of stagnation. The earliest conceptual approach that was used to provide a framework for Community integration was the theory of functionalism first constructed by David Mitrany in the inter-war years. While Monnet was often broadly described as a functionalist, this approach contains a number of contradictions as well as similarities with his ideas. A parallel between functionalist theory and Monnet's practice was their shared belief in functional agencies that would assume supranational authority across a range of specific policy areas. Coal and steel production, for example, could be removed from national control and decisionmaking authority given to a functional agency separate from any nation state. While functionalists and Monnet were both concerned with establishing conditions which would eliminate war and rejected nationalism as the basis for political organization and decisionmaking, functionalists (unlike Monnet) did not regard regional unification as superior to the existing system of nation states.[25] For Mitrany, the creation of new regional groupings would merely "change the dimensions of nationalism, but not its nature."[26] Consequently, Mitrany argued for a series of independent though complementary international functional agencies, not for the creation of a single supranational body—such as the Commission—with functional authority across several sectors. Functionalism, by definition, was to be a flexible mechanism or process that could accommodate both expansion and contraction in its scope depending on need, a characteristic that was not compatible with the purely integrationist aspirations of Monnet. Monnet's "political arrangement" (the prototype Community) on the other hand was more than a series of technical functional agencies. It was the combination of functionalist principles with the political objective of a form of federal government that prompted the development of theories that more closely reflected the Community reality.

Functionalism has made two significant and enduring theoretical contributions to the understanding of integration: its expansive logic of enmeshment or interdependencies, and its emphasis on attitudinal change.[27] This first aspect of functionalism—the assumption of its expansive logic suggests—that once the process of functional organization began, the power of nation states to act independently would be progressively reduced as a web of functional interdependent relations developed. This logic held true whether there were several independent or just one joint functional authority. Critics of functionalism have argued that any such systems of interdependence have not reduced disputes, but rather that functional integration has simply politicized more issues within and between states. Intergovernmental disputes have come to focus on functional problems, such as the international economic system, rather than on traditional topics such as territory or sovereignty. Functional integration has been no more successful in eliminating these tensions than was the previous system of autonomous states.[28]

The second aspect of functionalism as a process identified as central to integration is the gradual change in popular attitudes through the experience of cooperation transcending national borders. In Pentland's words, individuals "are gradually weaned away from their allegedly irrational nationalistic impulses toward a self-reinforcing ethos of cooperation."[29] This attitudinal change comes about through the experience of cooperative activity and through the conscious application of education and the media. It is the importance placed on mass attitudinal change that most clearly distinguishes Mitrany's work from the later neofunctionalists such as Haas and Lindberg, as well as from Monnet's strategy which tended to place a lower priority on this characteristic of integration. This commitment to attitudinal change by functionalists has been forcefully criticised. Taylor has noted a lack of empirical evidence to support the claim "that international institutions are capable of becoming the focus of loyalties at the expense of the state"[30] The French and Danish referendums of 1992 did nothing to undermine this conclusion. Thus, a divergence of opinion between pure functionalists and Monnet is clear. While Monnet was a vigorous advocate of a democratic Community, he saw the emergence of loyalties to the Community institutions developing as a *consequence* of elite agreements for the functional organization of Europe, not as an essential *prerequisite* to that organization. In a sense, it was integration through stealth rather than popular acclamation.

The practical reality of the Community drew critical attention to the inadequacy of the general theory of functionalism as an appropriate explanation of the process of integration. The response to this conceptual crisis was the development of the theory of neofunctionalism by Ernst Haas which was specifically designed to address the Community experience. Haas abandoned the central integrative role conferred on attitudinal change by Mitrany: integration is not initially dependent on mass support, although such support would, over time, become associated with its development. The question arises whether Monnet's approach can be better understood from a neofunctional rather than traditional functional theoretical perspective.

It was a new application of the "expansive logic of integration" that constitutes Haas' most significant theoretical contribution and remains the "hallmark" of his neofunctionalist theory. Haas argued that successful integration was dependent on the idea of "spillover." By this he means that integration by sector cannot be achieved in isolation: as one sector is integrated there will be consequences, both advantageous as well as disadvantageous, for related sectors and a "spillover effect" will occur, suggesting a kind of inevitability to the process.[31] Indeed, it is argued that even the original objective can only be realised through such spillover.

Monnet's approach certainly has sympathy with the logic of spillover, although he was far to pragmatic to ignore the political context of the process. He considers the generation of political will supporting integration was a necessity. Spillover is also reflected in the typical Community bargaining process whereby agreements across disparate areas are tied together. Decisionmaking does not take place in sectorial isolation, but rather concessions or agreements in one policy area will have implications and often direct consequences for other policy areas. Thus the logic of neofunctionalism was relevant, it was suggested, to both the general integration across functional sectors and to the functional and political aspects of Community decisionmaking.

However, just as functionalism was discarded because of its poor "fit" with reality, the events of the 1960s undermined confidence in the explanatory ability of neofunctionalism and led to a crisis in neofunctionalist theory. The initial expectations of a Monnet-inspired Community appeared largely unfulfilled and spillover and progressive integration did not seem to be occurring. The persistence of national self-interest indicated that the Community was closer to an intergovernmental grouping than any putative federation. The Commission appeared unable to fulfil its neofunctionalist role as the instigator of spillover due to the institutional imbalance that provided the Council with decisionmaking dominance. The Commission adopted a "mediatory conciliatory role rather than a creative one," arguably as a result of the inadequacies of the Treaty of Rome that placed it in conflict and at a disadvantage to the Council.[32] Political events in Europe continued to out pace academic theory.[33]

While the pace of events since the mid-1980s have been almost as frantic as those of the founding years of 1957-1963, this recognition of the role of political elites and the absence of the inevitability of spillover has led integration writers in the 1990s to reinterpret neofunctionalist theory in the light of practical experience. With the passing of the Single European Act (SEA) and the creation of the Single Market of 1992, the need for an adequate integration theory is perhaps more pressing than ever. As William Wallace has recently argued, "the greater the complexity of the processes of European integration, the more important it becomes to rebuild acceptable conceptual frameworks with which to order the mass of information."[34]

The idea that gradual integration by sector would lead towards a political union through the process of interdependence echoed quite accurately Monnet's own prescription for a united Europe. Monnet believed that successive functionalist forms of integration would progressively lead to a type of federalism. This process would be gradual, but cumulative as economic sectors were transferred from national to a Community level of competence. Consequently, central to neofunctionalist theory, as well as to Monnet's assumptions, was the automatic effect of the spillover process.

This assumption has recently been challenged by Keohane and Hoffmann.[35] The importance of their theoretical reformulation is the recognition that a prerequisite to any form of spillover (economic or political) is a successful intergovernmental bargaining process. Thus spillover *per se* is not an automatic procedure as commonly argued by neofunctionalist theorists. Once the inevitability of spillover is denied and the limitations on the process acknowledged, the disappointments of the 1960s and 1970s and the resulting theoretical disillusion can be overcome. Keohane and Hoffmann argue that the appropriate initial focus of analysis should, therefore, be at the intergovernmental level. This is not in conflict with either contemporary experience or Monnet's pragmatic "method." The deeper integration promoted by the SEA had its origins in an intergovernmental conference; and Monnet's willingness to make concessions in order to achieve or maintain consensus recognised the primacy of intergovernmental bargains. The expectation that spillover could be a sufficient explanation or stimulus for integration was unrealistic. The missing catalyst, it is contended, is the bargaining process characteristic of intergovernmentalism. To guide research, Keohane and Hoffmann provide a working hypothesis that does not conflict with Monnet's approach and centres on the notion that "successful spillover requires prior programmatic agreement among governments, expressed in an intergovernmental bargain."[36] The process they outline specifies external catalysts leading to an intergovernmental bargain, which in turn will result in task expansion for the Community and sectorial (political or economic) spillover internal to the EC. Spillover is stripped of its previously implied causal role and becomes a secondary, conditional consequence.

What insights do the approaches of these contemporary theoretical commentators provide for understanding Monnet's conception of integration? History has shown that it is wise to be cautionary with regard to the development of the EC. The theory of a supranational-style of decisionmaking where compromises enhancing common interests have superseded the veto principle of national protection, appears to be of utility once again. The process of spillover is a gradual one, but perceptible nevertheless.

The case for the re-evaluation of neofunctionalism is strong: with the demise of the Luxembourg Compromise and the qualitative leap of the Single European Act, European decisionmaking has become rather more decisive. The reality of Community politics has once again begun to resemble the predictive elements of neofunctional theory (after an absence of some two decades). While spillover ought to be rehabilitated, its role has to be clearly delimited. Similarly, functional theory remains instructive: as the Maastricht ratification process has reminded Europe, integration cannot be simply a technical exercise concerning markets and macroeconomics. To succeed, mass attitudes and loyalties have to be included. Without any such popular base, European integration will be built on sand. The consequential rather than causal role played by attitudinal change in Monnet's functional-federal approach remains an important limitation in an otherwise expansive and revolutionary concept of integration. Monnet was never restricted by the purity of theory but pragmatic in applying it as part of a wider search for European unity. As he observed, theory must always take second place to opportunity and circumstance in the construction of Europe.

Notes

The themes in this chapter are drawn in part from M. Holland, *European Community Integration* (London: Pinter, 1993), pp. 5-21.

1. F. Duchene, "More or Less Than Europe? European Integration in Retrospect" in C. Crouch and D. Marquand, eds., *The Politics of 1992: Beyond the Single European Market* (Oxford: Basil Blackwell, 1990), p. 21.

2. P. Fontaine, *Jean Monnet, a Design for Europe* (Luxembourg: European Documentation 5/1988), pp. 12-14.

3. R. Mayne, "The Role of Jean Monnet" in *Government and Opposition* (2: 1966), p. 350.

4. Ibid. p. 367.

5. J. Monnet, *Memoirs* (translated by R. Mayne) (New York: Doubleday and Company, 1978), p. 289.

6. S. Patijn, ed., *Landmarks in European Unity* (Leyden: Sijthoff, 1970), p. 33.

7. J. Monnet, *Memoirs*, pp. 273-3.

8. M. Burgess, *Federalism and European Union: Political Ideas, Influences and Strategies in the European Community, 1972-1987* (London: Routledge, 1989), p. 24.

9. J. Monnet, *Memoirs*, p. 298.

10. Ibid. p. 392.

11. M. Burgess, *Federalism and European Union: Political Ideas, Influences and Strategies in the European Community, 1972-1987*, p. 44.

12. J. Monnet, *Memoirs*, p. 343.

13. Ibid., p. 431.

14. The Spaak committee was set up at the Messina conference in 1955 by the foreign ministers of the ECSC. It consisted of representatives of each of the six governments and its brief was the establishment of the basis of the European Economic Community.

15. Ibid., p. 393.

16. R. Mayne, "The Role of Jean Monnet," p. 351.

17. Ibid, p. 367.

18. R. Pryce and W. Wessels, "The Search For an Ever Closer Union: a Framework For Analysis" in R. Pryce, ed., *The Dynamics of European Union* (London: Croom Helm, 1987), p. 24; R. Cardozo, "The Project for a Political Community, (1952-54)" in R. Pryce, ed., *The Dynamics of European Integration*, p. 73.

19. M. Burgess, *Federalism and European Union: Political Ideas, Influences and Strategies in the European Community, 1972-1987*, p. 20.

20. Ibid., p. 32.

21. Ibid., p. 46.

22. J. Monnet, *Memoirs*, p. 522.

23. F. Duchene, "Jean Monnet's Methods" in D. Brinkley and C. Hackett, *Jean Monnet: the Path to European Unity* (New York: St. Martin's Press, 1991), p. 187.

24. W. Wallace, ed., *The Dynamics of European Integration* (London: Pinter-RIIA, 1990), p. ix.

25. S. George, *Politics and Policy in the European Community* (Oxford: Clarendon Press, 1985).

26. D. Mitrany, "The Functional Approach to World Organisation" in C.A. Cosgrove and K.J. Twitchett, eds, *The New International Actors: the UN and the EEC* (London: Macmillan, 1990), p. 67.

27. P. Taylor, "Functionalism: The approach of David Mitrany" in A. J. R. Groom and P. Taylor, eds., *Frameworks for International Cooperation* (London: Pinter, 1990), p. 133.

28. Ibid., p. 135.

29. C. Pentland, *International Theory and European Integration*. (New York: The Free Press, 1973), p. 84.

30. P. Taylor, "Functionalism: The approach of David Mitrany," p. 133.

31. C. Pentland, *International Theory and European Integration*, p. 119.

32. R. J. Harrison, "Neofunctionalism" in A.J.R. Groom and P. Taylor, eds., *Frameworks for International Cooperation*, p. 145.

33. C. Pentland, *International Theory and European Integration*, p. 146.

34. W. Wallace, ed., *The Dynamics of European Integration*, p. x.

35. R. O. Keohane and S. Hoffmann, "Conclusions: Community Politics and Institutional Change" in W. Wallace, ed., *The Dynamics of European Integration*.

36. Ibid., p. 287.

6

Spinelli and European Union

Philomena Murray

The problem which must be solved in the first place, and without whose solution there will be no progress, is the definitive abolition of the division of Europe into national sovereign states. . . . The minds of people are already much better disposed than in the past towards federal reorganisation of Europe.

The Ventotene Manifesto, written by Altiero Spinelli
Ernesto Rossi and Eugenio Colorni, 1941.

Introduction

The early 1990s witnessed a revival of the controversy regarding Western Europe's political future. They were concentrated in particular on a 1990-1991 intergovernmental conference of the representatives of the European Community member states, the result of which was the Treaty establishing the European Union. The demand by some states and institutions for closer integration echoes a vision of the 1940s and 1950s for a political union which became known as "European Union," an imperative that is reminiscent of the initiatives of the 1940s and 1950s. Indeed the comparison with the 1950s period is useful. In the post-war period there was a desire for economic and even political reconstruction. In the earlier, the major actors in favour of European unity in the specific form of the European Coal and Steel Community (ECSC)—which was itself a blend of intergovernmentalism, whereby a central role is allocated to national governments and supranationalism, whereby a central role is accorded to institutions above the nation state—were the governments of Germany, Italy, France and the Benelux, that is, the six founding members of the European Community.

It was also in the 1940s and 1950s that the principle Italian federalist Altiero Spinelli put forward his vision of a united Europe. There are many parallels between the period of Spinelli's vision for a federal Europe and the debates in contemporary Europe. The postwar period was an era of recovery from the devastation of war. It was an era when blueprints for a new type of supranational political structure in Europe were written. Europe's future as a collection of independent nation states was also seriously under question. The realisation of the interdependence of nation states in a time of postwar recovery and reconciliation led to the desire for a transcendence of the traditional nation state. For idealists like Spinelli, supranationalism became a key concept of post-war negotiations on interstate cooperation, not least with the creation of the ECSC and the European Economic Community (EEC).

What became evident in the European Community of 1990-1991 was a reassessment of the political future of the European Community, especially its goal and new nomenclature as a European Union, that is, as a tighter, more cohesive organization of states, in the light of post-Cold War developments on the European and world stage. The debate on the creation of this political entity is not a new one. What is clear is that the ideas of the 1950s again came under scrutiny as the Community attempted to create a definitive economic bloc with the Single Internal Market of 1992 and a political superstructure of common foreign policy and an economic and monetary union that in some aspects was reminiscent of the Spinelli and Monnet projects. What is different is that, at the end of the twentieth century, the EU is already a common market, a customs union, and a single internal market. The European Union, as it has been called since the implementation of the Maastricht Treaty on European Union, is already a major negotiator in world economic issues—in the GATT and the World Trade Organization—and also in the UN. It is this very developed but still incomplete political entity that is under debate within the EU at present.

While the idealism of the postwar period was still manifest in the early 1990s, the desire for European unity is based on different premises from those of the 1940s and 1950s, such as the fear of disintegration in the wake of post-Maastricht reactions as well as the reawakening of extremist nationalism. The postwar fear of further war in Europe has been paralleled in the 1990s by the urgent need for a common foreign and security policy in the EU, an urgency intensified by events in the former Yugoslavia.

This chapter examines the Spinelli vision for European Union. First it looks at the post-war period, when Spinelli was instrumental in the creation of the federalist movement in Europe as an idealist who was not involved in politics. Second, it discusses the early-1980s phase of Spinelli's involvement in what he called his last battle, when he proposed his draft treaty on European Union. This later phase is more overtly political, with extensive contacts with politicians and governments, and is in many ways less visionary in approach.[1]

It is worthy of note that Spinelli's life history parallels the development of the EC, with the federalist phase of the 1940s and 1950s, and the 1980s need for common policies and even supranational European Union. It is clear from an examination of Spinelli's vision and of contemporary problems in European integration that the European Union still has not dealt with many of the original concerns of the federalists. These include the problems of the democratic deficit—the lack of democratic accountability in the EU—and the federalist-functionalist divide. The EU is still riven by the conflicting directions, of those who favour political and economic decisions above and beyond the state—known as supranationalists, and those who favour interstate decisionmaking among state bureaucrats and diplomats—commonly known as intergovernmentalists.

Spinelli and the Origins of the Federalist Movement

Spinelli was an active federalist in the first architectural phase of European unification in the 1940s, leading up to the creation of the ECSC. However, his role was not one of involvement in the actual creation of the Communities, but rather that of an intellectual idealist who favoured the replacement of the nation state with a constitutionally-based European federal system. He was not an active politician at this stage.

Spinelli's career began in 1924 when, as an antifascist communist, he was imprisoned for ten years by the fascist government of Mussolini.[2] He spent twenty years in active involvement in the European and Italian federalist movement. He was also an academic and author and taught at The Johns Hopkins University in Bologna and became founder and director of the Istituto di Affari Internazionali in Rome in 1966. He was personal adviser to Italian Foreign Minister, Pietro Nenni, from 1968 to 1970. He then was appointed a European Commissioner from 1970 to 1976, holding the portfolio on scientific, technological and industrial policy. In 1976 he was a member of the Italian Parliament and at the same time was delegated (by that Parliament) to the European Parliament (EP) and in 1979 he was directly elected to the EP. Looking back over Spinelli's long-standing commitment to European unity, it is primarily as the author of the Draft European Union Treaty (EUT) of the European Parliament that he may be remembered.

Ventotene

Spinelli had held a commitment to the creation of a federalist Europe since the World War II. In 1943, he was co-author of the *Ventotene Manifesto* along with Ernesto Rossi and Eugenio Colorni, who were fellow members of the Italian resistance. The Manifesto is a major document of European constitutional federalism and sets out clearly the ideal of a supranational state in which the nation state would be stripped of its powers and sovereignty. These would be pooled collectively, as a reaction to the failure of the nation state to defend democracy and human rights. The Manifesto constitutes what Delzell calls the first unmistakeably federalist group to organise itself on Italian soil.[3]

Inspired by the works of American, Swiss and British writers on federalism, Rossi, an anti-fascist journalist; Colorni, a socialist activist and philosophy teacher; and Spinelli, an anti-fascist, called for European federal union, as the highest priority for postwar Europe. During his years of imprisonment, Spinelli had read the work of the British federalists Lionel Robbins, Lord Lothian and Sir William Beveridge. The influence of continental European theorists was less pronounced in Spinelli's idealistic approach of federalism above the nation state, as they were not available to the resistance movement as readily as were the documents of the British Federal Union.

The Ventotene authors welcomed the entry of the United States into the War as a means of combating a possible Russian domination of Europe. In contrast to the Atlantic Charter, Spinelli urged a process of European integration based upon a tighter supranational organisation. Spinelli and his colleagues in the anti-fascist movement established the Movimento Federalista Europeo (European Federalist Movement) in August 1943 following the fall of the fascist regime in Italy.

The Nation State Under Question

Like other members of the resistance movement, Spinelli began to question the supremacy of the nation state, which was now closely identified with nazism and fascism; "to oppose these tyrannies" he wrote, "meant necessarily to oppose the state itself."[4] He saw clearly that the model of the strong state was no longer valid for continental Europe, and had maintained its validity only for Britain and to an extent, Russia.[5]

At the end of the war, Spinelli identified the resistance movement with "those who had placed other political and moral values above those of the nation state" and had now come into their own as a political force in European politics.[6] Lipgens has highlighted the sense of fellowship, transcending national boundaries, of the resistance members. The radical wing of the resistance, to which Spinelli belonged, called for a new type of democratic state and rejected the old forms of government. It called for an economic system based upon the free market to ensure continuous economic development and social justice and, lastly, a federal power. States would transfer to a European federal government the conduct of foreign policy, defence and the economic system, the areas in which Spinelli perceived that the nation state had failed. A European Constitutional Assembly would feature in this model.

Spinelli called for the abolition of the division of Europe into national sovereign states. According to the Draft Declaration of the European Resistances, the two world wars had produced anarchy and a federal union of the people of Europe was the means to solve that problem.[7] Federalism, for Spinelli, envisaged the construction of new political institutions to bring about a democratic Europe, with the surrender of certain powers of initiative, deliberation, decision and execution to a European executive, parliament and judiciary—a common political authority.[8]

This federal objective was not a central part of continental European experiences, which had not been predominently federal, but was a supranational solution to the dilemma of the re-emerging nation state in the 1940s, a solution which would focus on international cooperation above the nation state rather than on narrow national concerns. Spinelli saw that supranationalism required a philosophical act of faith for the peoples of Europe. He was cognisant of the fact that neither the peoples nor the political forces had adjusted themselves to this idea of common supranational action. Spinelli did, however, appear to believe that the adjustment to such a commitment could be made and there is considerable evidence to support this view.[9]

The Ventotene Manifesto was one of several calls for a transnational solution to the problems of a society which no longer had faith in the nation state. It was a manifestation of a desire to build Western European society on a basis of transnational cooperation, leading eventually to the creation of supranational political institutions and structures. Spinelli and Rossi even suggested that a peace treaty after the war should include proposals for a United States of Europe.[10] It was Spinelli who founded the initially clandestine Movimento Federalista Europeo in August 1943 in Milan.[11] The various resistance movements of Europe met in Geneva from March to June 1944. The European movements were to be split into the integralists or purist federalists, such as Spinelli and the Italian federalists and the gradualists, or incrementalists, such as Henri Brugmans.[12]

Spinelli later wrote of the circumstances in postwar Europe which rendered unification so pressing. The apparent denigration of the sovereign national state reinforced the movement for European unity and "the attainment of order which could replace the discredited and obsolete formula of national states." This theme recurs in Spinelli's speeches and writings throughout his long career. The nation state had failed the people symbolically and practically and so it no longer had sole legitimacy to deal with policy areas. So too had the national bureaucracies which were no longer able to satisfy the needs of the state.

The postwar shift in the international power system to the creation of two power blocs in the US and the USSR and resultant fears of Soviet strength lent new urgency—in Spinelli's eyes—to the need for an independent European power. The only way of giving Europe the necessary strength to preserve its strength was by forging European unity. The influence of the US and its federalism and the US desire "to see Europe forget its petty nationalism and unite itself in liberty as the American states had done" was, he felt, an aid for Europe to unite.[13]

Another declaration along with Ventotene, of publicity value, was the Geneva Declaration of the European Resistance, was called the European Charter of the Oppressed, and stated, inter alia, that a federal order must consist of

1. A government, not responsible to the governments of the individual member states, but to the peoples;
2. An armed force, subject to the orders of this federal government, and exclusive of all national contingents; and
3. A supreme court, responsible for the interpretation of questions referring to the federal constitution as well as for litigations between member states or between a member and a federation.[14]

Thus the desire for a creative solution, in part matching the national separation of powers, was impressed on a supranational agenda.

Functionalism, Federalism, and the Early European Community

The early proposals for cooperation such as the Schuman Plan for coal and steel cooperation, the Organisation for European Economic Cooperation, the Council of Europe and later the EC were proposals which came from crisis situations such as postwar reconstruction, economic recession, and the Korean War. As Schmidt points out, Schuman's proposal "was another child of the continuing postwar crisis." Spinelli contended, however, that it was only in times of crisis that definitive and bold steps to European Union could be made, calling these "moments of creative tension during which opportunities arise."[15] This contention was borne out by the proposals for European unity in the 1940s and 1950s and later in the 1980s.

Spinelli particularly considered the Monnet-Schuman plan for the ECSC had serious limitations as it involved two important raw materials, coal and steel, which could not be completely divorced from the national economies. For Spinelli, the Community needed to be a comprehensive economic and political system, and not a selective functionalist set of policies. Spinelli was at this stage critical of the functionalist and incrementalist approach of pooling of further markets and policies. He called for an alternative road to European unity—that of the six founder member states of the ECSC binding themselves "with a federal union pact with a common constitution and political organs." These suggestions, though, fell on deaf ears "at a time when the Marshall Plan and the Schuman Plan seemed to indicate the right road to European reconstruction."[16]

Spinelli thought the executive functions and the ECSC High Authority were too limited, as it was the member states in the Council who restricted these competences in the pursuit of national interests.[17] The High Authority, later the Commission, was to be regarded as restricted in its role by the fact that the Council held the power in the unequal balance of institutions within the Community. Spinelli considered there was a lack of inter-institutional balance among the Council, the Commission, and the Parliament which was contrary to federalist principles as well as democratic principles.[18] In addition, Spinelli lamented the fact that the Commission did not act as instigator of visions of European union, a role it inherited from federalist idealists.[19]

With regard to the democratic credentials of the Community, Spinelli was critical of the ECSC because its assembly, the precursor to the European Parliament, had no legislative powers at all. Rather a situation existed which analysts have called a democratic deficit. The people of Europe were not directly represented in the EP, with direct elections postponed by the Council until 1979 and the Council was not democratically accountable to the Parliament. Here too Spinelli called for increased powers for the EP, even involving co-decisionmaking of the Parliament and Council.[20]

The European movement after the war was split into two distinct streams with differing goals; Monnet was in one stream and Spinelli in the other. Monnet was part of what was later to be called the functionalist group, with emphasis on the ECSC rather than on the federalist ideals of the more radical Italian federalist movement. Monnet had close links with government officials in the Six, as well as with party leaders and trade unionists through the Action Committee for the United States of Europe.

The federal movement of Spinelli on the other hand, was an idealistic one with far-reaching goals involving individuals and intellectuals rather than parties or other movements and associations. Spinelli was never a member of Monnet's Action Committee for the United States of Europe, considering that the Committee, "in spite of its ambitious name," was concerned only with "the rapid promotion of an atomic pool"—a reference to the creation of the European Atomic Energy Community in 1957 at the same time as the EEC.[21] Monnet's Action Committee did achieve the gathering together of interested individuals and party representatives, including party leaders, in a regular exchange of views and it constituted a network of activists in government and non-government parties over two decades.[22]

Spinelli was critical of the creation of the EEC, as envisaged in the Spaak report on the Creation of an Economic Community, as unfeasible because it proposed "a merging of the various economies into a common market without, however, touching national sovereignty."[23] In 1966 he wrote

> It was the functionalists who won the race to create the first living unified European reality, and therefore, what there is of the united Europe which was born is neither a Europe of the peoples nor a Europe of states, but rather a Europe of supranational offices.[24]

Both Monnet and Spinelli were active in groups for a federal-style Europe, though both were elitist groups, and their aims and methods differed markedly. One of Spinelli's *Crocodile* newsletters expressed the differences in its portrayal of Monnet and his followers as functionalists and Spinelli as a federalist. The federalists, Spinelli explained in 1982, regarded the central issue in the 1950s as that of organising a new democratic political power structure in Europe, alongside the nation states.[25] The federalists considered this situation needed to have "certain limited but real authority and competence of its own, for its task of leading our peoples along the long and difficult road to unification of the economy, of international relations and of the armed forces." In contrast, the functionalists' central concern was what Spinelli called "the creation of "concrete" common commitments in economic policy, with its own administrative apparatus, while the power to decide not only on all further delegation of power should remain in the hands of the Member States governments."

The next quarter century saw the decline of federalist ideals as functional integration by economic sectors suited the revived nation state governments. Spinelli continued to call from within the EP, the new voice of the citizens of Europe, seen by many federalists as a true supranational institution, for federal political union. This "true union" of Europe would have responsibility for external and security affairs.[26]

Spinelli was thus not involved in the creation of the European Communities in the 1950s. That role and task fell in particular to Monnet and Schuman. Spinelli's role in the years of the formation of the Community was that of a visionary idealist rather than political negotiator. His activity was centred on the federalist movement, particularly the Italian one. Spinelli's European Federalist Movement (EFM) influenced Italian Prime Minister de Gasperi to the extent that he inserted a clause proposing European political union in the doomed European Defence Community Treaty of December 1951.[27]

Monnet had been active right from the start of negotiations with national governments after the war. Spinelli chose a different route to lobby for a united Europe, starting out as idealist and later getting involved as a politician in the last phase of his career. Spinelli was for many years critical of the ECSC, the EEC, and Euratom. He felt that the achievements of the 1950s fell short of his far-reaching ideal of European union.[28] While Spinelli was an idealist with a project for a federal state, Monnet was far from this world of abstractions, which he regarded as the prerogative of intellectuals rather than of men of action. Spinelli and the radical federalist such as the members of the Union Europeéne des Federalistes had hoped for a radical rejection of the nation state and its powers and prerogatives. This did not come about, and Spinelli himself began to realise this when he wrote in 1967, "the federalists had deceived themselves with regard to the speed with which the resistance of national traditions could be overcome."

The federalist movements exerted little influence on governments in the 1960s and 1970s, as intergovernmentalism and policy processes became the focus of the EC. Spinelli considered that federalism had its roots in the passions and dreams of the wartime resistance. Spinelli's vision was never fully achieved, but the trend had been set for an ideal beyond the nation state and beyond the European Communities which were established in the 1950s.

The vision of Spinelli and his contemporaries in the European Federalist Movement was one of a supranational entity, but also one that was democratic. The draft treaty on European Union which was Spinelli's brain-child was both federalist and also democratic. It was conceived as a means to redress the democratic deficit within the European Community, a problem that is not yet fully resolved today. It also aimed to bring into existence a supranational federal structure. Elements of both federalism (for instance, subsidiarity, common foreign and security policy, and single currency) and democracy (eg. increased power for the EP) are evident in the Maastricht Treaty on European

Union (TEU) and will no doubt continue to be the twin ideals of the federalist movement in Europe for the foreseeable future.

Spinelli, the European Parliament, and the European Union Treaty 1980-1984

It was in the EP that Spinelli became active again in advocating the creation of a supranational constitutional structure for the Community. As a member of the Italian Parliament in 1976 he was sent as a nominated member for Italy in the non-directly elected EP. He was elected to the first directly elected Assembly in June 1979. By this stage he was no longer a communist but was a member of the Communist and Allies electoral list and sat in the party group of the Communist and Allies of the EP.

From the mid-1980s onwards, the single most important initiative toward union was the draft Treaty on European Union, dubbed the Spinelli draft Treaty. Spinelli was the major proponent of European union, and a founder member of the EP Committee on Institutional Affairs.[29] He sent a letter to all members of the European Parliament in June 1980, suggesting that the parliament hold a major debate on the Community's institutional crisis, and proposed that a working party be set up to prepare a draft on institutional reform. He proposed this should be debated and voted upon as a draft treaty, and a recommendation put to the national governments and parliaments to adopt it.[30] Spinelli felt strongly that it was the task of the EP to initiate a constitutional move to European union. The group of parliamentarians behind this proposal (which continued after Spinelli's death in 1986), first met on 9 July 1980 in the Crocodile Restaurant in Strasbourg and became known as the Crocodile Club.

In 1981, after pressure from this group, the Committee on Institutional Affairs was set up in the EP, with the initial task of elaborating a draft Treaty on European Union.[31] The resultant treaty proposals were to come at a time of malaise in the Community, as institutions designed for a six-member Community required adaptation to cope with a membership of twelve, and limited policies needed expansion to apply to a wider range of tasks. In addition, since the Luxembourg Accord gave to member states the right to a national veto on decision making, the Council was not democratically accountable. The Council was also far from effective in decisionmaking and institutional inertia led to stalemates on many decisions. Spinelli phrased the problem thus:

... this arrogant oligarchy—epitomised by the protean Council—has become more impotent with the years because six, then nine, and now twelve distinct national systems are incapable of devising the longterm, forward-looking policies that Europe needs, or of providing the continuity needed for coherent development.[32]

The committee first met on 27-28 January 1982, with Spinelli as rapporteur-coordinator and parliamentarians Ferri, Nord, Jonker, and Pannella as its vice chairmen. The committee immediately set up six areas assigned to six rapporteurs, reflecting the EP agreement on aims for the committee and for the European Union Treaty. These were in the areas of internal and external economic policy; policy for society; political cooperation, security and development assistance; finance of the Union; the law of the Union and lastly the institutions of the Union. The committee consisted of members of all the political groups of the Parliament. The Committee held public hearings on the issue of European Union and used party political networks to circulate the drafts of its proposals.[33]

In September 1983, the committee resolution on the draft treaty's scope was adopted by the Parliament.[34] This resolution stated that in a world of change and crisis it was essential for the EC to assert its identity, thereby echoing the Tindemans 1976 report on European Union.[35] The resolution stated that the EC needed to make its voice heard among the two great powers, the US and the USSR, as well as to constitute a transforming force in North-South relations. The resolution formally instructed the Parliament's Committee on Institutional Affairs to draw up and submit for approval a preliminary draft Treaty establishing the European Union. The guidelines of the resolution called for a Union with the aim of helping "its peoples to develop the solidarity which binds them and to retain their historical identity" within the framework of freely accepted common laws and institutions whose aims were freedom and peace.

It further stated that citizens of the member states would be citizens of the Union, a claim to be echoed in the 1990 EP proposals on EU, especially the Martin and Colombo proposals. This issue of citizenship was also a feature to be of the discussion of the 1990-1991 Intergovernmental Conference (IGC) on European Union and featured in the final draft of the Maastricht Treaty on European Union.

Spinelli considered that a new Treaty was necessary because the objective of European Union in the Treaty of Rome was "caught up in the trammels of traditional diplomatic methods"[36] thus necessitating a new treaty to create a Union of greater political economic and social solidarity of its peoples in the "context of respect for human rights and democratic freedoms"—an echo of the language of the resistance movements of World War II.

The Committee on Institutional Affairs of the EP drew up a draft Treaty on European Union (EUT), adopted by the Parliament in February 1984. The Parliament urged the Commission and Council to support the creation of a government of European Union, with new powers transferred to it from the member states. The Treaty was divided into six parts: The Union (articles 1-8); Objectives, Methods of Action and Competences of the Union (9-13); Institutional Provisions (14-44); Policies, (45-69); Finances (70-81) and General and Final Provisions (82-87).[37]

The draft Treaty also drew up proposals for increased powers for the EP in co-decisionmaking with the Council of Ministers. It proposed that the Commission be transformed into a federal political Executive, along the lines of the 1950s proposals, with the EP-Commission relationship the strongest element of inter-institutional relations. The Treaty called for a European Union to take responsibility for economic and monetary policy, social policy, and foreign policy—including peace, disarmament, and security.

The legislature of the Union would be a bicameral system consisting of the EP and the Council of the Union, the latter continuing to consist of representatives of the member states. This in effect was a call for co-decision of Council and Parliament. The EP had called for the introduction of co-decisionmaking on all areas of EC policy in the second half of the 1980s and in the early 1990s, and some small measure of co-decision was accorded in the Single European Act and to a larger degree in the Maastricht Treaty. The Spinelli Treaty, as the EP draft became known, led to debate at national and intergovernmental levels as well as on the academic level regarding the implications of the treaty for the member states and for the political system of the EC.

Borchardt, in a report on European Unification written for the European Commission's *European Documentation* series, illustrates the political importance of the draft Treaty as follows:

> Although the draft treaty has no chance of being ratified by the national parliaments and thus becoming law, it presents a major challenge to the Member States, a public test of the seriousness of their commitment to real progress towards integration, forcing them to show their real colours.[38]

The draft EUT was never adopted as policy or as a treaty by the member states of the EC nor by its institutions, apart from the EP itself. However, it was part of a long line of initiatives for a community of states handing over sovereignty to the Community. It was not ignored, like the Tindemans report on European Union was in 1976, when adherence to national goals was particularly pronounced due in part to the oil crisis and economic difficulties at the national level. The draft

EUT led to full-scale debate on the Community's future, at a time of recognition of common economic problems, in the Dooge Ad Hoc Committee on Institutional Affairs and later the 1985 Intergovernmental Conference on the Single European Act.

Bieber *et al.* are correct in their assessment of the draft Treaty as "the most ambitious effort so far to achieve sweeping institutional and substantive reform in the European Community," re-opening the debate on reform of the Community at governmental and public levels.[39] The EUT goes beyond institutional reform, constituting a full comprehensive Treaty on the political power of the Community. It proposes a "single coherent structure" and does not attempt to amend the existing Treaties of the EC. Rather it "makes a fresh start and creates a new entity."[40] It does not create a fully fledged polity. It does however reflect a commitment to federalism which Spinelli held as an intellectual commitment, as well as constituting a legal and political system.[41]

Both the Spinelli Treaty and the Dooge Committee report agree on the following measures which were needed in order to achieve EU.[42]

1. The completion of the "Community venture" on monetary policy and freedom of movement;
2. The promotion of economic convergence;
3. Introduction of new policies especially technological developments and need for a cultural community;
4. The alignment of political cooperation and Community action and the incorporation of security aspects;
5. Reform of the institutions for democratic apparatus; and
6. The setting up of the basis for a genuine European citizenship.

There was a commonality in terms of identification of the problems of the Community. While the Dooge report is more federalist on the promotion of security policy, the EUT in general is more radical than the Dooge report in its call for a supranational set of democratic and accountable institutions and citizenship.

While Spinelli had been critical of the Community at the time of its foundation, he nevertheless came to appreciate its positive achievements. In 1986, he applauded the fact that a body of common interests, policies, common laws, common public expenditure, and common institutions existed.[43] He explained what his Treaty on European Union attempted to achieve in terms of broadening of the economic and political competence of the current Community. In this he was endeavouring to build on the existing Community structure, and not entirely replace it.

The Treaty attempted to "make the Union the legitimate successor of the Community"[44] and to introduce a federal government by giving the Commission the powers of an executive. It also attempted to render this government democratically accountable by giving the EP the powers of co-decision in the areas of the executive, legislation, taxation, and the budget. Thus the twin tenets of federalism and democracy are primary in the draft Treaty—tenets close to Spinelli given the origins of his ideas in the federalist movement. With regard to the redressing of the imbalances of the institution, Spinelli's treaty called for a reduction of "the excessive powers of the Council."[45] Spinelli regarded the draft Treaty as the new constitutional basis of the EC. He stated that in content it was a constitution or a fundamental law.[46]

This treaty was, according to Burgess, a means to an end for Spinelli as it was a step towards the federal structure of Europe which he had envisaged since the resistance years.[47] This view is correct, although it is clear that the EU envisaged in the Treaty was essentially federal in structure, in terms of state-centre relations and the federal control of matters of national sovereignty such as foreign affairs and political institutions in supranational decisionmaking. It was a qualitative and quantitative advance in the process of European integration.[48]

Spinelli was realistic in his assessment that the Union was too radical for some member states and so he proposed in the draft Treaty that the Union come into force even if some member states had no desire to join the Union. In this he effectively re-opened the debate on the two-tier Europe, or a two-speed Europe, which was to come under renewed scrutiny in the wake of the Danish "No" vote on the Maastricht Treaty in June 1992 and of the 1992 problems with the Exchange Rate Mechanism of the European Monetary System.

It is important to be aware that Spinelli worked for union in the 1980s from within the most federally minded institution of the Community, the EP. He was adamant that it was the work of a constituent assembly to draw up the Community's new constitutional and institutional basis in order for the Community to become a federalist entity. The EP is certainly proving to be the instigator of political initiative despite the fact that it had little formal power of initiative under the EC Treaties as this lay with the Commission. Nevertheless the Parliament has been a prime mover in putting the issues of the political future of the EC as a Union on the agenda of the nation states of Western Europe.

European Union objectives such as the Spinelli 1984 initiative saw that the EC legal system needed to change in order to be attentive to the problem which was tackled by the Single European Act. Spinelli's draft treaty on European Union, adopted by the European Parliament in February 1984, by 237 votes in favour and 31 against, with 43 abstentions, was significant for reopening the debate among the EC actors on the future of the EC as a European Union in political terms.

Spinelli utilised several distinct approaches and networks in his aim for political acceptance of the draft Treaty. Jacobs and Corbett[49] elaborate four channels used by Spinelli in order to gain support for the draft Treaty. The first channel was to approach governments in the European Council and individually. The second consisted of approaching national parties that had policy statements on the draft Treaty in their 1984 electoral programmes for the direct election to the EP in June of that year. Thirdly, contacts were established with national parliaments including the sending of EP delegations to every national parliament. Fourthly, there were contacts in interest groups, non-governmental organisations and academic circles, and use of the media interest in the draft Treaty. The initial reaction to the Treaty in government circles was support from the heads of state of Italy, the Netherlands, Belgium and Germany. The support of French President François Mitterrand was also crucial.

The Parliament, since it adopted Spinelli's draft Treaty in February 1984, has continued to advance the cause of European integration throughout the 1990s. It was this Treaty which was to lead to the setting up of the Dooge ad hoc Intergovernmental Committee [on Institutional Affairs consisting of national representatives] in 1985 on the instigation of the European Council. As a result of this Committee's report, urging the establishment of an economic area without internal frontiers, strengthened foreign policy to encompass security and defence and improved decision-making in particular, as a means of dealing with the 1985 White Paper on the Internal Market proposed by Lord Cockfield of the Commission, the Intergovernmental Conference (IGC) of representatives of all EC member states on the Single European Act (SEA) took place in late 1985.

The Spinelli initiative was thus quickly followed by an intergovernmental reaction on the part of the state actors with the creation of the Dooge Committee and the IGC on the SEA. This trend was to become the pattern in the EC over the last decade, of a supranational initiative followed by national responses by the intergovernmental actors, in the continuing conflict of intergovernmentalism and supranationalism.

The Dooge Committee officially did not regard its task as an examination of the Spinelli treaty but rather to produce a political document along the lines of the Spaak Committee of the 1950s in the lead up to the creation of the EEC and Euratom.[50] The Dooge committee produced a report to the European Council in Milan in June 1985. The report stated that there was a need for a new Treaty for the Community. It was in Milan that the heads of states and government of the Community decided to convene an intergovernmental conference to revise the EC Treaties, under article 236 of the EEC treaty, which was to result in the Single European Act.[51] The same year, the Cockfield White Paper on the completion of the Internal Market was circulated to the states and institutions. This White Paper went on the agenda of the IGC on the SEA, along with some of the issues raised by Spinelli's draft Treaty, as set out in the Dooge report.

Spinelli was not at all happy with the outcome of this Intergovernmental Conference on the Single European Act and in fact he suggested that the SEA would "almost certainly have proven its ineffectiveness within two years."[52] In this, he was in fact wrong, as the SEA was to constitute not the last but rather the initial step towards institutional reform and a move to European Union by the intergovernmental Council and permanent representatives.

The Legacy of Spinelli and European Union

Spinelli's career and vision can be divided into two distinct phases, the earlier idealistic federal one and later the political pro-active one in advocating the adoption of the draft Treaty on European Union. Spinelli was instrumental in setting up the European Federalist Movement and he was active in it for over forty years in keeping the federalist principle alive—a principle which he referred to as "Europeanism, now an ineradicable force in European political life."[53]

In addition, he had participant experience of the EC institutions from several perspectives, firstly as personal adviser to the Italian Foreign Minister Pietro Nenni and hence a knowledge of the Council of Ministers, secondly as a Commissioner in the 1970s and lastly as a member of the European Parliament, the most federally minded of the institutions, although Spinelli himself said, "The European Parliament is composed of impractical theorists and revolutionaries."[54] Spinelli was effective in gathering together the parliamentarians of differing beliefs in a common commitment to the greater good of the Community. He had a comprehensive view of the spectrum of institutions of the Community.

Wistrich sees Spinelli's lasting monument to the cause of federalism as the draft Treaty, the blueprint for European Union, which he "fathered and shepherded through to its adoption by a massive majority" of the first directly elected EP.[55] As Wistrich points out, "both Monnet and Spinelli saw that the key to their success lay in persuading those with influence and power to their cause."[56] Spinelli was also effective in bringing together several strands of European federalism in the Treaty and by proposing that the Community take on board an increased number of policies as common policies, that is, common to all constituent states and decided at EC and not national levels. He also dealt with the need for institutional reform of the Community, but did not simply rely on this reform as the panacea for the Community's ills.

He was concerned that issues of citizenship, monetary policy, and sovereignty all be dealt with in the Treaty by the Community, or the Union as he wished it to be called. He wished the Treaty to go beyond the functionalist model of integration, towards a federal one. This tension of functionalism, as perfected in the Single Market, and federalism, as proposed in the Spinelli Treaty, is a conflict which is still unresolved within the contemporary European Union at the end of the century. In addition, he called for the replacement of intergovernmentalism by supranationalism, a call issued, for example, in his discussion of the draft Treaty, when he asked that the Parliament be involved in the debate by member states' political elites on the Treaty.

While he recognised that the Intergovernmental Conference on the Single European Act was inevitable, he called for it not to be dominated by narrow national interests protecting national sovereignty to the full. The Intergovernmental Conference of September to December 1985, in the event, did not use the Spinelli Treaty as the basis of its negotiations, but rather produced an amendment to the existing Treaties entitled the Single European Act.

Spinelli was critical of the SEA as it did not take on board the principles of the EUT, but it nevertheless dealt with some of the issues of institutional lourdeur and stagnation of the European economy by setting a deadline for the completion of the Single Internal Market (SIM) and setting in place the decisional mechanisms for the SIM. The SEA was however stage one of what has now become an on-going process of intergovernmental negotiation on the handing over of sovereignty in the IGC on European Political and Economic and Monetary Union, a process which resulted in the Maastricht European Union Treaty concluded in December 1991, signed in February 1992 and ratified in October 1993.

The Maastricht Treaty provided for a further intergovernmental conference in 1996 on progress on the Maastricht Treaty. While the Commission and EP are involved in these negotiations, the fact remains that the direction of the European Union towards supranationalism is carried out in a largely intergovernmental forum, with proposals for supranationalism coming from the major actors in the European Union, France and Germany, with some Italian support. So there is still a need to deal with the fact that the EC, even while renamed European Union, remains an uneasy admixture of intergovernmentalism and supranationalism and federalism. Supranational proposals are dealt with in the most intergovernmental forum of the Union, the Council, even though they are proposed by the Commission and EP.

An examination of Spinelli and particularly his role in the formulation of the draft EUT illustrates that the EU still has to deal with the original concerns of its founders and the federalists of the postwar era. The EC is indeed the brain-child of men like Schuman and Monnet but the European Union initiative is the brain-child of Spinelli and his colleagues in the federalist movement and in the EP.

It is in the EP that Spinelli's influence is most evident. The Parliament has continued its commitment to the ideal of European Union and particularly the redressing of the democratic deficit. It is from within the EP that reports and resolutions have emanated on subsidiarity, European citizenship, and the desire for a supranational Community as a Union. The various Martin, Colombo (dubbed Spinelli 2), Duverger, Giscard d'Estaing, Haensch and Bourlanges reports are particularly relevant in this context as important blueprints for the Community's political future into the next century.[57]

Fontaine and Malosse see Spinelli's significance as attempting to bring about a revolutionary leap in the process of European Union in endowing the Community with a federal constitution establishing relations between the states and the Union, founded on the principle of subsidiarity.[58] They see the Treaty as the incentive to the governments to accept the principle of a revision of the Treaties, concretised in the SEA IGC in 1985. They point out correctly that the Spinelli proposal remains the doctrinal foundation of the strategy of the EP elected in 1989, a strategy carried out in the Institutional Affairs Committee in particular.

Spinelli foresaw the need for a thorough re-examination of the nation state and here in fact he expressed the dilemma of European Unity — the conflict between nation state and Europeanism. While he was adamant in his visionary phase (1940s and 1950s) that the nation state must be rejected as it had failed the people of Europe, he came to an acceptance of its durability in his desire to have national governments adopt the draft treaty, an acceptance which featured in his more overtly political phase of the late 1970s and 1980s.

Spinelli's vision also influenced a number of intellectuals in his writing as well as the *Ventotene Manifesto*. His draft treaty influenced politicians and governments. Both his vision and his treaty reflect in many ways the developmental stages of the European Community itself. The Community, founded at a time of idealism, was to become bogged down in a policy-making stalemate and in the resurgence of nationalism from the Luxembourg Accord of 1966 until the 1980s. The 1980s saw the revival of European union concepts at a time when the Single Market was the economic manifestation of that concept. Spinelli seized on the need to resolve the problem of the EC's institutional lourdeur and policy-making stalemate in the Council to launch his European Union Treaty ideal in the early 1980s. He also utilised the new democratic legitimacy of the popularly-elected EP since 1979 by using that institution as the launching pad for the proposed European Union, giving it democratic credibility. He built on the Tindemans and Genscher-Colombo proposals for European union, as well as the Italian government's federalist stance to build up his intellectual case for European unity and to implement his practical set of steps to achieve his goal.

The fact remains that the European Union Treaty draft was not accepted by the governments of the member states as its supranationalist elements were rejected by most member states in favour of increased economic cooperation in the Single Market Program. It was, however, the launching pad to the Single European Act and even Maastricht. The tension of the Union, of federalism versus intergovernmentalism, remains after Maastricht. The democratic deficit has still not been solved. Spinelli would have been less than satisfied with Maastricht but pleased that European unity is still prominent on the EU agenda in name as well as aspiration. The European Union agenda itself is now faced with new challenges. Dubois sees the Community edifice as being essentially functionalist, the Europe of Monnet, which lost contact with the other architects of European construction, such as Coudenhove Kalergi and Spinelli, and this functionalist Europe is now dead, as post-Maastricht Europe attempts to deal with its citizens' dreams and visions.[59]

Spinelli's vision of a federalist democratic European Union is still pertinent in contemporary Europe.

Notes

1. A. Spinelli, *Come ho tentato di diventare saggio* (Il Mulino: Bologna, 1987). Altiero Spinelli describes the six cycles of his action, each based on different hypotheses, as follows: 1943-1945 desire for a democratic renaissance and destruction of the nation state; 1947-1954 attempt to have moderate ministers construct a federation; 1954-1960 attempts to mobilise Europeanism against the nation states; 1960-1970 was a period of reflection rather than political action for the relaunch of federalist action; 1970-1976 represents an attempt to render the Commission as a motor of integration; 1978-1986 the EP was to draw up EU blueprint.

2. P. V. Dastoli, "Introduction" in A. Spinelli *Speeches in the European Parliament* (Brussels: Communist and Allies Group, European Parliament, 1987), p. 13.

3. C. F. Delzell, "The European Federalist Movement in Italy: First Phase 1918-1947," *The Journal of Modern History*, vol. 33, no. 3, September 1960, p. 245.

4. A. Spinelli, "European Union in the Resistance," *Government and Opposition*, 2, 1967, p. 322.

5. *Ibid.*, p. 323.

6. *Ibid.*, p. 324.

7. Quoted in Spinelli, "European Union in the Resistance," op cit., p. 327.

8. A. Spinelli, *The Eurocrats: Conflict and Crisis in the European Community* (Baltimore: Johns Hopkins, 1966).

9. It was in fact only in the 1980s that there was to be a desire for increased supranationalism. This was the first time since the failure of the European Defence Community and the European Political Community.

10. C. Webb, "Europeanism and the European Movements," in M. Kolinsky and W. E. Paterson, eds., *Social and Political Movements in Western Europe* (London: Croom Helm, 1976), p. 311.

11. C. Webb, "Europeanism and the European Movements," ibid., p. 312.

12. See Cornelia Navari's chapter in this volume for a discussion of the divisions among federalists.

13. A. Spinelli, "The Growth of the European Movement Since World War II" in C. Grove Haines, ed., *European Integration* (Baltimore: Johns Hopkins Press, 1957), p. 48.

14. H. Schmidt, *European Union: From Hitler to de Gaulle* (New York: Van Norstrand Reinhold, 1969), p. 103.

15. A. Spinelli, *The European Adventure: Tasks for the Enlarged Community* (London: Charles Knight, 1972), p. 17. He stated that "improvisation in response to the pressure of events is not enough. A strategy is needed," p. 186.

16. Spinelli, "The Growth of the European Movement Since World War II," 1957, p. 57.

17. The Council exercised the most power of decisionmaking within the EC, while the Commission and the Parliament were often portrayed as supranationalist opponents of the expression of national goals in the Council.

18. *Ibid.*, p. 56.

19. Spinelli was very critical of the limited role taken on by the "Eurocrats" of the Commission. See Spinelli, *The Eurocrats*, especially pp. 203-215 and Spinelli, *The European Adventure*, 1972, especially pp. 8-9.

20. Spinelli was thus later to call for substantial powers for the EP in his draft treaty, so that the EP, as the assembly of the Union, would be involved in co-decision and co-legislative powers with the Council.

21. Spinelli, "The Growth of the European Movement Since World War II," p. 62.

22. Author's discussion with Max Kohnstamm, former Secretary to the Action Committee for the United States of Europe, November 1992.

23. Spinelli, "The Growth of the European Movement Since World War II," p. 62.

24. Spinelli, *The Eurocrats*, p. 25. In his memoirs, Spinelli wrote of how, from 1970-1976, he worked on the hypothesis that the Commission could assume the role of political guide in the reactivating of the construction of political union. See Spinelli, *Come ho tentato di diventare saggio*, p. 348.

25. *Crocodile Letter*, a letter of the Federalists Intergroup of the European Parliament, 8 May 1982, p. 2.

26. Ibid., p. 3.

27. P. Ginsborg, *A History of Contemporary Italy* (London: Penguin, 1990).

28. See, for example, Michael Burgess, *Federalism and European Union* (London: Routledge, 1989).

29. See Cornelia Navari, Chapter 4, in this volume.

30. F. Capotorti, M. Hilf, F. Jacobs, J-P. Jacque, *The European Union Treaty* (Oxford: Clarendon Press, 1986), p. 11.

31. European Parliament Resolution of 9 July 1980 setting up a committee on Institutional Affairs, *Official Journal of the EC*, no. 234, 14 September 1980, p. 48.

32. Spinelli, Preface to R. Bieber, J-P. Jacque, J. H. H. Weiler, *An Ever Closer Union* (Luxembourg: Office for Offical Publications of the European Communities, 1985), p. 3.

33. F. Jacobs and R. Corbett, *The European Parliament* (Boulder and San Francisco: Westview, 1990), p. 250.

34. Resolution concerning the substance of the preliminary draft Treaty establishing the European Union, adopted by the EP at its session of 14 February 1983, *Official Journal of the European Communities* 277 of 17 October 1983, pp. 95-117.

35. The Report was drawn up by Belgian Prime Minister Leo Tindemans. It called for a Common European voice in international affairs and a clear EC commitment to creating a European Union which would be federal in nature as well as discussing the issue of a two-speed Europe.

36. *Crocodile Letter*, p. 9.

37. European Parliament, *Draft Treaty establishing the European Union* (Luxembourg: European Parliament, 1984). The Union would be created by the High Contracting Parties, and any democratic European state could apply to become a member of the Union. Citizens of members states could *ipso facto* be citizens of the Union. See especially Articles 1-3.

38. K. Borchardt, *European Unification: The Origins and growth of the European Community* (Luxembourg: Office for Official Publications of the European Communities, 1990), p. 73.

39. Bieber et al., *An Ever Closer Union*, p. 8.

40. F. Capotorti, M. Hilf, F. Jacobs, J-P. Jacque, *The European Union Treaty*, p. 17.

41. See, for example, R. Bieber, "Achievements of the European Parliament 1979-1984," *Common Market Law Review*, Number 21, 1984 and J. Lodge, "European Union and the First Elected European Parliament: The Spinelli Initiative," *Journal of Common Market Studies*, no. 234, 1984.

42. Here the author draws on Bieber et al., *An Ever Closer Union*, p. 10. See also EP Committee on Institutional Affairs, *Notice to Members*, Parallel between the Dooge Committee Report and the Draft Treaty establishing European Union, 13 December 1984.

43. A. Spinelli, Foreword, in J. Lodge, ed., *European Union: The European Community in search of a Future*. (London:, Macmillan, 1986), p. xii.

44. A. Spinelli, in J. Lodge, ed., *European Union: The European Community in search of a Future*, p. xvii.

45. *Ibid.*, p. xvii.

46. *Ibid.*, p. xviii.

47. M. Burgess, Altiero Spinelli, Federalism and the EUT, in J. Lodge, ed., *European Union: The European Community in search of a Future*, p. 174.

48. Burgess contends in this chapter and in his book, *Federalism and European Union*, that there is an intellectual continuity in the federal ideals of the postwar years and those of the 1980s.

49. F. Jacobs and R. Corbett, *The European Parliament*, p. 250. See also *Agence Europe*, 30 March 1985.

50. Discussion of author with Senator James Dooge, October 1992.

51. For an examination of the Single European Act, see P. Murray, "Who Legislates? Institutional Developments in the European Community and the Single European Act" in B. Nelson et al., eds., *The European Community in the 1990s* (Oxford: Berg, 1992).

52. Quoted in R. Keohane and S. Hoffmann, *The New European Community* (Boulder: Westview, 1991), p. 3.

53. Spinelli, *The Eurocrats*, p. 20.

54. Preface to Bieber et al., *An Ever Closer Union*, p. 3.

55. H. Wistrich, *After 1992: The United States of Europe* (London: Routledge, 1990), p. 149.

56. *Ibid.*

57. For a discussion of these reports, see P. Murray, "The European Community—Towards Political Union?" *Melbourne Journal of Politics*, vol. 20, 1991. See also the EP Reports preparing for the 1996 IGC and reviewing the TEU.

58. P. Fontaine and H. Malosse, *Les Institutions Europeenes* (Paris: Retz, 1992), p. 118.

59. N. Dubois, "L'Europe de Jean Monnet est morte! Vive l'Europe, federale," *EIPASCOPE*, European Institute of Public Administration, Maastricht, no. 1992/3, p. 13.

7

Conservative and Christian Democrat Debates on European Union

Richard Dunphy

Introduction

Since the emergence of Christian Democracy as a significant politi-
cal movement in many western European countries after 1945, Christian
Democrats have been to the fore of the movement for European unity.
In the decade following the end of the second world war, Christian
Democracy contributed many of the men with whose names the Euro-
pean movement has been associated ever since: Konrad Adenauer
(Germany), Alcide de Gasperi (Italy), Robert Schuman (France), Joseph
Bech (Luxembourg), Dirk Udo Stikker (Netherlands) and Paul van
Zeeland (Belgium). Several leading Christian Democrats—Adenauer, de
Gasperi and Schuman—came from frontier regions of Europe which had
repeatedly suffered from competing national ambitions and territorial
expansionism, and their political formation was moreover strongly influenced by Catholic internationalism.[1]

The hope of such leaders in the immediate postwar period was that
Britain would play a leading role in the construction of European unity,
of which Churchill had spoken at the Hague Congress in May 1948. In
the event, the Treaty of Rome (1957) embodied a much more modest
ambition—essentially the gradual creation of a common market—and
it was the incremental functionalism of Jean Monnet which proved a
more convincing path to European integration than the federalist idealism which many Christian Democrats shared with non-confessional
parties and forces, emerging from the ranks of the anti-Fascist resistance movements. Moreover, despite Churchill's return to power in 1951,

Britain chose to stand aside from the process. Influential Conservative Party figures such as Anthony Eden and Lord Salisbury, a leading light on the pro-Empire wing of the party, shared with the Labour Party political elite the view that Britain was still a world power, the future of which lay in close alliance with the USA rather than the states of Europe.[2]

The return to power in France of General de Gaulle in 1958, and perhaps also the absence of any mass Christian Democratic party which might have challenged nationalistic hegemony on the Right during the lifetime of the French Fifth Republic, meant that the French approach to the Community continued to reflect concerns with economic functionalism, national self-interest and the sovereignty of the nationstate. For de Gaulle, the European project above all involved increasing French prosperity and keeping Germany in check. During the first decade or so of the Community's life it was above all German Christian Democracy, loyal to the vision of Konrad Adenauer, which kept alive the dream of a Europe which would be economically integrated, politically unified, and firmly anchored in the Western camp—though capable of approaching the USA, within the NATO alliance, on more equal terms. Germany's Christian Democratic Union (CDU) could generally count upon the support of Alcide de Gasperi's Italian Christian Democracy (DC), although it has been often argued that Italy's Christian Democrats showed little pro-active interest in the European project in the years following the demise of de Gasperi, invoking European federalist rhetoric more as a weapon in domestic political struggle against the Italian Communist Party, whilst in reality being more concerned with a functionalist and narrowly economic approach to integration.[3]

Britain's first two applications to join the European Community—the first by Macmillan's Conservative Government in 1961 and the second by Wilson's Labour Government in 1967—both fell foul of a French veto. The principal EC Christian Democratic parties—the German, the Italian and the Belgian—all voiced support for British membership. No doubt, their motives had much to do with geopolitical considerations and the internal balance of power within the Community. But their support also indicated that, although the Christian Democratic vision of Europe might owe part of its inspiration to Papal encyclicals, and the movement can be regarded as confessional in the sense of enjoying Catholic Church support and reflecting broad Catholic values, it can in no way be branded as Catholic in a sectarian sense. (The German CDU and the Dutch Christian Democratic movement have always enjoyed substantial Protestant support.)

When Edward Heath eventually succeeded in taking Britain into the Community on 1 January 1973, the Conservative Party essentially "sold" the decision to the British public on grounds of economic expediency: Britain's economy was in severe crisis, the period being one of social and political tension; the country was soon to fall victim to the international oil crisis. Its future, Heath argued, lay in acceptance of the "end of empire" and the pursuit of new markets in Europe. This so-called realistic view of Britain's situation was shared by the intellectual and political elite in the centre of British politics: the pragmatic or "modernising" wing of the Conservative Party, the social democratic wing of the Labour Party, and the Liberal Party.

However, despite joining the Community, no real effort was made by either major political party in Britain to effect a sea-change in traditionally hostile British attitudes towards "the continent." No effort was made to temper, let alone supplant, British nationalism with any concept of a new European identity. The debate over Europe remained largely an affair of the elite. Only two years after joining the Community were the British people allowed to vote on the matter in a referendum—conceded by Labour prime minister Harold Wilson largely as a means of neutering his own Left-wing—and the conduct of the referendum campaign by both Labour Government and Conservative opposition was revealing: people were invited to vote in favour of what was by now the status quo, and warned of the economic disruption which would follow withdrawal from the EC. In other words, the appeal was to the conservatism and self-interest of the British electorate; the themes of European federalism were almost entirely absent from the debate.

It was really only from the mid-1970s, with the extension of the Community's financial scope and the approaching direct elections to the European Parliament (EP), that the debate about the nature and future direction of the Community got under way once again. Many of the issues which have been to the fore in that debate ever since—Community financing, enlargement, institutional reform, democratisation, Community competence and the question of supranationality—have cut across traditional Left/Right political cleavages. The EP has become a forum in which European federalism has emerged as the issue around which a new political cleavage, at least at the elite level, is taking shape. Nowadays, there is much talk in Europe about the erosion of traditional Left/Right certainties and the emergence of a new political agenda. The contours of that agenda are not entirely clear, and predictions about the future shape of European politics would be hazardous. At present it seems likely that political forces will increasingly respond to an agenda set by the "three Es"—Europe, Environment, and Ethnicity (or racism).

In fact, "Europe" has long been an issue around which an "historic compromise" has been forged, inside the EP, between pro-federalist forces of both Left and Right—against nationalistic forces, also of both Left and Right. When one considers that the dominant features of the contemporary political era include the unprecedented internationalisation of both economy and culture, the break-up of the USSR and some of the former eastern and central European states with the revival of age-old ethnic and national conflicts, and the emergence of an alarming degree of political malaise in western Europe—expressed partly through the medium of protest parties and movements, many of which are overtly racist or nihilistic—it is not surprising that the theme of European union should be central to the strategic debates taking place on both Right and Left.

On the Right of the traditional political spectrum, European Christian Democrats and British Conservatives have, more often than not, displayed marked differences of emphasis if not outright disagreement on key questions about Europe's future. The purpose of this chapter is to examine the emergence of competing discourses over Europe in the Conservative and Christian Democratic camps in recent years; and to raise the question of whether, in the light of contemporary debates on Europe's future, and the admission of the British and Danish Conservatives to the Group of the European People's Party (Christian Democrats) in the EP in May 1992, a true *rapprochement* is now taking place between Conservatives and Christian Democrats on the terrain of European union.

British Conservatism and European Christian Democracy: Two Ideologies, Two Traditions and the Idea of Europe

It is a moot point as to whether Conservatism and Christian Democracy can be regarded as reasonably coherent ideologies or philosophies. Both terms have been used to cover a wide variety of political positions. In mainland Europe, considerable differences of emphasis and of outlook have been noted between the Left and Right of Christian Democracy; between Protestant and Catholic, confessional and more "lay," variants, as well as between national Christian Democratic parties. In Britain, it is commonly acknowledged that the Conservative Party has long been host to a number of disparate tendencies, which might well break up into different political parties given another electoral system. Moreover, the longterm processes of change which have affected the social structure, political cleavages and political culture of western European countries throughout the postwar period have not merely challenged traditional ideologies of the Left. The Right has also been forced to respond to the challenge of restructuring its political project to meet the demands of an increasingly post-Fordist and post-modern society.

Many of the problems which have confronted both Christian Democracy and Conservatism have been similar: how to maintain or build a consensus capable of sustaining a bloc of social and political forces which is electorally successful at a time when the crisis of the welfare state is straining social solidarity; how to articulate the concerns of those strata and groups which feel that traditional values, identities and beliefs are being undermined and eroded by secularisation, modernisation and societal diversity; how to respond to the clear limitations of the nationstate, above all in the economic sphere. The nature of the responses, however, have often been very different, and the differences have been underlined by the hegemony of the Thatcherite New Right within British (and not only British) Conservative politics since the mid-1970s. Although Thatcherism has had its admirers within the ranks of European Christian Democracy, and the broader centre-Right in Europe, its overall strategic project has not won many converts in terms of parties or Governments. The "Thatcherisation" of the western European Right—which the lady herself hoped for—has, on the whole, not materialised. It is this very failure which prompts the observer to look again at the sources of the European Christian Democratic and British Conservative traditions. At a time when the Thatcherite project appears to be exhausting itself in Britain, might Christian Democracy offer a possible alternative route forward, as some Conservatives—including former party chairman, Chris Patten—appear to think?

It therefore seems sensible to locate Conservative and Christian Democratic debates about the future of Europe against the background of a very brief survey of these two political traditions.

Stephen George has argued that within the contemporary Conservative Party one can detect three major tendencies: the old "high Tory" tradition of paternalism, the "pragmatic modernisers" and the free market neoliberals.[4]

Traditional Tory paternalism has its roots in an organic conception of society which sees relations between social groups and categories as reflecting a "natural" social order. Profoundly conservative and reactionary, such a view sits uneasily with the myths of upward social mobility and a classless society associated with Thatcher and Major respectively. Traditional Toryism concerns itself with the defence of traditional values, the preservation of a strong state, above all in the sphere of "law and order," the defiance of modern "decadence," and the cult of British nationalism. Imperialist and nationalist to the core, traditional Toryism has extolled the legacy of the British empire and clung to a frankly unrealistic view of Britain's position in the post-1945 world. Representing, as it does, something of a compromise between the aristocratic Britain of a pre-democratic and pre-liberal era—the Britain which never experienced a modern bourgeois-democratic revolution— and the Britain of the industrial revolution and advent of universal suffrage, it has never accepted fully that economic transactions should be governed exclusively by the market, or that governments should withdraw from all but a supervisory and custodial role in economic and social affairs.

George is right to argue that it is the traditionalists who have been most hostile to the project of European integration since 1945. Nostalgic and nationalistic, convinced of the innate superiority of Britishness (or Englishness), and concerned with respect for, and deference towards, British institutions and traditions which are seen as threatened by "alien" European political traditions, this wing of the Conservative Party has long produced politicians who are amongst the most "Europhobic": Enoch Powell, the late Nicholas Ridley and William Cash, to name but a few. In so far as they have an equivalent on mainland Europe, it is undoubtedly those elements on the nationalist Right—including Le Pen's Front National (FN) in France—who likewise reject the project of a federal Europe as "threatening' to national traditions.

The neoliberals have generally been inclined to go along with European unity in the economic sphere so long as it adheres to free market principles. Hence, their support for the Single European Act, but opposition to any move towards political union or social harmonisation which might impose costs on British industry. They are at best reluctant Europeans, for whom an ideological attachment to the market overrides any attachment to the idea of Europe. Again, their nearest European counterparts are probably found within freemarket liberal parties, rather than within Christian Democracy, although the recent formation of Silvio Berlusconi's *Forza Italia* movement in Italy may have provided them with new allies.

The pragmatic modernisers, according to George, are the most pro-EC/EU, even favouring a measure of central control from Brussels when such is deemed beneficial to the British economy. This group also contains those most open perhaps to the reform and relaunch of the Conservative Party along mainstream European centre-Right lines, and the regeneration of British democracy. George includes both Harold Macmillan and Edward Heath in this category. The same is probably true of Chancellor of the Exchequer, Kenneth Clarke, and was even held until recently to be true of John Major—although Major has notoriously wavered between the three tendencies. Yet the modernisers' very pragmatism has meant that they have tended to extol the practical advantages of EC membership for Britain rather than elaborate the idea of Europe itself.

Of course, British Conservatism involves a constant balancing act between these three tendencies, and actual approaches to Europe at any given time tend to reflect an ideological mix (witness, for example, the increasingly desperate attempts made by John Major in 1994 and 1995 to keep his party united on the subject by sending out contradictory signals to different constituencies). Throughout most of the Thatcher period, a nationalist and imperialist rhetoric went hand-in-hand with an emphasis on the defence of the free market. This was usually articulated ideologically in terms of Britain's mission to "save" Europe from statist interventionism and "Brussels bureaucracy" as it had "saved" Europe from Hitler in 1939-1945.

Under John Major's leadership, since November 1990, two noticeable shifts occurred. During the first phase—which lasted until roughly the summer of 1993, when debates over ratification of the Maastricht Treaty on European Union threatened party unity visibly—the pragmatic modernisers seemed to be in the driving seat, and Europhiles from within the ranks of the Conservative MEPs even interpreted the change in leadership as an encouragement to explore further the party's, and Britain's, "European vocation." However, from mid-1993 onwards, Conservative divisions over Europe assumed ever more critical and bitter forms. Internecine warfare over the Maastricht Treaty, severe losses in the European Parliament elections of June 1994 when the party lost 14 of its 32 MEPs, the withdrawal of the parliamentary whip from nine anti-European Conservative MPs in late 1994 (which technically left Major leading a minority Government), and finally open warfare between members of the cabinet over a single European currency and related constitutional issues in early 1995, revealed a party in real danger of falling apart over the central issue of European political union. Major found himself more circumscribed than ever by the need to unify his party. Hence the continuing use of nationalist rhetoric (albeit in more dulcet tones than Thatcher), and an insistence on freemarket principles which seems to belie the promise of a more caring and more Christian Democratic Conservatism.

For the nationalist wing of the Conservative party, fronted by such figures as Employment Secretary Michael Portillo and Social Security Secretary Peter Lilley, Europe is again a dark cloud hovering over the white cliffs of Dover. In February 1995, for example, the junior government minister Charles Wardle resigned his post, citing the spectre of a flood of illegal immigrants engulfing Britain as a result of free movement of peoples within the European Union (as the Community became known, following ratification of the Maastricht Treaty in November

1993). Significantly, within Conservative ranks the defence of the European ideal by figures such as Kenneth Clarke or Trade and Industry Secretary Michael Heseltine has continued to be couched in pragmatic terms, leaving Conservative exponents of European federalism to bemoan the fact that the idea of Europe is not yet publicly proclaimed as the terrain on which a reconstruction of both British society, and of the Right in British politics, may take place.

Although countries such as Germany and the Netherlands have produced Christian Democratic movements of a Protestant inspiration, Christian Democracy really has its roots in the encounter between political Catholicism and modernity—and in particular mass democracy—since the late nineteenth century. According to Irving, the authoritarian and anti-democratic nature of the Roman Catholic church made it extremely difficult for Catholics to be "good liberal democrats," and consequently for Christian Democracy to emerge as a significant mass movement, before 1914: "they [Catholics] could be good social workers, but not good democrats."[5] Indeed, in a sense this remained the case until 1945. There were, of course, many politically active Catholic democrats; but they tended to have a semidetached relationship with the Church hierarchy, regarding themselves as "social Christians" or "Christian socialists," rather than Christian Democrats. As Clemens points out,[6] these Christian socialists were often much more radical than their Christian Democratic successors. In 1945, with authoritarianism discredited, and with the Church itself severely embarrassed by its association with Mussolini's regime in Italy and with the anti-democratic Right elsewhere, Christian Democracy was favoured as the organisational, ideological and strategic model for the future.

Christian Democracy, inspired by Catholic social teaching, set itself the goal of plotting an alternative course in human affairs to both Marxism, with its emphasis upon class politics and its historic tendency to assimilate public ownership to state ownership, and to freemarket capitalism, which was seen as rooted in a theory of human nature which reduces one's worth to one's market value, and which promotes a materialistic consumerism which threatens human spirituality. In practice, the pursuit of a social order which transcended both capitalism and socialism has long been abandoned by all but a few idealists and intellectuals. Encouraged by the fanatically anti-Communist Pope Pius XII, Christian Democracy, during the Cold War years, accommodated itself to the capitalist order. Since the 1950s, it has sought to stabilise and consolidate capitalism in western Europe and to provide the European Right with a model capable of resisting the hegemony of the Left, both communist and social democratic.

Christian Democracy itself has faced a multiple crisis of identity for some years. The process of secularisation has confronted Christian Democracy with the challenge of articulating its concern with conservative "family values" in language which does not alienate liberal and non-confessional centre-Right voters. These voters are nowadays of greater electoral significance. Too close an identification with the Catholic church can impose electoral costs, as the Italian DC learned during Italy's divorce and abortion referendums of 1974 and 1981 respectively. The crisis of the welfare state has also affected the viability of the Christian Democratic model of a social market economy; this makes it more difficult to maintain the cohesion of the bloc of social forces which constitutes Christian Democracy's cross-class political base, above all its "popular" component. Christian Democracy is not immune to pressure for a neo-liberal approach to capitalist restructuring, from its own Right flank. And some Christian Democratic parties—above all the Italian DC—have succumbed to corruption and political degeneration to such an extent that the outside observer could be forgiven for questioning what exactly, if anything, is especially "Christian" or "democratic" about their politics.

Nevertheless, one can attempt to delineate the contours of a specifically Christian Democratic politics in western Europe since 1945. Four aspects of these politics deserve mention here: the Christian Democratic attempt to develop and apply a theory of the individual, society and the state; the concept of a social market economy; the emphasis on combating class politics through the construction of a cross-class bloc of forces; and the rejection of nationalism.

Christian Democrats have tended to emphasise the importance of a strong civil society, guided by "Christian principles," as a counter to the power of the state. Although the family is extolled as the most important unit—which inclines Christian Democracy towards a highly conservative position on family policy and sexual politics—recognition is also given to the multiplicity of citizens' organisations which comprise civil society. The principle of subsidiarity enshrines what Christian Democrats regard as the proper balance between individual, society and the State. This principle states that power should be exercised at the most appropriate level—local, regional, national or European Community—with regard to effectiveness and closeness to the people. In theory, it should make of Christian Democrats natural "federalists" and "decentralisers." In practice, it can on occasion, as in Italy, be a camouflage for clientelist activities which take place within the "para-state" sector. What is clear is that Christian Democracy is far removed from Mrs.Thatcher's famous declaration that "there is no such thing as society, only individuals and their families."

It is the German CDU which has developed the concept of the social market economy to the greatest extent, although it is now paid lip service at least by most if not all Christian Democratic parties. The social market economy in essence means three things: that the State should guarantee a private sector-led market economy rather than "distort" market conditions through "unnecessary" nationalisations; that the State should regulate competition, taking tough action against cartels; and that market-generated wealth should lay the basis for a comprehensive system of social security—the "social State."[7] Although recessionary times have taken their toll of the social market economy, as they have of the more social democratic-inspired welfare State, the concept retains its power for the German Christian Democrats especially. That party's programme contains the rhetorical flourish: "We would be in favour of the social market economy even if it were to provide less material wealth than other systems. It would be intolerable to acquire goods at the expense of freedom."[8]

Characterisations of Christian Democratic parties as "bourgeois" or "conservative" fall short of the reality implied by Christian Democracy's quest to construct an interclass bloc capable of meeting the challenge of Left-wing class politics. In practice, this has usually meant that Christian Democratic parties—certainly the most successful—have enjoyed a substantial popular or workingclass base. What is involved here is much more than the phenomenon of "working class conservatives" familiar to students of British politics. Christian Democrats have generally sought to "co-opt" organised labour, complete with affiliated trade unions and workers' recreational associations. In the absence of a recourse to nationalism, Christian Democracy has generally sought to maintain its popular support base through the doctrine of social solidarity. In general, this means that such parties are more inclined towards a substantial degree of state intervention, social welfare expenditure, cooperation with the trade union movement (or at least part of it) and political compromise than such a confrontational and arguably "classist" approach as that of the British Conservatives under Mrs Thatcher.

Finally, Christian Democracy, in the postwar period, has presented itself as an alternative ideological model for the political Right to nationalism. The Christian Democratic parties have been strongest—in Germany and Italy—where nationalism and imperialism have been discredited as options for the Right by the Nazi-Fascist experience. Conversely, in France, the crisis of the Fourth Republic and the relegitimation of strong, quasi-authoritarian nationalism following de Gaulle's return to power, marked the contraction of any political space for the Christian Democratic movement. Eschewing any recourse to nationalist populism, preaching instead a message of solidaristic "popularism" rooted in Catholic internationalism, Christian Democracy has been almost naturally inclined towards the idea of Europe, beyond the confines of the nationstate.

The European People's Party: the Christian Democratic Group in the European Parliament

From the creation of the European Parliament (EP) in 1958 until 1973, the Christian Democrats "held the largest single share of seats in the European Parliament and were viewed as the motor of European unity."[9] Of course, the EP was as yet chosen from within the ranks of national parliaments rather than directly elected, altogether powerless, and out of sight as far as the majority of Europeans were concerned. The Christian Democrats also benefited from the exclusion of the powerful French and Italian Communist Parties.[10]

From 1958 until 1976 the Christian Democrats operated inside the EP as a fairly loose-knit group. In preparation for the first direct elections to the Parliament, the Christian Democratic parties of the member-states formed a federation—the European People's Party (EPP) on 29 April 1976 in Brussels, under the chairmanship of the influential Belgian politician and ex-Prime Minister Leo Tindemans. It was hoped that such a move would enable the Christian Democrats to coordinate their European policies and continue to play a leading role in the future evolution of the European Community. This was important, not only because direct elections were likely to lead to an increase in Left-wing representation within the EP; but also because the evolution of the major western European Communist Parties—and especially the Italian—in the direction of Eurocommunism was perceived by some to threaten the Christian Democrats' hegemony in the field of pan-European strategic thinking. Indeed, the PCI's electoral lists for the 1979 direct elections featured none other than Altiero Spinelli, the prominent European federalist and former Italian EC Commissioner, who was to be the chief architect of the Draft Treaty on European Union, approved by the EP in 1984.

In July 1979, one month after the first direct elections, the Christian Democrats inside the EP became formally constituted as the Group of the European People's Party—i.e., the European parliamentary group of the Community's then only self-defined transnational political federation. The Group of the EPP has distinguished itself by its almost total support for the principle of European political and economic union. The influential German component, in particular, has adhered strictly to Konrad Adenauer's vision of a united Europe, allied to the USA but also possessing the necessary internal coherence to compete with the USA on less unequal terms. By contrast, the British Conservatives, from 1973, joined with the small Danish Conservative Party to form the European Democratic Group (EDG) which effectively mirrored British Conservative Government policy during the Heath years. According to Pridham,[11] the Conservative MEPs from the outset maintained close contact with Downing Street and followed Heath's directive to advocate reform of the EP along the lines of Westminster's parliamentary procedure, whilst adhering to a cautious approach to supranationality. Indeed, when the Conservatives were led back to power by Margaret Thatcher in 1979, after Labour's four-year spell in office, the Conservative MEPs were encouraged to press for a reform of the Common Agricultural Policy, to support Thatcher's demands for a reduction in Britain's contribution to the Community budget, and to resist the EP's Draft Treaty on European Union—in short to echo the new British Government's defence of "British national interests."

The late 1980s, however, saw growing dissatisfaction and unease on the part of many Conservative MEPs with the stonewalling attitude of the Thatcher administrations towards European political union. There are several possible reasons why this should have been so.

First, the exposure of Conservatives MEPs to the debates and dialogue taking place within the European political mainstream over Europe's future, and their own vested interest in securing a bigger role for the EP, undoubtedly increased the "Europhilia" of the Conservative Strasbourg Group. In Mrs. Thatcher's eyes, many were in danger of "going native"—if they had not already done so. Rudolf Hrbek[12] has written of German MEPs that they "have developed or achieved some European or Community outlook; many of them can be regarded as belonging to a new European elite. But the members of this elite have remained isolated from their political base in the member-state; they have not yet succeeded in generating an EC-mindedness at home." This is certainly true, to a greater extent if anything, of British MEPs, Conservative and Labour.

Second, Mrs. Thatcher's decision to sign the Single European Act at the end of 1985 undoubtedly had the unintended effect of helping to legitimise a more positive approach to European union on the part of her MEPs.

Third, the rules of the European Parliament itself—which reward maximum consensus and condemn to impotence small and dissenting groups—meant that throughout the 1980s an effective coalition between the two biggest groups—the Group of the EPP and the Socialists—set the pace in formulating Parliament's decisions on European union. The British Conservative MEPs, isolated in their EDG, grew increasingly restless with their marginalisation. Pressure grew from the most "Europhile" elements, such as Lord O'Hagan, for a realignment of the EP's centre-Right which would bring the Tories into the mainstream of the European centre-Right, increase their influence within the EP accordingly, and offer the possibility of an alternative majority to the Socialist-EPP informal alliance. In practice, this meant an application to merge with the Group of the EPP—which was made, with Mrs Thatcher's approval, if not her enthusiasm, after the EP elections of June 1989.

The request was at first denied, a two-year long period of "intense dialogue" being stipulated by the EPP Political Office. This reflected EPP concern at the British Conservatives' record of opposition to European political union and social policy harmonisation. It may also have reflected concern on the part of the Left-wing of European Christian Democracy—most committed to social legislation to protect the low paid and marginalised groups, to democratic reform of the Community institutions, and to cooperating with the Socialists to build a "Community Europe" as opposed to a mere "market Europe"—at what the Group of the EPP had denounced in 1988 as "Conservative Liberalism which is dominated by the power of wealth and through which the weak are systematically victimised."[13]

In April 1991, a meeting of the Christian Democratic heads of government in Brussels set out final conditions for British Conservative admission to the Group of the EPP: a clear commitment to a united, federal Europe based on the principle of subsidiarity and support for the European Community's Charter of Workers' Rights (the so-called Social Charter). It should be noted that for the Christian Democrats, the principle of subsidiarity implied that political decisions should be taken at the European, national or regional level, depending on political effectiveness and the practicality of keeping decisionmaking as close to those affected by the decisions as possible. This was not exactly the interpretation of subsidiarity which the British Conservatives would insist upon during the Maastricht negotiations (see below).

At the same time, the Christian Democratic leaders acknowledged what they regarded as a clear change of attitude on the part of the British Conservative Party since John Major acceded to the leadership in November 1990. This reflected the satisfaction of a majority of Christian Democrats that almost two years of dialogue had seen the Conservative MEPs, led by Sir Christopher Prout, move closer to the political positions of the Group of the EPP. In June 1991, the EPP also recorded its satisfaction with the EDG's "growing interest in the intellectual and historical principles underlying Christian Democracy."[14] The same communique recorded:

The Conservative British Euro MPs hope that, after a two-year waiting period, during which they did everything possible to prove their good will, their capacity for consensus and how close they are to Christian Democracy, they will be allowed to join the EPP fraction. They do not make any conditions with regard to the programme, the policies or the identity of the fraction which they wish to join. On the contrary, they emphasise that they wish to join the EPP fraction because of its special Christian Democratic and European federalistic identity, with which they themselves and, in the medium term, their party wish to identify.

And, despite the fact that the Conservative Party itself would not, for the time being, join the European People's Party proper: "the new [Conservative] party leadership does not exclude the possibility that, in the long term, with their political programmes coming closer together, integration in the EPP may occur."

Such sentiments have provoked the opposition of the so-called Eurosceptic, or Europhobic, wing of the Conservative Party; not least because the EPP proper is a federal party (albeit a rather weak one as yet) which makes no secret that its goal is the creation of "a democratic and federal European Union" which "cannot be achieved without the development of real European parties which are present throughout the entire community (union)."

In May 1992, the EDG finally merged with the Group of the EPP. The merger followed a vote by the Group of the EPP on 9 April in which 72 members of that Group voted in favour of the merger, 32 voted against and three abstained. The vote, though decisive, showed continued scepticism on the part of a substantial number of Christian Democratic MEPs at the prospect of an organic relationship with the British Conservatives which might affect the ideological and political profile of European Christian Democracy, as well as its strategic European project.

The rather disingenuous argument used by the Conservative Party to "sell" the merger to rank and file Conservatives in the UK was that it was intended to "counteract the Socialists" and would strengthen the hand of the centre-Right as a whole in combating "the forces of collectivism in Europe."[15] The British Euro-Conservatives' leader, Sir Christopher Prout, was to claim that "the two most successful anti-collectivist political movements of modern Europe have too long been separated by unnecessary misunderstandings."[16] In fact, Conservative propaganda, for domestic party consumption, exaggerated the extent to which the EP is divided along Left/Right lines. Within the EP, as mentioned, an effective informal coalition of Socialists and Group of the EPP has spearheaded the movement for greater European union. Of course, the delicate balance of forces within the Conservative Party in Britain prevented any admission that one effect of the adhesion to the Group of the EPP might be to involve the British Conservative MEPs in this "historic compromise" between Left and Right in the cause of European federalism. Moreover, the portrayal of Christian Democracy as "anti-collectivist" masks the fact that Christian Democracy is an infinitely more integrative and solidaristic ideology that Conservatism— above all, the neo-liberal variety of Conservatism which was hegemonic under Thatcher and remains dominant under John Major.

The procedural device which facilitated Conservative admission to the Group of the EPP at Strasbourg, without the Conservatives joining the wider EPP federal party, was the redefinition of the status of the Group of the EPP as a parliamentary Group of Christian Democrats and their "allies." The Danish and British Conservatives thus joined as "allies"—insisting that their separate identity had thus been preserved. This delicate balancing act was aimed at satisfying the Europhobic wing of the Conservative Party in Britain—at a time of considerable internal party pressure on prime minister John Major—and simultaneously satisfying many European Christian Democrats that the distinctiveness of Christian Democracy was not being compromised by Anglo-Saxon neoliberalism: the clear message was that the final stage in Conservatism's "encounter" with Christian Democracy had by no means been reached; further evolution lay ahead. The ambiguity of this message lay in the fact that it remained far from clear just who would evolve most in the other's direction. However, in the run-up to the 1994 EP elections, the Europhobic wing of the Conservative Party had gained sufficiently in strength to block any possibility of the British Conservatives and European Christian Democrats agreeing on a common electoral platform. The Conservatives remained a semidetached associate of the European People's Party.

At the time of writing (February 1995), the Group of the European People's Party in the EP consisted of 21 parties from 13 countries which were, or were in the process of becoming, full members of the EPP federation:

Austrian People's Party (OVP)	Austria
Christian People's Party (CVP)	Belgium
Social Christian Party (PSC)	Belgium
Christian Social Party (CSP)	Belgium
National Coalition Party (KoK)	Finland
Social Democrat Centre (CDS)	France
Christian-Democratic Union (CDU)	Germany

Christian-Social Union (CSU)	Germany
New Democracy (ND)	Greece
Fine Gael (FG)	Ireland
Italian Popular Party (PPI)	Italy
Pact For Italy	Italy
South Tyrol People's Party (SVP)	Italy
Christian Social Party (CSV/PCS)	Luxembourg
Christian Democratic Alliance (CDA)	Netherlands
Centre Democratic Party (CDS)	Portugal
Basque Nationalist Party (PNV)	Spain
Catalan Nationalist Party (CiU)	Spain
Popular Party (PP)	Spain
Christian Democratic Party (KdS)	Sweden
Moderate Party (M)	Sweden

plus MEPs from the following 4 parties who sit as allied members of the Group of the EPP without, however, their parties being full members of the EPP federation:

Conservative People's Party (KF)	Denmark
Union for French Democracy (UDF)	France
Conservative and Unionist Party	UK
Ulster Unionist Party	UK

Conservatives and Christian Democrats on the Future of the European Union: Unity in Diversity?

Following the return to power of the British Conservative Party under the leadership of Margaret Thatcher in May 1979, a renewed emphasis was noticeable upon an essentially negative and minimalist approach to the European Community. British membership of the European Community was accepted as an accomplished fact. But Mrs. Thatcher's own sense of British nationalism (some would say English nationalism) and her suspicions of EC membership which had never quite abated meant that the pragmatic Europeanism of Edward Heath gave way to repeated propaganda about the need for Britain to defend its national sovereignty, if necessary by standing alone in resisting further moves towards European political and monetary unity. Despite the adoption of a softer rhetoric by John Major, who succeeded Thatcher to the leadership of the Conservative Party and the prime ministership in November 1990, the hopes of European Christian Democrats for a "new beginning" in Britain's relations with Europe have as yet been largely unfulfilled. Under Major, the Conservatives have continued to display their preference for "loose intergovernmental cooperation between the EC states and caution towards monetary union."[17]

Since 1979, five themes have featured prominently in Conservative discourses on the European Community.

First, the Conservatives have stressed the need for Britain to get "value for money" by reducing its contribution to Community's budget. This was the prelude to a tenacious fight from 1979 to 1984 which eventually succeeded in reducing British financial inputs: a rebate was agreed in December 1984. Indeed, the stubborn resistance which the Conservative Government offered to any further progress towards European unity during these years helped produce a reaction to the perceived institutional stalemate in the form of the 1981 Genscher-Colombo Plan (named after the German Liberal and Italian Christian Democratic foreign ministers), which sought movement towards political unity through institutional reform.

Allied to British demands for a financial rebate was an assault upon the management of Community policies, with demands for a massive revision of the Common Agricultural Policy and the spending priorities of the Community. Mrs. Thatcher certainly succeeded in the short term objective of saving money. But she greatly alienated many other European countries—including France, whose farmers have benefitted from the Common Agricultural Policy; Italy, which has depended on redistribution of resources through the social and regional funds to pour money into the underdeveloped Italian south; and the poorer countries, such as Spain, Portugal, Greece and Ireland, which hoped for a redistribution of resources within the Community through additional spending on Regional and Social funds. Indeed the conflict between John Major and the poorer EC countries, at the Edinburgh summit of the European Council in December 1992, was once again precisely over this point: should not the wealthier countries which enjoy the benefits of the single market compensate the poorer countries through a redistribution of money?

Second, a popular Conservative line of attack upon the Community has been to portray "Brussels" as a huge and monstrous bureaucracy, wasteful of resources and destructive of entrepreneurial energy. Of course such claims are massively exaggerated. In fact, the EU employs fewer bureaucrats than Whitehall. Nevertheless, given the popular distaste for bureaucracy and red tape, the fact that the British by many accounts are the least pro-European of the nations in the Union now, and the Union's own tendency to shoot itself in the foot with ridiculous directives on the trivia of daily life, the Conservatives could count upon attacks on bureaucracy as a good crowd-warmer.

Third, the Conservative governments, especially under Thatcher, linked this portrayal of the EC/EU as a huge bureaucracy to another link of critical attack: the allegation that the EC/EU was attempting to force Labour Party-style socialism upon the British people through the back door. This was a central theme of Mrs. Thatcher's speech in the Belgium city of Bruges in September 1988 (see below), after which the so-called Bruges group of Conservative MPs hostile to European political unity was named. The argument was that Thatcher had defeated socialism in Britain; but that "Brussels" was creating a new super-State which would revive all that Thatcherism had fought against in Britain. In fact, of the other eleven EC countries, nine then had conservative— or centrist-dominated governments; only two—France and Spain—had Socialist governments and in both cases, very moderate Socialist governments. However, Mrs. Thatcher's case did contain a grain of truth, which is that most conservative or Christian Democratic parties in Europe are firmly committed to a greater degree of public spending and welfare provision than the British Tories. What the allegation that the EC was Socialistic was really saying is that Thatcherism had not caught on in mainland western Europe, or convinced European Christian Democracy of its superiority as an ideological, political and economic project for the Right, as Mrs. Thatcher had hoped it might.

Fourth, the period since 1979 has seen a repeated emphasis upon an enduring myth of British political culture—the Anglo-American "special relationship." The Thatcher governments were absolutely unwilling to exchange this for a closer relationship with European partners. Therefore every move towards common defence, security or foreign policies in the Community brought forth strenuous protests. At the time of the Westland affair, in 1986, the then Defence Secretary Michael Heseltine's preference for a European deal to rescue the ailing British helicopter firm was held suspect, and ultimately caused his resignation. Mrs. Thatcher was absolutely committed to a US deal instead. Although some commentators have argued that the real issue at stake was the principle of state intervention to aid industry,[18] the public and political perception was that an ideological battle had taken place within the Conservative Party around the question of Europe versus United States of America, with Europe emerging as the loser.

Finally, Mrs. Thatcher's most emotional blast against the vision of a politically united, economically integrated and socially harmonised Europe has been rooted in the myth of British national sovereignty. Moves towards political union or the harmonisation of social protection legislation and citizens' rights have been resisted as eroding British independence. The EP has been held in particular contempt as any increase in its powers might enhance the EC's democratic legitimacy.[19]

Perhaps the emphasis on British sovereignty also masks a fear of Scottish and Welsh independence—a fear that greater moves towards European union might also encourage pressure for a break-up of Britain. Certainly, recent general election results—which have seen the Conservatives in 1987 and 1992 poll between 20 percent and 25 percent of the popular vote in Scotland, and between 25 percent and 30 percent in Wales—cast doubt upon the extent to which the Conservative defence of British sovereignty against European encroachment sets the valleys of Wales or the mountains of Scotland alight with enthusiasm. However, the quintessentially Catholic and Christian Democratic principle of subsidiarity has been effectively redefined by British Conservatives to mean little more than "keeping Europe at bay" whilst upholding the institutions of a highly centralised British state.

And yet, in December 1985, Mrs Thatcher's Government signed the Single European Act (operative in July 1987), which aimed to create a European Single Market by 1 January 1993. Mrs Thatcher seemingly believed that the project of a European common market—a cherished Conservative goal, to which her Government had indeed made a substantial contribution—could be separated from political and monetary union. As Greenwood puts it, Thatcher was prepared to accept "that the objective of a free market by 1992 would require a revision of the Treaty of Rome and was prepared to go along with what appeared to be innocuous statements on eventual European unity and the development of the EMS."[20] But the pressure for further unity and institutional reform was gaining momentum, centring on demands for the creation of new supranational institutions to serve the integrated economy, and the extension of qualified majority voting within the Council of Ministers. The latter had been provided for in the Single European Act for measures designed to speed the completion of the Single Market.

Incredible though it may seem, such an astute and decisive politician as Margaret Thatcher must have been unaware of the full implications of the Single European Act, to judge by her subsequent actions and statements. Certainly, when concrete proposals emerged from 1988 onwards for a Central European Bank and a single currency (the ECU), Thatcher was horrified. Some of Mrs. Thatcher's closest admirers, such as Lord (formerly Mr Norman) Tebbit were also to claim later that she would never have signed the Single European Act had she known of some of the constitutional implications, such as eventual removal of national controls over passport and border checks, which the European Commission pressed for in early 1995.

It was in this context that she made her speech at Bruges in September 1988, which seemed to mark an important step backwards from the Single European Act towards a neo-Gaullist vision of a *Europe des patries*.

According to some commentators,[21] this speech marked a turning point. Thereafter, the Christian Democratic leaders of the EC responded by accelerating proposals for European union.[22] The last years in the Thatcher bunker, 1988-1990, witnessed an unprecedented deterioration in relations between her Government and most of the other EC governments—above all those Christian Democrat-led (or dominated) governments of Germany, Italy and the Benelux states. This was notwithstanding Thatcher's reluctant agreement, under internal British Government pressure, to take sterling into the exchange rate mechanism (ERM) of the European Monetary System in 1989—while vigorously insisting that this in no way implied support for a single currency or political union.

In 1988, the Christian Democratic parties of the Group of the EPP reiterated their demands for a federal European union in language which was unambiguous and which underlined the vast gulf which separated the Christian Democrats from the British Conservative Party under Thatcher—even if Conservative MEPs were closer to the EPP position. Indeed, in a sense, the crystallization of the EPP's position served to enhance the EPP as an alternative pole of attraction for many Conservative MEPs to the message coming from Downing Street.

The Christian Democrats pledged their support for the introduction of a common currency—the ECU; the harmonisation of fiscal, economic and monetary policies; and the development of common industrial, environmental and technology policies. They also called for the harmonisation of social policy, better legal protection for workers, and the right of workers to be consulted about decisions affecting their employment or their company. The British Conservatives could indeed take comfort in the demand for "direct and secret elections for workers' representatives"—perhaps an echo of Mrs. Thatcher's famous trade union reforms—but the central thrust of a common social charter of workers' rights was anathema to Mrs. Thatcher and the Conservatives. Again, whilst British Tories would have no problem identifying with the deeply conservative and traditionalist defence of "family values" and the "right to life of the unborn," support for a concept of European citizenship was quite another matter. On the major political issues, the EPP was even more at odds with the Conservative Government: "Through European Union [we wish] to arrive at a true European Federation endowed with institutions having sufficient authority so that in all areas of interest to our daily lives, there will be a common vision and a common policy. We want an elected Parliament reflecting the views of the people, a Senate representing the legitimate interests of the Member-States, a European Government capable of deciding within the context of the competences (sic) transferred to the Union."[23]

In November 1988, the 7th Congress of the EPP, meeting in Luxembourg, approved a five year programme for the period 1989-1994 (the life-span of the 3rd directly-elected EP) entitled "On the People's Side." This document—to which the Conservative MEPs assented upon merging with the Group of the EPP in May 1992, a point specifically noted by the conference of Christian Democratic Heads of Government and party leaders in April 1991—was an elaborate 65 page manifesto for a federal Europe.

The Christian Democrats echoed Socialist and Italian Communist calls for a major institutional reform in a federalist direction: "The EPP wants the progressive realisation of the United States of Europe, with a government responsible to the democratically elected European Parliament and endowed with all the powers of lawmaking and control of the administration. The efficiency of the political decision making process and the administration must be improved." The document called for the EP to gain the power to initiate legislation jointly with the Council of Ministers, and the power to name the members of the European Commission. In this way, the Commission would be effectively transformed into a European Government, while the Council of Ministers would evolve into a second chamber—a Senate—in which each state would have a seat.

The Community should gain its own powers of taxation—to be exercised by both Parliament and Council of Ministers (Senate). In accordance with the principle of the Community gaining financial autonomy from member-states, the EPP called for ". . . a step by step development of a relationship between the taxpayers and the Community, which would make the European Parliament directly responsible to the taxpayers."

The Christian Democrats also called for the Parliament to draw up another new treaty for a European Union which would then be ratified by national parliaments and national governments and would form the Constitution for a federal union. In a clearly critical reference to Britain, the document claimed that ratification would "lead to a situation where the more reluctant parliaments or Governments will not be able to stand aside from the construction of European Union. Only a decisive step, not influenced by those who wish to prevent unity, can move the opponents of union towards sensible compromise."[24]

The Christian Democrats also redefined their vision of a social market economy—a capitalism, led by the private sector, but involving both a considerable element of corporatist relations between the "social partners" and a "European social area" to protect the weakest social groups.

The replacement of Margaret Thatcher by John Major in November 1990 was followed by 12 months of intense negotiations between Britain and the other EC member-states about a new Treaty on European Union which would meet the perceived need for further economic and political integration. Such an agreement, involving a treaty on economic and monetary union and a treaty on political union, was eventually reached at the Maastricht summit of the European Council in December 1991, signed by the foreign ministers in February 1992, and finally ratified by all 12 member-states in November 1993.

The intense debate over the Maastricht Treaty has exposed the full extent of the differences between British Conservatives and their European centre-Right allies. In some respects, the Treaty represents a victory for the Conservatives; the Europe it enshrines is uncomfortably close to Thatcher's vision of a community of nationstates driven by free market priorities for many Christian Democrats as well as Socialists. Yet the perceived wisdom in most European capitals at the time was that such a victory was partial and short-term: that Maastricht represented an important step forward—which could never have been achieved under Thatcher—and a starting point from which further movement in the direction of federalism could take place when domestic Conservative Party pressure on John Major eases. In this respect, one can appreciate Helmut Kohl's declaration in May 1991 that "John Major is the best thing that could have happened to Europe."[25]

In June 1991, the conference of Heads of Government and party leaders of the EPP issued a statement outlining the Christian Democrats' "absolute priorities" for the forthcoming European Union Treaty. These included: a European Government; a single currency; common defence and foreign policies; the foundation of the European Union on "a federal Constitution derived from a mandate given to the European Parliament"; and protection of "Community rules" from encroachment by "intergovernmental procedures." The EPP leaders also repeated calls for the EP to "share legislative decisionmaking power on equal terms with the Council," to be given powers of co-decision on all acts of a legislative nature subject to majority voting, to elect the Commission "on nomination by the Council, by means of a dual investiture procedure," and to enjoy a effective veto, by absolute majority of the EP's members, on any revision of the Community's treaties.

The statement also called for moves towards a common foreign and defence policy "according to the rules and principles of federal unity"; and for a timetable for movement towards monetary union and a European Central Bank. In addition, the call for a Community citizenship was repeated.

The Maastricht Treaty which emerged represents a compromise between these positions—shared also, of course, by most Socialists and European Left forces—and the British Conservative position. Five questions were at stake: the social dimension, monetary union, subsidiarity and the competence of the Community, institutional reform, and foreign and defence policies.

British insistence effectively removed the Social Chapter from the Treaty on European Union, leaving the other 11 states to agree under a Protocol to pursue its objectives. This sets back an extension of Community competence in industrial relations and labour policy. The British Conservatives insisted that "the Social Chapter would centralise in Brussels key issues of employment policy," it would "greatly increase union power," "return Britain to corporatism" and "sharply increase the costs to employers" of creating jobs.[26] The agreement to delete the Social Chapter from the Treaty certainly represents a setback for all—Socialists and Christian Democrats—who believe that the new European Union must go beyond mere free market rationale, and it has been furiously attacked as such. Nevertheless, Britain's decision to "opt-out" also leaves open the possibility that a future British Government—even, possibly, a future Conservative one which is less constrained by the Thatcherite legacy—might decide to "opt in." That has been the hope expressed by Christian Democratic leaders. Britain remains bound by the Community's existing social dimension.

Likewise, on economic and monetary union, Britain agreed conditions for strict monetary and economic convergence which must precede monetary union. The timetable agreed at Maastricht envisaged completion of the current stage by 1997, followed by a decision then to proceed to a single currency by 1999. The Treaty also proposes a European central bank, independent of all political control—modelled on the German Bundesbank. The other member-states (except Denmark) agreed to automatically proceed, assuming they satisfy convergence conditions; Britain, it was said, would require a vote in the House of Commons in 1997. This allowed the Major Government to ease Conservative backbench pressure against any movement towards a single currency. However, the issue of the single currency exploded on to the political centre-stage in Britain in 1994 and 1995 with Conservative critics demanding a popular referendum on the subject and threatening to vote against the Government should it agree to precede. Major sought to gain time by insisting that there was now no chance of a single currency by the end of the century and that additional criteria to those laid down in the Maastricht Treaty might have to be insisted upon at the Intergovernmental Conference of the EU scheduled for 1996 (when a review of progress towards union is due to take place). The cabinet is deeply divided over whether one can proceed to a single currency without "surrendering" national sovereignty or not, and over whether—if a constitutional issue is at stake—a referendum should be held. Barring a change of government, it is increasingly unlikely that the Conservative Party will be able to deliver British adherence to a single currency and survive with its unity intact.

An almost theological debate on the definition and practical application of the principle of subsidiarity produced the following clause in the Maastricht Treaty:

> The Community shall act within the limits of the powers conferred upon it by the Treaty and of the objectives assigned to it herein.
>
> In areas which do not fall within its competence, the Community shall take action, in accordance with the principle of subsidiarity, only if and in so far as the objectives of the proposed action cannot be sufficiently achieved by the Member States and can therefore, by reason of the scale or effects of the proposed action, be better achieved by the Community.
>
> An action by the Community shall not go beyond what is necessary to achieve the objectives of this Treaty.[27]

What this actually means is open to question. The reference to "Member States" certainly seems closer to a Conservative than a Christian Democratic definition of subsidiarity. But who decides what "cannot be sufficiently achieved"? It is certainly the view of the Christian Democrats that subsidiarity "must not be used as an alibi to bring into question the *acquis communautaire*, nor to put a brake on future development. The aim of subsidiarity is not to spread responsibility more widely, but to lay down rules as to exercise of that responsibility."[28] In other words, the emphasis should be upon a supple interpretation of the principle which aims to ensure effectiveness and closeness—rather than simply protecting the sanctity of the nationstate. This point has been repeated by Chancellor Helmut Kohl who has pointed out that nationstates, pursuing their own selfish interests, are often to blame for many of the regulations emanating from Brussels.[29] There can be little doubt that the debate on subsidiarity and the competencies of the EU is destined to continue.

On institutional reform, the Conservatives conceded an extension of the Commission's role in education, health and consumer protection. Moreover, the Commission will henceforth take office to coincide with the five year term of the European Parliament. The EP gains more power to call the Commission to account, including the right to negotiate directly with the Council of Ministers and to reject bills which do not satisfy it. But it remains powerless to legislate or to elect the Commission. The Treaty requires the EP's assent to the objectives of the structural fund which decide on regional funds, and its agreement to a definition of European citizenship, a harmonisation of electoral systems for EP elections, and international treaties. This falls far short of the proposals of the EPP and the Socialists, and it brought a stinging rebuke from the European Parliament in a resolution of 7 April 1992, to which the EPP assented. Moreover, Christian Democratic leaders have pledged to fight on for a true reform of the institutions in the direction of a federal United States of Europe. Again, Maastricht looks like being a staging post rather than the conclusion of the debate.

Finally, it was agreed to proceed with the development of a common foreign and defence policy. The implementation of the principles of such a policy will be decided by a qualified majority vote of the Council of Ministers, although the principles themselves will require unanimous agreement.

Conclusion

The British Conservative Party sought to portray the performance of Margaret Thatcher and John Major, in the negotiations over both the Single European Act and the Treaty on European Union, as a masterly triumph of Conservative freemarket thinking and national sovereignty over collectivist-inspired "creeping socialism," supranationalism and "Brussels bureaucracy." As a corollary, the party's inclusion in the Group of the European People's Party has been trumpeted within the party as a necessary realignment of the Community centre-Right with the aim of out-gunning the Socialists at Strasbourg. For the majority of European Christian Democrats—and most EU Governments—the reality is somewhat different. The hopes raised by Thatcher's replacement by Major—for a much more positive approach to Community development in a federalist direction—have not as yet been realised, by any means. However, Britain's partners have shown a greater degree of sensitivity to the severe political constraints under which Major must operate as a result of continuing resistance within Conservative ranks to European union.

The Treaty on European Union represents above all a compromise between the agendas of British Conservatism and European Christian Democracy, in which each side has sought to allow movement forward. The Treaty has not eased the fears of many Christian Democrats that too much has been conceded to a vision of the Community as an intergovernmental body, rather than a democratic federation; nor the fears of some Tories that a decisive step has been taken towards a European superstate. In many respects, the Treaty is significant for what it leaves unresolved, and for the ambiguity of its language—as much as for its actual provisions. Conservative and Christian Democrat debates on European Union are destined to continue and gather pace, both before and after the 1996 Intergovernmental Conference, when questions of institutional reform (including the powers of the European Parliament), monetary union, and expansion of the EU to the east must be addressed. The next few years may well be decisive, not only for the future of the European Union, but for the nature of the European centre-Right.

Notes

1. P. Ginsborg, *A History of Contemporary Italy: Politics and Society, 1943-1988* (London: Penguin, 1990), p. 159.

2. S. George, *An Awkward Partner: Britain in the European Community* (Oxford: Oxford University Press, 1990), p. 40.

3. C. Merlini, "Italy in the European Community and the Atlantic Alliance" *The World Today*, April 1975, p. 160.

4. S. George, *Britain and European Integration since 1945* (Oxford: Basil Blackwell, 1991), pp. 67-73.

5. R. E. M. Irving, The *Christian Democratic Parties of Western Europe* (London: RIIA, 1979), p. 28.

6. C. Clemens, *Christian Democracy: The Different Dimensions of a Modern Movement* (Brussels: European People's Party, 1989), pp. 8-9.

7. C. Watrin, "The Social Market Economy: its Significance for the Economic Development of the Federal Republic of Germany in the Early Years of the Konrad Adenauer Administration" in *The Konrad Adenauer Memorial Lectures, 1978-1982* (London: Konrad Adenauer Foundation, 1983), p. 43.

8. CDU. (1979), pp. 29-30.

9. C. Clemens, *Christian Democracy: The Different Dimensions of a Modern Movement*, p. 24.

10. The Communists were excluded by their national parliaments, on prejudicial grounds, for many years. The Italian Communist Party (PCI) entered the Strasbourg chamber in 1969, the French Communist Party (PCF), not until 1973.

11. G. Pridham, "Transnational Party Groups in the European Parliament," *Journal of Common Market Studies*, March 1975, p. 273.

12. C. C. Schweitzer and D. Karsten, eds., *Federal Republic of Germany and EC Membership Evaluated* (Pinter, London: 1990).

13. EPP, 1988, p. 13.

14. *EPP Bulletin*, June 1991.

15. *Euro Briefing*, April 1992.

16. C. Prout, "Working Together," *The House Magazine*, 3 June 1991.

17. S. Greenwood, *Britain and European Cooperation Since 1945* (Oxford: Basil Blackwell, 1992), p. 120.

18. S. George, *An Awkward Partner: Britain in the European Community* (Oxford: Oxford University Press, 1990), pp. 171-173.

19. Perhaps the emphasis on British sovereignty also masks a fear of Scottish and Welsh independence—a fear that greater moves towards European union might also encourage pressure for a break-up of Britain. Certainly, recent elections results—which have seen the Conservatives in 1987 and 1992 poll between 20 percent and 25 percent of the popular vote in Scotland, and between 25 percent and 30 percent in Wales—cast doubt upon the extent to which the Conservative defence of British sovereignty against European encroachment sets the valleys of Wales or the mountains of Scotland alight with enthusiasm.

20. S. Greenwood, *Britain and European Cooperation Since 1945*, p. 113.

21. M. Thatcher, *Britain and Europe*, text of speech delivered at Bruges on 20 September 1988, Conservative Political Centre, London 1988.

22. S. George, *An Awkward Partner: Britain in the European Community and Britain and European Integration since 1945*; Sean Greenwood, *Britain and European Cooperation Since 1945*.

23. *CD-Europe*, February 1988.

24. EPP, 1989a, pp. 15-19.

25. H. Kohl, "Our Future in Europe" (London: Konrad Adenauer Foundation, 1991), p. 16.

26. "Britain at the Heart of Europe," special issue of *Politics Today*, Journal of the Conservative Research Department, 7 February 1992.

27. C. Jackson, "Whose Job is it Anyway? Decentralisation (or Subsidiarity) in the European Community" (London: Conservatives in the European Parliament, undated), p. 15.

28. "Subsidiarity Between Birmingham and Edinburgh," (Brussels: October 1992), p. 14.

29. H. Kohl, "United Germany in a Uniting Europe" (London: Konrad Adenauer Foundation, 1992).

8

Nationalist or Internationalist? Socialists and European Unity

Philomena Murray

Parties' national organizations, even if not hostile to the movement towards European unification, did not see in this a favourable ground for action and intervention: the citizens as a whole, the "masses," only had a superficial knowledge of this movement, its aims and its means: the coming of a European power was a myth. What interested parties was to gain (or keep) national power: to this end, they mobilized the electorate.

Agence Europe, 10 November 1993, p. 1.

Introduction

The fact of the creation of the European Socialist Party in late 1992 may have led observers to assume that its member parties, socialists, socialist democrats and labour parties, are in favour of supranational politics and a supranational political system. However, the socialist and social democratic approach to the idea of European unity has never been unambiguously one of support and enthusiasm. Unlike the Christian Democrats, the various Socialist parties of Western Europe have exhibited varied responses to European unification. While transnational co-operation and an internationalist stance have been a feature of socialist discourse, this has not always overcome nationally-oriented concerns.

The issue of internationalist involvement in the European Community (EC) and European Union (EU) has been a very contentious one within the ranks of these parties. The Socialist, Social Democratic and Labour parties of Western Europe have frequently demonstrated ambiguities in the positions they have taken about the ideal of a United

States of Europe and its variants. While some parties favoured European Unity from the interwar period, others manifested a more complex set of approaches. There is thus no readily discernible socialist ideological vision of European Unity. The socialist parties in Western Europe did not exhibit a domestic preoccupation with the EC/EU and it seemed as if only those members who were avowedly "Europeanists" in the parties were delegated to the European Parliament. In the past, Europe was not often a platform on which to fight a national election.

It is true that there is a discernible trend of an increase in support for European integration among the Socialist parties in Western Europe over the last few decades.[1] The reasons for the socialist initial unwillingness to embrace wholeheartedly the ideal of European Unity have not yet been fully explored in the literature on the socialist and social democrat parties. Apart from the excellent account from Featherstone and some studies such as Newman, there has been relatively little academic coverage of the socialist parties and European integration, on a crossnational level.[2] The Christian Democrats have been far better documented and dissected, if only because it is a task that is less frustrating for the analysts than attempting to understand and document socialist inter party and intraparty differences over time on policy towards the issue of European integration.

There are several reasons for the ambiguities in the socialist positions. They depend, for example, upon such factors as the relative strength of nationalism, the existence of a sizeable Communist party or rival Social Democratic party in the domestic political setting. The uneasy alliance of nationalism and internationalism has been a prominent feature of the socialist debate on European unity. While some socialist parties or individuals have been to the fore in the move for European unity, others have taken a distinctively individualistic or nationalistic approach to the issue. For some, like the French Socialists, nationalism was an important brake on internationalist tendencies in the European domain, as was the case with the French Communists. For others, like the German Social Democratic party, the EC and especially the European Coal and Steel Community (ECSC) were regarded at first as a system of institutions and market regulation which would benefit the capitalists rather than the workers, although the party was to come out in favour of the EEC in 1957, in recognition of economic benefits to the German people. The priority of German unification placed all other issues, including membership of the ECSC in the early 1950s, lower on the party's agenda.

This is not to state that many socialists were not active in the European unity movement—it was not a movement identified with any single political tradition within Europe. The socialists were, like the

Communists and Christian Democrats, active members of the resistance movements against fascism and actively involved in postwar cooperation and reconstruction as they questioned the role and nature of the nation state. It was a socialist, Paul Henri Spaak, who was prominent at the Hague Congress in 1948 and urged its creation of a European Assembly and who headed the 1955 Messina meeting of intergovernmental representatives to lay down the guidelines for what became the European Economic Community (EEC).[3]

The socialist tradition is an internationalist one and this tradition of course was evident in many of the ideals and pronouncements of the socialist individuals and parties who were in favour of European Unity. The experience of dissent in the First Socialist Workers' International had left a legacy of division among the member parties.[4] In addition, the British Labour party's reluctance to lead the new International, proposed by the French, German, Austrian, Dutch and Italian socialists, after the World War II led to a lack of a cohesive socialist approach to many issues, not least European integration. Dreyfus suggests that while the European socialist movement can pride itself on its relative success in the fight for universal suffrage, it can be far less proud of its action in the fight against nationalism.[5]

During the interwar years many European Social Democratic parties were in favour of the rather vague ideals of European unity current at the time. There was even some support from the British Labour party at this time for European integration. The Social Democratic parties of Italy and the Benelux actively promoted European unity ideals at the Hague Congress in 1948. Both the Danish Social Democrats and the Labour party in Britain were split very deeply on this issue.

The Socialist International by 1947, after many disagreements and the eventual decision to exclude East European parties, agreed to the "basic theme of international socialist conferences" by supporting the reconstruction of Western Europe under the Marshall Plan.[6] The parties most in favour of the decisive creation of a European federation were the French and Dutch socialists followed by the Belgian socialists and the Socialist party of Italian workers. The Labour party was opposed to binding obligations on this issue. Due largely to this British reluctance, the Socialist International remained split over the issue. The Socialist conferences, while attempting to be internationalist, saw little cooperation among the British and continental parties who incidentally soon expressed themselves as pro-Western alignment.

The creation of the European Coal and Steel Community and the Europe of the Six (France, Germany, Italy, the Netherlands, Belgium and Luxembourg) led to what amounted to an inner core of pro-integrationists, consisting of those parties from the Six countries which became the EC, and an outer circle of those parties who were outside the initial European integration process. The Socialist International in 1951, although it passed a basic resolution on the need for European union, had no stated or agreed position on the issue of the creation of the ECSC or the initiative for a European Defence Community.[7] By the time the EEC was created in 1957, the socialist and Social Democratic parties of the Six were firmly in favour of the EC and European integration. In fact it is the socialist parties of the six founding countries of the EC that have consistently, since 1958, called for radical proposals for increased European unity, while the parties of the newer countries were to be more hesitant in their support of the EC, if not downright hostile. For example, the Fouchet plan for French-influenced coordination of foreign and defence policies and the Franco-German Treaty of 22 January 1963 were attacked by the Socialist parties of the Six founding states of the EC "for putting at risk the trust that had developed within the Community and for seeking to return to the 'outworn concept of the absolute sovereignty of states.'"[8] Opposition to the European Community was especially apparent among the socialist parties of those countries that joined the Community in 1973, the Community's first enlargement of membership, namely the United Kingdom, Ireland and Denmark. The later enlargement, to include Greece in 1981, saw the Greek socialist party PASOK change its outright opposition to a cautious acceptance of the European Community and its benefits to Greece by the middle of the 1980s. The socialist parties of the 1986 enlargement of the EC, Spain and Portugal, expressed a clear preference for joining the European Community and an appreciation of the benefits of Community membership, particularly the means to achieve a certain democratic credibility and sustained economic development.

Socialists have featured prominently within the Community in the institutions, such as Piet Dankert in the European Parliament (EP), who laboured for increased powers for the European Parliament and utilised its budgetary powers extensively and David Martin, author of European Parliament reports on European Union as well as Klaus Haensch, president of the European Parliament since 1994. In the Commission, Roy Jenkins as well as Jacques Delors have raised the stature of the Commission in their commitment to a social agenda. In the EP, it was a socialist, Hank Vredling, who first proposed a common market of parties at the EC level as early as 1971 and he was also the author of the initiative for industrial democracy in the EC in the so-called Vredling directive.[9] Even before Vredling, the idea of the creation of a European Socialist party came from Andre Philip in his article in 1950, entitled *Socialism and European Unity*.[10]

It should not be very surprising to analysts of the history and development of European integration that the Socialists were not the main creators of the EC. The Communities, especially the EEC, were not radical or socialist in the manner that they were created. Socialists were not in government in five of the six founding countries to sign the EEC Treaty. The EC was created by the political establishment of the time. Spinelli has illustrated in 1972 that the political elites, such as parties and governments, absorbed the ideas of European unity and the conversions to the idea of the EC, itself a radical plan, was made first and foremost made by those in the political centre.[11] The Christian Democrats are an example of this centrist adherence to European integration. Further, the appeal of anti-communism and of Europeanism as a defence against the Soviet Union, was one echoed by Christian Democrats rather than socialists or social democrats.

Spinelli points out that the Left in Europe "although originally internationalist," had for a long time been largely nationalist in orientation.[12] The European Union (EU) is not Socialist, although elements such as the social provisions in the EEC Treaty of Rome are social democratic in nature or design. Far more is achieved by the EU for farmers and capital in the freedom of movement of capital and enterprise than the free movement of workers. The EEC was long regarded as a means to achieve prosperity for farmers and business and was seen by many socialist and Social Democratic parties at the time of its creation as a tool or instrument of the larger firms and multinational corporations. While the ideal of European Unity was often a radical one, even envisaging the destruction of and replacement of the nation state by a supranational body, the actual EC that was put into operation in the 1950s lost a great deal of its idealism by the time that nationalism began to reassert itself in the late 1950s and this was firmly in place by the time of the Luxembourg Compromise. The EC/EU did not become a Europe of the Peoples. Neither did it evolve as a *Europe des patries* as envisaged by de Gaulle. In the first two or three decades of the Community's existence, it certainly was not a Europe of the Workers but a European Community benefitting farmers, industrialists and traders in general.

The expansive logic of integration, as espoused by the functionalists and also the neofunctionalists like Ernst Haas did not include the issue of workers rights to any great degree. The logic appealed to bureaucrats, politicians of the government of the day, and to industry. The integration of sectors envisaged by the functionalists, the neofunctionalists and even federalists, dealt with sectors of the economy such as industry. This integration was not horizontally based on sectors of society, nor on socioeconomic differentiation of class. The issue of class division or class conflict was not an EC/EU issue. Class differences in fact are rarely alluded to in the EU rhetoric and EU councils and Summits. They tend to be subsumed in issues like the social aspect of the Single Market, or the much diluted Social Charter. Also, in terms of interest politics and corporatist influences on EC policymaking, the multinational corporations, the farmers' organisation and companies like FIAT and IBM have had far more influence on legislation, along with the representatives of business and employers, in the Union of Employers and Industry of the EC (UNICE), than representatives of trade unions in the European Trade Union Confederation has ever had.

Nevertheless there were leaders who were in the socialist camp who favoured integration from the beginning. Monnet for example was a socialist voter and very keen on involving trade unions and socialist parties in the Action Committee for the United States of Europe and he adopted a dirigiste approach to state control of the economy. As Chapter 5 points out, he was also a pragmatist.

Socialism, Social Democracy and Labour: Trends and Traditions

For the purposes of demonstrating the multifaceted approach of socialist and social democratic parties to politics in the European Community and European Union, it is important to draw out the distinctions of the various traditions within what is sometimes referred to as the Socialist grouping. The Social Democrats have tended to be pro-EC/EU and in favour of promoting further European unity while the Socialist parties were more reluctant to embrace the European unity ideal. The Labour parties have been divided on this issue.

Social democrats can be defined as pragmatists who see pragmatism as more important than socialist ideology, who have a strong commitment to democracy and its rules, and who, in the European context, have largely had experience of coalition partners in government. They are in the Keynesian tradition and committed to the welfare state. They are at home, like the socialists, with an increased role for the state in economic and fiscal organisation of the state. Padgett and Patterson describe social democracy as a "hybrid political tradition composed of socialism and liberalism" and consisting of those who seek to realise socialist goals within the institutions of liberal capitalist society.[13] Wide variations are evident within the tradition along national lines, with the British Labour commitment to nationalisation in the 1950s contrasting with the German party's Marxism until the late 1950s, though most would broadly support Crosland's five central values of social democracy of political liberalism, the mixed economy, the welfare state, Keynesian economics and a belief in equality.[14]

By and large Social Democrats are pro-European integration, although there is evident the tension between the fundamental idea of social democracy, namely controlling the market in order to achieve political ends, and the EC/EU aims of according a much less constrained role to the markets operations. Peter Glotz, when general secretary of the German Social Democratic party, noted in 1985:

> Social democracy and democratic socialism can *only* be achieved as European concepts; in national terms these ideals become more illusory and hopeless every day (his emphasis).[15]

He saw the need to recognise transnational interdependence and to have a European unity based on social justice.[16]

> Europe, even with its history, can only advance as a political concept, if Europeans respect a minimal moral standard—social justice.

Labour Parties

The only parties in Western Europe which are called Labour parties are the British and Irish Labour parties and both have been on record as antimarketeers in the past. They have very close links with the trade union movement and were in fact each Labour party was founded as a political wing of the Trade Union movement. Unlike their continental colleagues, they are the only parties in their national contexts to have links with the Trade Unions. Traditionally, they have seen themselves as representatives of British and Irish Labour. Both have come, over the years of EC/EU membership, to admit that the EU has some distinct advantages for the worker and both parties contain tendencies that are avidly federalist and those who oppose federalism in any form.

Socialist Views of European Unity

The socialist parties of the Benelux countries (Belgium, the Netherlands and Luxembourg) supported the ideal of European integration most strongly in the 1950s, when the three communities of the EC were established and they reflected their national elites' support for the creation of the European Community. The French socialist party[17] was split on the issue of the creation of the European Defence Community in the early 1950s and by the late 1950s was to support the EC as it felt that it was in the French national interest. The German Social

Democratic Party, the SPD, also opposed the EC, at first, as it felt that it deflected from the goal of German reunification. From the time of the creation of the EEC and Euratom, the six founding countries of the Community had social democratic parties who were all in favour of the Community. The British felt that national sovereignty would be undermined by participation in the EC. The veto by de Gaulle of the British applications to join the Community was to be opposed by the social democratic parties of the Six founding member states of the EC.

The socialist and social democratic parties of the EC did not engage in passionate commitment to the vision of a United States of Europe. Their approach to European integration in the national arena was to be far more muted than that of their Christian Democratic counterparts. The EC was not an electoral issue for them nationally. Further, when these parties were in government, in the 1960s and 1970s, they did not perceive any need to enunciate a clear Europeanist vision, and they were under no pressure to create one during those decades of nationalism and deriving of economic benefits from the EC. The federalist movement was far removed from the centre of political power and was not actively working on its socialist and social democratic comrades to support the creation of European political Union. The major report in the 1970s on European Union, although drawn up at the request of the Heads of State and Government of the Community, written by a Christian Democrat, Leo Tindemans, was ignored by the Summit leaders of all political persuasions and was not to be replaced by other such initiatives for some time.

Early Transnational Links

In January 1957, a conference took place of the socialist parties (that is members of the second International) of the six founding member states of the ECSC, with the aim of setting up a common platform "for public action and developing joint concepts for the impending European Economic Community"[18] and building on earlier cooperation since 1951. The parties involved were the German Social Democratic Party (SPD), the French SFIO, the Belgian Parti Socialiste Belge (PSB), the Dutch PvdA, the Italian Social Democratic Party and the Luxembourg POSL. A Liaison Bureau was established for the parties and this was to meet at least twice a year. This conference followed the SPD's alteration of its position from anti-ECSC to pro-EEC. The SPD's scepticism on European integration was based on opposition to the EC as a capitalist structure. At this Luxembourg conference, the EEC was recognised as being "unfavourable to the development of a socialist European Community, but it was finally accepted that it would not rule it out altogether."[19] The grouping of parties in 1962 at is fifth conference adopted a "Common Action programme for the Social Democrat parties in the European Community." The socialist position as expressed in this programme and socialist group documents was in favour of a single body for the Communities, uniform institutions and the direct election of the EP. In addition, there was a desire for foreign affairs, defence and cultural policies to be transferred to the EC as quickly as possible, according to Herbert Maier.[20]

The 8th Congress held in April 1973 saw the Dutch member Alfred Mozer produce a report calling for a supranational structure of European Social Democratic forces. The Liaison Bureau, it was hoped, would become a Union of Socialist parties of the European Community with the authority to make binding decisions. The result, however, was the establishment of a Confederation in 5 April 1974, in Luxembourg. The Confederation was not a resounding success, due to a fear by the national party elites of a loss of power to the Confederation, and the limitations to freedom of action of some of the larger parties, as well as differences of approach among the socialist as distinct from the Social Democratic parties.[21] National differences were also evident.

The programmes of the parties in cooperation in the EP and the confederation of the 1970s were the following: the attainment of social equality, support for the Third World, a policy of creating full employment within the EC, the elimination of regional differences and the democratisation of the EC economy.[22] These programmes remained largely programmes of ideals and not a framework for action. Differences were evident in, for example, the fact that the cooperation among the parties tended to be elitist cooperation at leadership level only. Further, while the SPD could not disagree with the CDU/CSU policy of anti-communism, their French counterparts were actively cooperating with the PCF (French Communist Party).

Democratic control of the EC institutions and the need to make the EC more relevant to the worker were themes that all the parties under discussion in this chapter had in common. The need for an articulated social policy and a developed regional policy also featured high on the Social Democratic/socialist agenda relating to the EC. So too, the relationship of the Community to the Third World was important, in order to avoid exploitation of the resources of the latter.

The French Socialist Party

The French Socialist Party has had within its membership differences on European policy. Some elements regarded the EC/EU as a means to

express French interests on a larger scale, seeing Europe as "a necessary dimension of socialism."[23] Other elements regarded the EC as a
capitalist plot, and this view was expressed by the more left wing members of the party, notably members of the CERES, the Centre d'Etudes,
de Recherches et de l'Education Socialiste.

The SFIO was initially opposed to the ECSC due to fears of Franco-
German cooperation on the revival of capitalism and an awareness that
the British would be excluded. However, they did come to support the
Treaty of Paris establishing the ECSC.

A reluctance to embrace supranational elements of the EC was evident in the French Socialist Party in the years up to Mitterrand's presidency and even Mitterrand's first three years or so were not
characterised by a supernationalists stance. The change in attitude
by Mitterrand came about in 1984, with the expression of official French
support for increased powers of the EP, for example. As Bell wrote in
the 1970s, "the questions though is not whether socialists are for or
against Europe," but "what kind of Europe"?[24]

The issue of European integration was one of two issues, the other
being *autogestion* (workers' control) which divided the French Socialist
Party in the 1970s.[25] The left wing CERES faction, later controlled by
Jean Pierre Chevenement, who was also to lead a faction against the
ratification of the Maastricht Treaty in France in September 1992, saw
the European Community as a capitalist organisation and for this reason opposed supranationality as it was identified with institutions that
had vested interests in capitalism. The EC, or EEC, as it was commonly
regarded at this time, was seen by the CERES faction in the 1970s as
an expression of American economic imperialism and hence incompatible with socialism although the other members of the PSF favoured
the EC.[26]

The difference between French Socialists and the British Labour party
has been expressed by Newman in terms of differing perceptions, as
follows:

> . . . to a typical member of the Labour left it is manifest that the EEC is
> wholly devoted to the furtherance of capitalism and is undemocratic while,
> to his counterpart in the French Socialist party, whose general conception
> of socialism may be very similar, it is equally obvious that, although the
> Community has many faults, it is only on the European level that social
> justice, internationalism and independence from the USA can be estab-
> lished.[27]

Michel Rocard in an interview in 1993 put the priorities for European Socialists as the following:

. . . employment, that is a different kind of organisation of work in our societies; a Social Europe; industrial policy; immigration and management.[28]

British Labour

The approach of the British Labour party to membership of the EEC and to the intensification of European integration in general has been largely negative in the past and opposed to cooperation in, and membership of, the EC. Indeed, they did not take their seats in the European Parliament until after the June 1975 referendum on EC membership. However, it is important to keep in mind Byrd's caveat that there are difficulties in talking about the party as if it were a cohesive whole, given its internal division on the issue of European integration.[29] Thus it is hardly surprising that the British members of the Socialist group in the EP have in the past been criticised for their lack of "Europeanness." For example, *The Guardian* reported in 1984 that:

The most serious charge against the labour group is that they are obsessed with national politics, and pay scant regard to the European issue which should properly concern them.[30]

The Labour party came under criticism in 1984 for refusing to deal with the EC issue at all, and Walter Cairns called this the "Trappist monk" approach of removing the issue from all discussion. He called for a Labour strategy of reform of the EC from within rather than a withdrawal from the EC.[31]

As in 1980 and 1981, the Labour party had in July 1982 set out a policy statement entitled "Withdrawal from the EEC" and this was overwhelmingly endorsed at the party's national conference later that year.[32] It was agreed by delegates at the conference to take Britain out of the EC as soon as possible without a referendum. In 1975, the year of the Labour-organised referendum on continued membership of the EC, the party conference and the parliamentary party had a majority in favour of withdrawal from the EC.[33] The party was divided among those who had a nationalist view of Europe, and those who, like the eventual breakaway Social Democratic Party, saw the European Community as an important focus of Labour policy.[34] The Labour opposition was based on the perception of the EC as a rich man's club, which did not relate to British people. Barbara Castle expressed the view thus:

I don't disagree with the Market of the Six. I can understand why they got together. It was historically and economically relevant in the aftermath of war.[35]

Tom Nairn regarded the Labour party, in its opposition to the EC, as having sold out class interests for the sake of the nation.[36] Featherstone has illustrated the confusion in the Labour ranks over the EC's institutional structure and the party's stance on European integration. The party saw the EEC as a diminution of national sovereignty, a block to the progress towards socialism and a potential weakening of the link with the Commonwealth.[37]

Ken Collins, a Scottish Labour MEP, pointed out the irony of the Labour position; "the idea of sovereignty and socialism in one country hardly appears on any other left-wing party's agenda."[38]

The leadership of Neil Kinnock saw a change of Labour emphasis on the Community as Kinnock engaged in active collaboration with the European Parliament's Socialist Group and he advocated a European-wide policy to deal with unemployment and the rejection of a nationalist approach to international relations. Byrd describes this change of approach:

This new-found commitment to internationalism represents a staggering reverse from Labour's attachment to the nationalist/autarchic economic policies which had dominated after 1979.[39]

Meanwhile the breakaway Social Democrats under Roy Jenkins, David Owen and Shirley Williams were from the more pro-EC wing of the party. Like their current party partners, the Liberals, the social democrats have always promoted the deepening of European integration and especially the redressing of the democratic deficit.[40] However, they have no representation at the European Parliament level.

The Danish Social Democrats

The Danish Social Democratic party was against the creation of the ECSC and the EDC in the 1950s and was of the opinion that the EEC should have been a looser structure on a broader geographical basis than the EEC of the Six, such as the European Free Trade Association.[41] Paterson and Campbell's description of Scandinavian social democratic parties holds for the Danes:

The social democrats in Scandinavia have traditionally followed a policy similar to that of their British counterpart: sympathy towards certain forms of European cooperation but antipathy to integration as represented by the European Communities. The original attitude taken by most social democrat leaders in Scandinavia to the EEC was one of guarded hostility; for them the Communities represented a Catholic, conservative, capitalist bloc whose policies could vitally affect Scandinavia's trading interests.[42]

When negotiating Danish entry to the EC, most members of the party were in favour of membership. The party, before joining, engaged in extensive debate on the need for the EC to be guided by social democratic principles, such as workers' co-determination, worker's protection and environmental health. It also called for an increase in democratic control of the EC institutions. However, it opposed the involvement of Denmark in close military or political alliances.[43] The EC was regarded as a means to achieve social democracy, not an end in itself.[43] Thomas notes:

> There is a general suspicion of anything that might result in the formation of another superpower, and it is certainly not the party's aim to see a realisation of high-flying dreams of a United States of Europe,[44]

In common with most European Social Democrats, the Danish party feels that it has a better chance of achieving its ideals from within the European Union than from outside it.[45]

Poul Rasmussen, the current leader of the Danish Social Democrats, when interviewed in 1993, saw the five priority areas for European Socialists as follows: ". . . employment and growth initiatives; enlargement; environmental questions; social affairs and the social dimension of the internal market."[46] These concerns reflect the issues on which the Socialists consistently concur as EU-related goals within the Socialist group and the confederation of Socialist parties of the EU. However, when asked about the 1992 change of name of the Confederation of Socialist parties to the European Socialist party, he said that he did not see much difference. He added: ". . . although the name of the party of European Socialists indicates the opposite, our national parties still form the basis of any political action undertaken."[47]

German Social Democratic Party

The SPD was to become over the years more integrationist than many of its counterparts in other member states, although in the 1950s it strongly argued against the rearming of Germany and it vehemently opposed the creation of the ECSC, regarding it as a French plan to con-

trol Germany and keep it on an equal footing in Europe. It also opposed the initiative for a European Defence Community. At this time,
its position was that German reunification should be the primary objective of the German government.

It dropped a great deal of its ideological baggage, to coin
Kircheimer's' phrase, namely Marxism, in the Bad Godesberg conference in 1959. Since then, it supported Christian Democratic governments
in pro-EC initiatives, although on the issue of NATO, the SPD opposed
this at first as it did not wish Germany to be part of a military alliance. The SPD altered its anti-European cooperation stance in 1955 and
supported the creation of the EEC and Euratom in 1957. Paterson points
to the peak of the SPD's pro-European phase in 1965 when the party
deeply supported the Commission in its showdown with de Gaulle at
the time of the Empty Chair crisis and Luxembourg compromise.[48]

The SPD position since the 1970s has been far more overtly in favour of a vision of European Unity than its counterparts in other countries. The Schmidt declaration in 1974 was, in many ways, a continuation
of Brandt's policy:

> We declare ourselves for the political unification of Europe, in partner-
> ship with the United States of America. For this the European Commu-
> nity is an irreplaceable basis . . . The Goal of a European political union
> appears more urgent than ever. Together with our partners in the Euro-
> pean Community we shall seek to achieve this goal.[49]

Friedrich illustrates the continuity by Schmidt of Brandt's policies
when he shows that Schmidt explicitly endorsed a Brandt definition of
political union as "less than supranationality but more than conventional
cooperation."[50] The theme of Schmidt's approach to the EC was "the
only hope is in partnership," a partnership based on the fact that the
EC was in Germany's interest and that Europe's interest was an
atlanticist one.[51] Patterson shows that Brandt was however far more a
visionary in his plans for a European Social Order than Schmidt, whose
approach was more pragmatic in style.[52] Schmidt was also of the opinion that close relations with France must be cultivated and that intergovernmental relations were more important than relations with the
Commission. He also is regarded as having had a profound impact on
ensuring budgetary stability in the Community through the transfer of
resources to the Community.[53]

The SPD has always maintained its stance in favour of European integration and its emphasis on employment, with slogans in the 1994
European Parliament elections including "Jobs, Jobs, Jobs" and "Secu-

rity instead of fear: Beat the Mafia in Europe" as well as the more na-
tionally-minded "We can better represent German interests."

Italy's Socialist Parties

Until the early 1990s, Italy had two parties that could be called
socialist, the socialist party, the PSI, and the social democratic party, the
PSDI and both were members of the Socialist Group of the European
Parliament. The Social Democratic Party has always supported the
EC, the ECSC and EDC, while the PSI was opposed to the creation of
the ECSC and the EDC in the early 1950s. It was only in 1961 that the
PSI fully accepted Italian membership of the EC.[54] The PSI had
been opposed to Italian participation in the ECSC and feared that this
would lead to American dominance in Europe. They also feared that
national industries would be dominated by that of their partners. The
party abstained in the parliament on the national vote on the EEC in
1957.

The former Italian Communisty Party (PCI) changed its name to
the Democratic Party of the Left and joined the Socialist Group in
1993. It has often cooperated with that group in the past and its
platform had been more Eurocommunist than communist for several
decades.

The Italian Enrico Ferri said that the three parties in the Socialist
Party cooperated in the Party but not in Italy. The Italian Social Democrat Party, the Socialist Party and the former Communist party the PDS
all collaborate in Europe but not in Italy.[55]

Spanish Socialist Party (PSOE)

The Socialist party has always been pro-EC and after the October
1982 election Prime Minister Gonzalez approached President Mitterrand
about the possibility of Spain joining the EC, which it eventually did
in 1986. The party was also in favour of joining NATO but this did not
reflect public opinion in the early 1980s, when a referendum was called
on NATO membership. Like the Portuguese Socialists, the party has
been in favour of the deepening of European integration, especially the
clarification of a type of European citizenship, an initiative of Prime Minister Felipe Gonzalez at the intergovernmental conference on the Treaty
of European Union in 1991. Featherstone correctly suggests that both
the Spanish and Portuguese Socialist parties saw the EC as a means of
consolidating and strengthening their national democratic institutions
as well as modernising their economies.[55] The issues of Europeanism and
modernization have been closely linked for these parties.

Irish Labour Party

The Irish Labour party, like the Congress of Trade Unions, campaigned against Ireland's entry into the Community in 1972, due to a fear of loss of national sovereignty and fear of increased consumer prices. Its stance was still very sceptical in the 1979 direct elections to the EP. This has, however, altered since direct elections and, if only for nationalist interests, the party is in favour of the Community/ Union for its regional and social policies, for example. It has often been at odds with the other Irish parties in the EP in its support for the Socialist group's proposals for reform of the Common Agricultural Policy.[56]

Transnational Linkages and the
Socialist Group in the European Parliament

The Socialist group in the EP was founded in 1952, at the same time as the Christian Democratic and Liberal party groups were formed, reflecting the transnational nature of the Assembly of the ECSC and the desire to transcend national rivalries and concentrate on common ideological alignments. The Socialists were perceived as the most internationalist grouping within the Assembly at that time. Since 1973, the Socialist group has reflected the conflicts of pro and anti-EC members. However, until the Community's first enlargement of member states in 1973, to include the UK, Ireland and Denmark, the Socialists were probably the most far-reaching in their designs for a United States of Europe. Indeed as early as 1962 they produced a Common Programme for direct elections to the Assembly, elections which were to be stalled by national governments until 1979.

It was the Socialist group which acted as the main proponents of European Unity and advancing European integration in the Community, from within the EP. It was the Socialist group which first instigated clear-cut policy proposals in the form of formal group documents and programmes in the Assembly. It also took upon itself, in the early years in particular, to criticise the High Authority, the precursor to the Commission, for what it considered the Authority's failure to prompt further integration and progress in the field of social policy.

It was the socialists who for the first time ever threatened the use of the European Parliament's power of censure over the Commission and utilised this threat in the early years with some effect. For the first two decades in the EP, the Socialist group's commitment to advancing the ideals of European Unity served as an impetus to the other groups to define their EC policies. In fact Fitzmaurice suggested that only the

Socialists, by the dissolution of the Assembly in 1958, "had gone any way towards the formulation of clear-cut positions at the European level, and that this alone had been the catalyst to the politicisation of the Assembly."[57]

The group was quite homogeneous in membership and program orientation until 1973 and had a reasonably united front among its six member country representatives. When the British Labour party joined the Group, it became, for the first time, the largest group in the EP, outstripping the Christian Democrats for the first time. It has been suggested that there had been a remarkable degree of unity of common ideology and shared economic policies among the socialist parties of the Six.[58] The British, unlike their more Social Democratic continental counterparts, did not share the latters' faith in a mixed economy. After 1973, the Group was to be clearly divided among pro- and anti-marketeers, as they were dubbed, especially when the British Labour members ended their boycott of attendance of the EP in 1975 when the British referendum on UK membership resulted in the majority of the British population being in favour of continued membership of the Community. Thus, the group was often riven by internal difficulties and found it difficult to be united on issues relating especially to furthering European integration.

The Socialist Group founded the first socialist European confederation on 5 April 1974. This confederation consisted of parties from eight member states, to be joined by the British Labour party in early 1976. It was part of the Socialist International and built on transnational links established in the 1960s which had an institutionalised machinery and had held regular meeting since the 1960s.

The new Party of European Socialists was created from the Confederation of Socialist parties of the European Community in November 1992, at the Hague. This party was not just a gathering of EC member parties, but is also open to the parties outside the EC. In fact, the Austrian and Finnish parties as well as the Swedish Social Democratic party joined at that time.[59] The aim of the new Party was to "have some structural power at the European Community level" and organise the campaign for a social Europe and other goals in common.[60] This is seen as particularly important in post Maastricht Europe, given that the Maastricht Treaty for the first time recognises the existence of "political parties at the European level" as being important for integration and to further help form" a European awareness, and to expressing the political will of the citizens of Europe."[61] The Socialist group of the European Parliament changed its name officially on 21 April 1993 to the "Group of the Party of European Socialists" and in January that year 20 Italian members of the former Italian Communist Party, the Democratic Party of the Left, left the Group of the European United Left and joined the Socialists.[62]

Claes correctly perceives that it is the national parties which will give the necessary organisational development to a European party. Such a party, according to Claes, a former member of the EP, needs to work with national parties and with colleagues in the other EC institutions, especially given that there are socialist ministers in six of the twelve member states at present.[63] The Party adopted a clear approach to the Edinburgh Summit of December 1992 in calling for a European-wide program of economic recovery, with a social Europe and an EC which is even closer to its citizens and the application of subsidiarity. It is also in favour of the Community's enlargement of membership to include all countries who accept the Maastricht Treaty. This was in the context of being a grouping which is "brought together by the common threads of European social-democratic ideology."[64] Claes, former deputy prime minister of Belgium and President of the Party of European Socialists and later Secretary General of NATO, further set out as part of the Party's agenda the strengthening of the powers of the European Parliament and suggested that there would be much soul-searching assessment of social democratic ideology on the eve of the new millennium. He saw the need to "take up the challenge of new political culture— which is essentially a Europe federalism in the face of the diminishing role of the nation state."[65]

It was on the issue of workers' rights and workers' participation in company boards that the Socialists and Jacques Delors, as President of the Commission, distinguished themselves as being in favour of a Europe of the Workers especially in the context of the Single Market. The Socialist group was so dissatisfied with the diluted Social Charter of 1989-90 that it even considered censuring the Commission.[66] Jacques Delors had been the main protagonist of workers' rights in the context of the Single Market but had been unable to persuade the UK to accept these principles.

Socialists and Maastricht

The position of socialist parties in the EC/EU towards the Maastricht Treaty on European Union was positive in general, even if some were of the opinion that the Community needed a further redressing of the democratic deficit.

While the domestic British Labour party was split on the issue of the Treaty on European Union, the Labour members of the EP were in favour and advocated its acceptance by the British parliament. The Labour Campaign for a Social Europe stated:

> The Treaty of European Union is supported by all other European Social-
> ists parties, including those of countries seeking EC membership. If La-
> bour opposed Maastricht, we would be isolated from our European
> colleagues, and our about-turn would make us look ridiculous in the eyes
> of the electorate.[67]

This was of course addressed very much at the Labour MPS who
would vote on the Maastricht Treaty in the House of Commons.

The socialists expressed themselves in favour of Economic and Monetary Union (EMU) in the Maastricht Treaty because it supports the
framework for coordinated budget action, which is a "key demand of
the Left since the 1970s."[68] They are in favour of coordinated action as
it creates the possibility of economic expansion and not a go-it-alone
policy of one nation state. A European currency and closer coordination of economic policy-making in the EC "open up the prospect for
even more radical shifts in economic power."[69] Given that the multinational corporations play off one country against another, according to
Ford and Reed, a European level negotiating approach is considered
necessary and the Maastricht is regarded as going in this direction.
While it supports the economic aspect of EMU, the French and Danish
parties have been fearful about monetary policy, as Ford and Reed
explain. They called for a "Maastricht Plus policy" as Maastricht has
many imperfections and needs to supplemented by a radical socialist
approach to the achievement of EMU.[70] Indeed, David Marquand has
reflected such an approach in a 1994 New Left Reviews article which
stated that the Treaty did not go far enough as it "was rooted in
the technocratic economism of the Community's salad days." He called
on the European Left to "embrace a new version of the federalism of
the forties, based on the good Christian Democratic principle of
subsidiarity."[71]

Among the issues on the post-Maastricht TEU agenda of Socialists
are a revision of the Social Chapter of the treaty, with a strong legal
base and the inclusion of employment, pay and social security and right
of association and collective bargaining under qualified majority voting
provisions in the Council of Ministers. In addition, they support co-
decision of the European Parliament and Council to include a new social chapter and secondly the right should be accorded to the EP to
initiate legislation on social issues. Hughes suggests that, for the longer
term, "the left needs to begin now to define the sought-after scope for
EU action on broader citizens' rights; the right to decent housing, education, health care and other strands of social policy" and a division of
responsibility for these among local authorities, regions, the member
states and the EU.[72]

The electoral platform of Party of European Socialists was a platform with three important messages: a vote for European Union, a vote against racism and nationalism and a vote in favour of the establishment of new priorities in Europe. The Party was however divided among its member parties on the issues of a sharp reduction in the working week. Gerd Walter, who drafted the platform, elaborated on the priorities announced in the platform as job creation, social progress and cohesion, equality for men and women, environmental and consumer protection, peace, efforts to combat racism, xenophobia and organized crime and the development of greater democracy, including relations with national parliament.[73]

Conclusion

The socialists and social democrats within the European Union are increasingly involved in Study Days and cooperation within the European Parliament and they also have contacts with party counterparts who are Minister at the Council meetings. In addition, the Confederation of Socialist parties, founded in 1974, provides the opportunity for leaders of parties to meet in opinion-forming settings such as annual conferences to decide on policy on EU issues.

The question that is, however, rarely asked about these parties is why they were less than passionate in their commitment to European Unity, although individuals do serve to remind us of the commitment and dedication of some. Spinelli was in many ways a socialist and his vision and Draft Treaty on European Union have been supported by the Socialist groups of the EP. Willy Brandt was a supporter and promoter of European Union and also a member of the newly-elected European Parliament for a short time. Roy Jenkins was a supporter of European integration although his position in the EC Commission came at a time of disillusionment with the Community. He did not provide a strong intellectual leadership of the European Unity movement among social democrats in the 1970s. The analyst is sometimes struck by the fact that the most committed socialists to European Unity are the core parties of the Six founding member states of the Community and the Iberian socialist parties. In fact the Spanish Socialist party was regarded as being ahead of public opinion in its embracing of the Community.

If there is a socialist or social democratic vision of Europe, it is a desire for a socially committed European Union. This involves a reform of the Common Agricultural Policy so that funds are allocated to other needs, such as the cohesion funds of social and regional policy. The EEC Treaty is committed to dissolving the imbalances in society in general terms, in Article 123, and the Single European Act attempted to give a social dimension of the Community in the cohesion funds. So too, the social dimension of the Single European Market project was promoted by the socialist President of the Commission, Jacques Delors and in the publication of a book of socialist views of Europe entitled *Europe Without Frontiers* in the late 1980s.[74]

Since the 1980s, the Commission has been actively promoting a social dimension and especially the Social Charter, agreed on by all member states except the United Kingdom, in 1989 and incorporated, in an amended form, in the Maastricht Treaty as a Protocol, by all but the UK. The Socialist group in the EP was particularly active in promoting the need to create a Social Charter, in a ". . . revolt against what they saw as the unbalanced 'Thatcherite' liberalism underpinning the Single market initiative."[75]

The Socialist group came under criticism in the European Parliament for putting forward too many proposals on the Social Charter, many of which would not be successful, and without a clear list of priorities.[76] Thus the most comprehensive, if unprioritised, set of principles on social policy in the European Union has come from the Socialist group in the largely limited forum of the European Parliament, which has narrow scope in terms of decisionmaking within the EU.

It appears that the socialist vision of Europe is thus a social one of reduction of working hours and improvement of living and working standards and the achievement of the aims of the Social Charter. It features little debate on the creation of a supranational political system, although democratisation is a recurrent theme, despite its support of European integration. European Parliament reports like the Martin reports make it clear that the Socialist group is committed to the achievement of increased integration in the European Union and that Maastricht did not go far enough in this regard. Perhaps this focusing on the social dimension is the clearest way forward for the socialists in their vision of European unity.

Notes

I would like to thank William E. Paterson for his comments on an earlier version of this chapter.

1. K. Featherstone, "Socialist Parties and European integration: Variations on a Common Theme," in W. Paterson and A. Thomas, eds., *The Future of Social Democracy: Problems and Prospects of Social Democratic Parties in Western Europe* (Oxford: Clarendon Press, 1986), p. 243.

2. However, R. Ladrech's "Social Democratic Parties and EC integration" attempts to fill this gap. *European Journal of Political Research*, vol. 24, 1993.

3. D. Urwin, *The Community of Europe* (London: Longman, 1991), p. 33.

4. W. Loth, "The Socialist International," in Walter Lipgens and Wilfried Loth, *Documents on the History of European integration*, vol. 4 (Berlin: Walter de Gruyter, 1991), p. 437.

5. M. Dreyfus, *L'Europe des Socialistes* (Bruxelles: Editions Complexe, 1991), p. 305.

6. W. Loth, "The Socialist International" in Walter Lipgens and Wilfried Loth, *Documents on the History of European integration*, vol. 4, p. 440.

7. Ibid., p. 442.

8. D. Urwin, *The Community of Europe* (London: Longman, 1991), p. 107.

9. See H. Vredling, "The Common market of Political Parties," *Government and Opposition*, no. 3, 1971.

10. A. Philip, "Socialism and European Unity, September 1950," Walter Lipgens and Wilfried Loth, *Documents on the History of European integration*, vol. 4, pp. 311-314.

11. A. Spinelli, *The European Adventure* (London: Charles Knight, 1972), p. 10.

12. Ibid., p. 11.

13. S. Padgett and W. E. Paterson, *A History of Social Democracy in Postwar Europa* (London: Longman, 1991), p. 1.

14. P. Glotz, "Europe—The Helpless and Silent Continent" in *New Statesman*, 20-27 December, 1985.

15. Ibid.

16. Called the French Section of the Workers' International, or SFIO, until the creation of the French Socialist party, the PSF, in 1970.

17. S. Padgett and W. E. Paterson, *A History of Social Democracy in Postwar Europe*, p. 3.

18. H. Maier, "Socialist and Social Democrat Parties" in T. Stammen, *Political Parties in Europe* (London: Martin, 1982), p. 229.

19. Ibid., p. 230.

20. Ibid., p. 230.

21. Ibid., p. 231.

22. Ibid., p. 232.

23. D. S. Bell, "The Parti Socialiste in France" in *Journal of Common Market Studies*, vol. 13, Number 4, 1975, p. 429.

24. Ibid., p. 430.

25. Criddle, 1977, p. 41.

26. Criddle, 1977, p. 43.

27. M. Newman, *Socialism and European Unity: The Dilemma of the Left in Britain and France* (London: Junction Books, 1983), p. 14.

28. M. Rocard, quoted in *European Labour Forum*, Summer 1993, p. 13.

29. P. Byrd, The Labour Party and the European Economic Community 1970-1975, *Journal of Common Market Studies*, vol. 13, no. 4, 1975, p. 469.

30. D. Brown, "Labour Raises a Point of Order" in *The Guardian*, 23 November 1984.

31. W. Cairns, "Labour's Search For a New Europe," *Guardian*, 2 November 1984.

32. Editorial Comments, "Labour's Love's Lost" in *Common Market Law Review*, vol. 18, no. 4, November 1981, p. 443.

33. P. Byrd, "The Labour Party in Britain" in W. E. Patterson and A. H. Thomas, eds., *The Future of Social Democracy*, p. 69.

34. Ibid., p. 69.

35. B. Castle, "There is no sense of equality for us in Europe—none at all" in *Europe 81*, Delegation of the Commission of the EC (London: December 1981), p. 19.

36. K. Featherstone, "Socialists and European integration: The Attitudes of British Labour Members of Parliament" in *European Journal of Political Research*, no. 9, 1981, p. 408.

37. K. Featherstone, "Socialist Parties and European Integration: Variations on a Common Theme" in W. Paterson and A. Thomas, eds., *The Future of Social Democracy: Problems and Prospects of Social Democratic Parties in Western Europe*, p. 247.

38. K. Collins, "The Left faces isolation over Europe," *Europe 81*, Delegation of the Commission of the EC (London: December, 1981), p. 13.

39. P. Byrd, "The Labour Party in Britain" in W. E. Patterson and A. H. Thomas, eds., *The Future of Social Democracy*, p. 70.

40. For further discussion of the issue of parliamentary sovereignty see S. Williams, "Sovereignty and Accountability in the European Community," *The Political Quarterly*, vol. 61, July-September 1990, pp. 299-317.

41. EFTA has the aims of establishing the free trade of industrial products among its member countries and the creation of a free trade area. It excluded agricultural goods from this area.

42. W. Paterson and I. Campbell, *Social Democracy in Postwar Europe* (London: Macmillan, 1974), p. 58.

43. A. Thomas, "Danish Social Democracy and the European Community" in *Journal of Common Market Studies*, vol. 13, no. 4, 1975, p. 464-467.

44. Ibid., p. 467.

45. Ibid., p. 468.

46. P. Rasmussen interviewed in "Building the Party of European Socialists," *European Labour Forum*, Summer 1993, p. 13.

47. Ibid., p. 15.

48. W. Paterson, "The German Social Democratic Party" in W. Paterson and A. Thomas, *Social Democratic Parties in Western Europe*, eds. (London: Croom Helm, 1977), p. 197.

49. Schmidt's government declaration of 17 May 1974, quoted in P. Friedrich, "The SPD and the Politics of Europe: from Willy Brandt to Helmut Schmidt," *Journal of Common Market Studies*, vol. 13, no. 4, 1975, p. 434.

50. Ibid., p. 434.

51. Ibid., p. 437.

52. W. Paterson, "The German Social Democratic Party" in W. Paterson and A. Thomas, *Social Democratic Parties in Western Europe*, p. 200.

53. Ibid.

54. K. Featherstone, 1983.

55. *Agence Europe*, 8/9 November 1993.

56. K. Featherstone, "Socialist Parties and European integration: Variations on a Common Theme," W. Paterson and A. Thomas, eds., *The Future of Social Democracy: Problems and Prospects of Social Democratic Parties in Western Europe*, p. 246.

57. P. Murray, "The European Parliament and the Irish Dimension" in P. Hainsworth, ed., *Breaking and Preserving the Mould: The Third Direct Elections to the European Parliament (1989): The Irish Republic and Northern Ireland* (Belfast: Policy Research Institute, 1992).

58. J. Fitzmaurice, *The Party Groups in the European Parliament* (London: Saxon House, 1975), p. 36.

59. For example, see M. Palmer, *The European Parliament: What It Is, What It Does, How It Works* (Oxford: Pergamon, 1980), p. 151.

60. W. Claes, "What's in a Name?" *European Labour Forum*, no. 10, Summer 1993, p. 9.

61. Ibid., p. 8.

62. Article 138a of the European Union Treaty.

63. EP Bulletin 21 June 1993, PE163.6006, p. 30 and EP Bulletin 8 February 1993, PE163.602, p. 30.

64. W. Claes, "What's in a Name?" p. 11.

65. Ibid., p. 12.

66. Ibid., p. 12.

67. D. Urwin, *The Community of Europe*, p. 239.

68. "Labour Campaign for a Socialist Europe," *European Labour Forum*, no. 8. Summer 1992, Socialist Group, European Parliament, p. 27.

69. G. Ford and D. Reed, "The Socialist Case for Maastricht," *European Labour Forum*, Winter 1992-93, p. 35.

70. Ibid., p. 35.

71. Ibid., p. 37.

72. D. Marquand, Reinventing Federalism: Europe and the Left, *New Left Review*, no. 203, Jan/Feb. 1994.

73. S. Hughes, "Beyond the Social Chapter," *European Labour Forum*, Winter 1994-1995, no. 14, p. 10

74. *Agence Europe*, 8/9 November 1993.

75. P. Dankert and A. Kooyman, eds., *Europe Without Frontiers: Socialists on the Future of the European Economic Community* (London: Mansell, 1989).

76. Ibid., p. 173.

77. Ibid., p. 175.

9

The Transformation of the European Ideal Since World War II

Paul Rich

The ideal of European unity which developed in the course of the twentieth century contained a number of internal tensions which have still not been satisfactorily resolved. Was the envisaged union of European states to be supranational in nature, one that would override the sovereignty of existing nation states? Or was it be intergovernmental in nature leaving many important decisions in matters such as defence and foreign policy to national governments? Was the envisaged European political entity to be a superpower that could compete with other superpowers such as the USA and, before its demise, the USSR? Or was it be a looser confederation that would lack any major military capacity and would work in tandem with other international organisations like the United Nations? What also was to be the role of this new European polity in global affairs? Was it be another imperial bloc anxious to protect its existing economic and security interests? Or was it to be a different kind of political force dedicated to the promotion of world peace and even a way station to eventual world government?

This chapter will discuss these questions in terms of the postwar debate on a united Europe and its external relationships to other states in order to see how far the ideal of a supranational European political entity prevailed. It will examine the reasons for the failure of the "grand design" for a European superstate in favour of the more limited functionalist model. Finally, the chapter will look at the continuing relevance of the older debates for the contemporary one on European unification in the context of the end of the Cold War and the collapse of the Soviet Union.

The Phases of Postwar Debate

As previous chapters have pointed out, the ideal of European unification grew out of the hopes of intellectuals and political visionaries stretching back to the early nineteenth century who looked towards building a new kind of political order that would break with the system of international power politics. These failed to gell into any sort of major mass movement before World War II. It was the European resistance to Hitler which acted as a major turning point in the ideal of European unification. By 1945, a new mood began to prevail that looked towards a different kind of Europe emerging out of the ashes of fascism.

The 1940s served as the first major "architectural" phase of the debate over European unification, characterised by the establishment of the ECSC in 1950, the shelving of the European Defence Community in 1954 and the signing of the Treaty of Rome in 1957. The more utopian hopes for a federal Europe gave way to a more functionalist strategy of progressive integration of the states of Western Europe into an economic bloc. The process of European integration from the middle 1950s until a second "architectural" phase in the 1980s was only partially "supranational" since it was mainly driven forward by the will of an administrative elite rather than popular political pressure.[1] Under the dominating aegis of the bipolar superpower confrontation of the Cold War, Western Europe failed to emerge as a third superpower in its own right.

By the late 1980s, a second effort towards European integration suggests that a critical phase in European unification has been reached. For the first time, a major pooling of state sovereignty began to appear possible with the passage of the Maastricht Treaty, with its provisions for a common currency and banking system as well as a European defence and foreign policy. This has also led to a major political reaction in favour of a looser model of European cooperation based upon intergovernmental bargaining.

Those who championed the federalist cause did much to make the idea appear feasible and pragmatic at a time of rising tensions between the superpowers. This endeavour lacked credibility for many sections of informed opinion in Europe. As Alan Milward has cogently shown, European federalism had only marginal support among the political elites of postwar Europe, who remained preoccupied with the revitalisation of the nation state. The work of a scholar such as Walter Lipgens is thus flawed by a basic failure to investigate the relative political significance of the pro-Europeanist opinions that he has copiously documented. It is by no means evident that this sort of idealist opinion had any major long term impact on the policymaking elites of national governments.[2] The basic problem was that federalism contradicted the tenets of state-centric realism which came to dominate European foreign policies as the Cold War intensified. This realism drove the superpowers to reconstruct the new European system after 1945 on the basis of spheres of influence. Under the over-arching canopy of this system, the old European nation state system survived and flourished once the German issue appeared to have been solved by the country's partition into two separate states.[3]

The Resurgence of Debate on European Unity

The various sources of idealism generated by the European resistance did not in any case all flow into a single federalist channel. An analysis of the extensive series of documents produced by the resistance in the 1940s indicates a considerable variety of attitudes on eventual European unification. For some the idea of a united Europe appeared to be the logical historical outcome of a continent-wide struggle against fascism. In France, the *Combat* manifesto drawn up in July-September 1943 by Henri Frenay, Claude Bourdet and Andre Hauriou saw the war ushering in a revolution which would lead to the "dawn of a new civilisation." "History teaches," the manifesto continued, "that frontiers are constantly widening." A "United States of Europe" was a "stage on the road to world union" and would "soon be a living reality for which we are fighting."[4]

This optimism reflected a common error among those idealists of the 1930s and 1940s whose belief in the desirability of creating one world led them to assume that this oneness actually existed in fact.[5] Not all French intellectuals shared this sense of historical destiny, while even many federalists took a sober view of the chances of a European federal state being achieved. Ernest Pezet and Robert Buron, for instance, warned in December 1943 that European nation states could not be compelled to federate without the risk of another war. Federation, they argued, would not occur under the hegemony of a single European power but "by way of agreements between nations which are form in purpose and possess genuinely equally rights, to surrender some of those rights for the sake of forming an association."[6] Some intellectuals stressed the likely continuation of great power politics after hostilities were terminated. In January 1944 Raymond Aron cautioned that "in the shorter term for some years after the war, there can be balance in Europe without the active participation of the US. In the longer term the western *entente* will be the more influential in proportion as the huge reservoir of US strength can be felt behind it."[7]

This debate was echoed in other resistance movements in Europe. In Germany, the resistance to Hitler was divided between a group centred upon the Beck-Goerdeler-Hassall group and another group, the Kreisau Circle, which contained more idealistic and utopian thinking. The Beck-Goerdeler-Hassall group accepted the framework of the nation state system and wanted to revive the traditional role of German foreign policy as a "third force" between Britain and the USSR. It broadly saw Germany playing a leading economic role in Europe rather than one based on conquest and racial extermination, although it underestimated the capacity of the western allies during the war to understand this distinction.[8]

By contrast, the Kreisau Circle was important for its more idealistic rejection of the European nation state system. At the centre of this group was Graf Helmuth James von Moltke, who by April 1941, saw the defeat of Germany as ushering in a new European sovereign state extending from Portugal to "as far east as possible." But even Moltke envisaged Britain as having rather looser ties with this federation compared to other European countries given its global empire. In contrast to the ideas of the Round Table Group in Britain he thought a federal European structure would be attractive for Britain since it would secure a stable base in the rear and allow Britain to play a major intermediary role with the United States.[9]

By 1943-1944 the two groups exercised growing influence over each other. Carl Goerdeler moved towards the idea of a European federation in which Germany's forces would be put under supranational command. In July 1944 he wrote of the need for a European currency, economic assemblies and an "arbitral system" so that the continent could be "integrated into new world wide arrangements." Germans should not, he continued, "be outdone by any other state in readiness to cooperate effectively. We must not lay claim to power or prestige, but must regain our influence and the respect of others by correct behaviour and efficient performance."[10] The destruction of the two groups after the July coup attempt wiped out a major input into the debate by postwar Germany and ensured that the initiative came from other resistance groups.

It was in Italy that some of the clearest visionary statements of the federalist design emerged in the wake of the *Ventotene Manifesto*, one of the corner stones of the European Federalist Movement, launched in August 1943. The Manifesto urged that European unity was needed in order to preserve what was left of the continent's civilisation after the war's end. It considered that the collapse of state structures in Europe as a result of Nazi occupation placed "the destinies of the European populations on common ground." With suitable propaganda it felt it possible that a single Europe-wide movement could be formed to over-throw the corporatist and autarchic economic structures that were the backbone of the totalitarian regimes that currently dominated European politics. Unions in particular had to be excluded from corporatist structures of decisionmaking since otherwise a "kind of feudal anarchy in the economic life of the country" would be created.[11]

There was an anarchic theme in some of this utopian federalism that was probably derived from the ideas of Pierre Joseph Proudhon. Those who drafted the *Ventotene Manifesto* later spelt out in more detail the kind of political strategy necessary to advance its ideas. Altiero Spinelli wrote that the federalist revolutionaries had to seek as wide a base of political support as possible. The federalist idea needed in fact to be "flexible enough to become, in a revolutionary situation, a touchstone of existing passions and political elements, not opposing itself to them but impregnating them with itself and thus immunising them against the fatal defects of the old attitudes." Federalists, moreover, needed to:

> have the skill to make it clear to these political elements and to impassioned nationalists, democrats and socialists, who are profoundly disoriented, that the only way of fully meeting their desires is to set up a few simple federal institutions, which must be solid, irrevocable and easily understood. It will not be necessary to trouble with individual national problems. The federation would provide the necessary internal order to which progressive forces would naturally adjust and from which they would derive their future character.[12]

The revolutionary movement that Spinelli envisaged as the vehicle of the federalist project was going to require acute political insight into the mood of its potential allies. Given the likely balance of political forces, Spinelli suggested an initial attempt at a limited federal structure. If this was easily enough understood at the popular level, it would be able to build on its political achievements. It would, he hoped, eventually acquire a momentum sufficiently wide-ranging as to eclipse in importance the problems of individual nation states.

By the end of World War II it would be untrue to say that the resistance fully supported the breaking down of state structures in favour of a European federation.[13] There was certainly considerable ideological momentum behind the idea, but it needed more concrete form after the disparate statements and manifestos issued during the war itself. This began to occur in 1946 with the founding of the European Union of Federalists, though an actual congress of this organisation only took place at the Hague in 1948, some three years after the war. By this time the onset of the Cold War had reinforced superpower domination in

Europe whilst the beginnings of Marshall Aid from the US hastened the reconstruction of the old nation states of Western Europe. The hoped-for European revolution clearly had not arrived and it was to prove an infinitely more difficult and protracted process than many of the visionaries in the resistance had imagined.

The Failure of the
Federal Grand Design

For pro-federalist scholars such as Walter Lipgens, the failure to achieve federation in Europe after the war is due to a series of lost opportunities. Lipgens has stressed a multiple set of factors concerning the role of external intervention in European politics by the superpowers, the failure of senior European statesmen to provide real political leadership to the movement and the loss of impetus by the federal movement itself.[14] Critics of this thesis argue that it is necessary to look more closely at the longer-term durability of the European nation state system. One of the major features of European history has been its continuing pluralism and resistance to a single political form.[15]

The Europeanist cause might well have benefited had it been promoted by a major European political figure in office such as the British Foreign Secretary Ernest Bevin. The main figure to align himself with the idea of a "United States of Europe" was Winston Churchill, who was now out of power. Churchill's Europeanism owed little to the ideas of the European resistance during World War II for he saw a united Europe as secondary to the "special relationship" between Britain and the United States.

Churchill outlined his own vision of European unity in a speech at Zurich on 19 September 1946. He stressed postwar Europe's incapacity on its own of standing up to Soviet aggression; the continent was, he declared, a "vast quivering mass of tormented, hungry, careworn and bewildered human beings, scanning the horizons for the approach of some new peril, tyranny or terror." The "remedy" for this state of affairs was to "recreate the human family" by trying to build a "United States of Europe." He envisaged applying the model of the British Commonwealth to Europe since it was already a "natural grouping in the Western hemisphere." The Commonwealth would help to create a "European group which could give a sense of enlarge patriotism and common citizenship to the distracted people of this mighty and turbulent continent." As a first step, Churchill suggested a Council of Europe which would include France, Germany, Britain, the British Commonwealth and the USSR. Churchill's Europeanism, however, found little support from Britain's postwar Labour Government, though it was viewed rather more positively in Washington and helped stimulated ideas for the economic recovery of Europe leading to the Marshall Aid programme in 1948. Churchill avoided spelling out any detailed programme for European unification and when he returned to power in Britain in 1951 failed to provide any lead on the Europeanist cause.

The federal cause was mainly espoused at an elite level, though even here it met a mixed reception. By the time of the first congress of the *Union Europeene des Federalistes* in Switzerland in August 1947 there were only 100,000 paid-up members in the forty affiliated associations. The Congress launching the idea of a European "estates general" which met the following year at the Hague.[16] It gained the support of such prominent figures as Churchill, Leon Blum, Paul Henri Spaak and Alcide de Gasperi and became the focus for the European movement which was launched with a national council in each member state.

By the time the Council of Europe was established in 1948 the superpower balance in Europe had become frozen. The Council of Foreign Ministers (consisting of the US, USSR, France and Britain) that had been established at the end of the war broke down in London on 15 December 1947 after failing to reach agreement on a joint policy for Germany. In February 1948 a communist coup in Czechoslovakia brought that country into the Eastern bloc, while later the same year an airlift began to assist the beleaguered inhabitants of West Berlin. The growing polarisation in Europe forced the states of Western Europe to look for a common system of security and this led to the establishment of NATO in 1949.

American Marshall Aid policy after 1948 encouraged a wider economic outlook among Western Europe and led to the establishment in 1948 of the Organisation for European Economic Cooperation (OEEC). The European Recovery Programme (ERC) was geared to the reorganisation of the European economies into a single integrated market export that would purchase US-made goods and help stabilise the west European political order. Some US officials in the State Department and the Economic Cooperation Administration also hoped the ERC would eventually transcend national sovereignty and facilitate the development of a new supranational bureaucratic elite.[17]

Most West European governments welcomed the programme, though in Britain there was suspicion among the governing elite at a scheme that threatened to end national control over economic decisionmaking. The Labour foreign secretary Ernest Bevin opposed a European regional organisation and only supported looser arrangements based on intergovernmental cooperation.[18] Between January 1948 and January 1949 Britain ceased being in the forefront of proposals for "Western Union" to being one of the main obstacles to European integration, a position it has continued to hold more or less consistently in the decades since.[19] This loss of political initiative by Britain also led to the emergence of a rather more functionalist vision of European union centred on progressive economic cooperation.

The roots of the Schuman Plan lay in the continuing British obstruction to French proposals to increase the supranational authority of the OEEC whilst the revival of the German economy revived the pre-war threat to France or German dumping of low-cost steel. The effective partition of Germany into two states by 1949 meant that it was no longer possible to forge a postwar European system which excluded the Germans, whose growing economic power had to be controlled. It was feared that if Germany was totally excluded it might threaten the stability of Central Europe by becoming neutral and seeking a rapprochement with the Soviet Union as it had in the late 1930s.

The Schuman Plan, which led to the creation of the European Coal and Steel Community (ECSC), was in some respects a European version of trans-national corporatism that had first been tried out through the OEEC. Monnet conceived the plan in April 1950 as a way of preventing renewed German economic domination of Europe by getting both the victors and the vanquished in postwar Europe to pool their sovereignty. He then secured the approval of Robert Schuman, the French foreign minister, who was able to present the plan to the US Secretary of State, Dean Acheson, while he was visiting Paris. The British government was only informed after the plan had been announced in the French National Assembly and Bevin angrily felt that the scheme was designed to exclude Britain.[20]

The way in which Monnet conceived the scheme reduced the chances of an agreement being reached with the British. Monnet persuaded Schuman to insist that the participants of the proposed Coal and Steel community pool their resources and accept the decisions of the new High Authority as binding. There was little chance of Britain being able to modify the scheme and this increased the opposition of ministers in the Attlee Government. The acting Prime Minister, Herbert Morrison commented that the scheme was "no good, we can't do it, the Durham miners won't wear it,"—a remark that strongly exemplified the power of organised labour on postwar British government policy.[21] Britain refused to be included in the scheme, which was accepted by six European governments on 3 June 1950. This in turn led to a full treaty on 18 April 1951.

The successful creation of the ECSC was not due simply to the idealism of the European federalists since it conveniently dovetailed with the desire of the French government to ensure that the return of German sovereignty did not lead to its economic and political domination of Europe. The continuing centrality of state self-interest revealed the limits of this Europeanist idealism. Some leading French politicians hoped that the ECSC would lead to a European Defence Community (EDC) providing for a European army. In May 1952 agreements were signed in Bonn and Paris providing for the establishment of a European army on lines similar to that of the ECSC while at the same time restoring full sovereignty to West Germany. The Gaullist opposition in France attacked the measure as amounting to "protocols of surrender." This was a time of political crisis in France following the French army's defeat at Dien Bien Phu in Vietnam. A Gaullist alliance with the Communists proved effective in forcing the French National Assembly to reject the scheme in August of 1954, though it was accepted by the other five European members. The British Foreign Secretary Anthony Eden proposed a new solution whereby Germany joined the Western European Union (WEU) which had been established at the time of the Brussels Treaty. This meant that Germany would join NATO and its forces would be placed under the control of the Supreme Allied Commander Europe (SACEUR).[22] This enabled Germany to join NATO and WEU failed to become a significant force in West European politics.

Despite the failure of the EDC, many prominent Europeanists still hoped that a united federal Europe could emerge as a "third force" between the superpowers. As Chapter 5 pointed out, Jean Monnet's *Action Committee for the United States of Europe*, founded after he resigned from the Presidency of the ECSC's High Authority in 1954, helped mobilise support for a Common Market on these grounds. Monnet hoped that an evolutionary strategy would lead to some form of consensus emerging between functionalists and federalists in the form of functional integration. Political integration would emerge in this conception as the final outcome of a cumulative process of economic integration.[23]

It proved impossible to isolate these moves towards European economic integration from external political pressures. The three governments—Germany under Adenauer, France under Guy Mollet and Belgium under Paul Henri Spaak—initially agreed in May 1956 to work on the two areas of an economic market without frontiers and an atomic energy authority. It was now clear that British policy would not be shifted from its basic commitment to the Atlantic Alliance, the Commonwealth and independent role of sterling.[24]

The success of the negotiations which resulted in the treaty of Rome setting up the EEC owed much to timing and diplomatic skill, especially on the part of Paul Henri Spaak, who insisted that the two areas of economic integration and the creation of an atom pool be treated as a package deal. This overcame many French reservations since there was a strong interest in developing a European atomic energy industry. At the same time French concerns for the inclusion of overseas colonial territories was met by providing for associated status. The gradualist approach eventually appeared to have paid off over the more elaborate federalist design and the Treaty of Rome creating the EEC and Euratom was finally signed in 1957.[25] At the same time, though, they had owed much to the diplomatic skill involved, a factor that was rather poorly recognised in the academic scholarship of the period. Ernst Haas saw the process of European integration as more or less inexorable in *The Uniting of Europe* in 1958 and failed to recognise the possibility that a single member state could do much to hamper this process over the following decades.[26]

The timing of the Treaty in fact proved to be crucial. The downfall of the Fourth Republic in 1958 and the return of de Gaulle as President of France in the midst of the Algerian crisis might have sunk the negotiations. As it was, de Gaulle chose to work within the terms of the Rome Treaty and attempted to turn it to his political advantage at a time when the Cold War seemed to be thawing. But this only indicated that the political basis to the EEC was rather more fragile than the integration theorists supposed.

Gaullism and Re-emergence of the Federal Design

If nothing else the Treaty of Rome underlined the loss of impetus behind the federalist vision of European unity. The immediate issue of European security was taken care of by the rival alliances of NATO and the Warsaw Pact. Some visionaries such as Monnet continue to hope that European unification would be a first step towards a wider Atlantic community involving the United States.[27] Western Europe became inward-looking as it defined its role largely outside great power politics, being termed a "civilian power."[28]

The notion of a European civilian power was really the only feasible vision given the failure to develop any alternative that could command widespread political acceptance. By the early 1960s the European federalist ideal came under sustained attack from General de Gaulle who had a rather looser notion of a *Europe des patries*. The Gaullist vision made considerable headway following the two French vetos on the British application to join the EEC in 1963 and 1967. De Gaulle tried to assert French leadership over what he perceived as a "concert of European states" while at the same time disengaging Europe from American hegemony.[29]

The fact that de Gaulle was only partially successful in this strategy should not detract from his longer-term impact on the debate on European unification. Even though NATO proved strong enough to survive French withdrawal in 1966, de Gaulle's ideal of a European of nation states has endured within European political debate and may indeed become of increasing relevance in the post Cold War era as the EU takes in new members. De Gaulle has proved to be essentially correct in his prediction that European populations would be extremely reluctant to abandon the mythology of the nation state.[30] His own vision of French national destiny, like that of Enoch Powell in Britain, was strongly mystical and continues to exert a major ideological influence in French politics. He professed to imagining France as "the Madonna in the frescoes" acting as a biological organism which stretched back into the past and forward into the future. He opposed any supranational entity which could weaken this French national organism.[31]

Nevertheless, the departure of de Gaulle in 1969 and the admission of the United Kingdom, Denmark and Ireland to the EC in 1973 gave renewed hope to those who championed a European federal super state. By the early 1970s, the arguments in favour of federalism had begun to change. A united Europe was seen as important not so much in terms of the defence of the west against communism than as protection of European economies from international, and specifically US competition. The outflow of dollars from the United States during this period particularly gave reason for concern. As the assets of the overseas branches of US, banks grew from US\$47 billion in 1970 to \$166 billion by 1975 there was a growing fear that Europe was going to come under increasing economic domination by the US. The French politician Jean Jacques Servan Schreiber described this in his famous book as the "American Challenge" which threatened to make American industry in Europe the third greatest industrial power after the US and USSR unless the European political elite fail to achieve at least a minimal form of federal integration.[32]

Political leaders in the EC largely lacked the political will to make a major new federal initiative. Despite Monnet's efforts to merge functionalism with federalism, functionalism won by default in the European debate. The main impetus behind integration appeared to be an increasingly technocratic one with little or no popular political mandate.[33] The paralysis was partly induced by external international factors such as the fourfold increase in the price of oil by OPEC in 1973. There were continuing doubts over the direction of European Unity: in the case of Britain, these doubts over EC membership were only resolved by a referendum held in 1975 which resulted in Britain remaining in the Community. Gaullist sentiments remained strong in the EC throughout the 1970s. The German historian Fritz Stern discerned in 1980 a "Gaullism by default, a selective Gaullism, without

grandeur, an improvised, depressed adaptation to selective circumstances."[34]

The creation of the European Monetary System demonstrated that it
might be possible to achieve European economic solidarity when under pressure from one of the superpowers. It hardly amounted to a new
vision of European union built on the original hopes of Monnet and
Schuman for European monetary and economic union. If the EC was
to get itself out of the despondency that had set in by the early 1980s,
a major political initiative was imperative. By the middle 1980s a second "architectural" phase began as the European Parliament approved
in 1984 a Draft Treaty on European Union. This gained the approval of
the Belgian, Dutch and Italian Parliaments, though there was rather
more resistance to the idea from the British government of Margaret
Thatcher.[35] This was followed in 1986 by the Single European Act, in
1989 by the Social Charter and finally the Maastricht Treaty at the end
of 1991.

The End of the Cold War and the
Future of European Unification

The pattern of European unification under the umbrella of superpower domination during the Cold War has not left the EU in a particularly strong position to respond to the challenges of a new and more
unpredictable era following the collapse of communism in Eastern Europe. The debate on European unification pivoted around the EEC/EC/
EU increasingly emerges as parochial in orientation and limited in its
vision of the scope and nature of a united Europe. The idea of "Europe" in this debate remained largely confined to the states of Western
Europe as the states of Central and Eastern Europe disappeared behind
the iron curtain. To some critics such as Johan Galtung, the whole
scheme of European unification really represented the continuation of
older imperial traditions rather than the forging of something intrinsi-
cally new. If it did eventually lead to the emergence of a European
superstate, it would be in defence of a dominant structural power in
the global economy, centred on an international division of labour. Faced
with growing political and ideological challenges, the purpose of such
a united European bloc would be to defend this dominant position by
military as well economic means.[36]

Such a defensive bloc has begun to appear rather more feasible in
the post-Cold War era. The hopes of the postwar generation of European visionaries look increasingly redundant as newer threats to European security emerge on its southern flank in the form of fundamentalist
Islam in such states as Algeria and Egypt, while the Russian experi-

ment with democracy is threatened by an alliance of extreme nationalists and former communists. Some realist analysts have seen this new situation leading to a return of old-fashioned balance of power politics. John Mearsheimer has argued that following superpower withdrawal Europe will return to its normal historical pattern of interstate rivalry. The bipolarity of the Cold War would be replaced by multipolarity with a small number of powers emerging as the dominant ones. Since the EU was the product of Cold War pattern of security enforced by the superpowers, then the EU too may well decline in significance if not disappear altogether or at least become severely undermined by the rival suspicions of its larger members.[37]

It could be argued that instead of a balance of power a concert of powers might emerge on the pattern of the Holy Alliance after the Treaty of Vienna in 1815. Such a concert would be led by Germany and include France, Britain and Italy. It would be forged in response to potential breakdowns in security in North Africa, the Balkans and Eastern Europe and would help orchestrate the widening of the EU to include some former Eastern bloc states such as Hungary, Poland and the Czech Republic. The concert could in turn operate through the structures of the EU and provide a major political base to its emergent foreign policy.

A concert of powers would also reflect the fact that the nation state is not likely to be readily superceded in post-Cold War Europe. The nature and extent of the continent had begun to be reconceptualised by intellectuals even before the collapse of the Berlin Wall. For some years Eastern European intellectuals such as Milan Kundera have pointed to the separate identity of "Central Europe." While this is only an imaginary conception, it has nevertheless had an enormous impact on the way that the continent as a whole is conceived. The disappearance of "Central Europe" reflected the ending of the idea of Europe as a cultural unity. Kundera has seen Central Europe playing a potentially major role to play in the resurrection of the idea of a common European culture since it straddled the Eastern and Western parts of the continent.[38]

The growing importance of Central and Eastern European intellectuals in European political debate will probably exert an impact on discussion over European unification. There are enormous difficulties with the notion that there can be a distinct "middle way" for Central Europe. Many of the small nation states there will in all likelihood be forced to accept the hegemonic domination of rising German power, especially as they become drawn towards trying to emulate the model of the German social market economy. They are likely to bring a strong commitment to the survival of the nation state, which they managed to defend during more than four decades of authoritarian communist control. The challenge for German diplomacy in the decades ahead may well be that to craft institutions that go beyond the nation state it may well be necessary to help consolidate the nation state in the first place.[39]

The project of European unification is also likely in all events to be considerably slowed down as the EU grows to twenty or more members. The challenge of rival free trade blocs in the form of NAFTA in North America and APEC in the Asia Pacific may act as a further stimulus to concentrate upon building a free trade zone and restricting the bureaucratic powers of the European Commission. To this extent, the social engineering designs of the earlier generation of European visionaries such as Schuman and Monnet are likely to be replaced by nongovernmental agencies such as those within an emerging European civil society. In this respect the revolution in Eastern Europe against an all pervasive state have given new life to the notion of a distinct and independent civil society, out of which in time a political liberalism may take root. It is within the civil society realm that a renewed idea of a common European cultural identity is likely to emerge with a concomitant set of demands for civil and political rights; it is unlikely though to go again down the road of political utopianism in the form of a grand ideal of a European federal super state.[40]

The nature and form of European unification will need to be radically rethought in the years ahead. It is likely that there will be no immediate consensus on goals at the 1996 review of the Maastricht Treaty. Given the complexities of multilateral diplomacy that accrues from such an expanded membership, the only chance for the original federalist vision to survive is in the form of a "two-tier Europe" that may eventually prove to be self-defeating. An easier option is to move towards a free trade area on the NAFTA and Asia Pacific model. European executives feel increasingly pessimistic about the longterm chances of the continent being able to stand up to competition from the Asia Pacific.[41] This looser model may well have increasing political credibility—especially if the EU fails to solve the economic crisis on its eastern and southern fringe.

A rather more dismal scenario is a global order defined by a series of rival trade blocs on lines rather like George Orwell's *1984*. If global negotiations to free up world trade through the World Trade Organisation (the successor of GATT) fail, then it will bepossible to envisage a series of more introverted trade zones developing. In this instance, the EU would be well placed to assert its independence compared to its competitors. Trade among its members grew by 75 percent during the 1980s and the prospect of bloc rivalry would doubtless encourage moves towards EMU since this would give it a massive advantage over NAFTA or APEC where anything similar is hard to imagine.[42] However, the globalisation of production and investment makes this sort of bloc rivalry increasingly anachronistic as the ownership of multinationals is spread over different continents. It seems indeed far more likely that a European "bloc" centred on the EU is likely to take the form of a free trade area as it expands in membership and will become increasingly subject to German economic and political hegemony. The vision of a European federalist superstate still seems a very distant one.

Notes

1. F. Rosentiel, "Reflections on the Notion of 'Supranationality,'" *Journal of Common Market Studies*, vol. 11, no. 4, 1963, pp. 127-139.

2. A. S. Milward, *The European Rescue of the Nation State* (London: Routledge, 1993). See also A. Hartley, "How the European Community Really Came About," *The World Today*, 50, 1 (January 1994), pp. 19-20.

3. A. W. dePorte, *Europe Between the Superpowers* (New Haven and London: Yale University Press, 1986), esp. pp. 115-141.

4. C. Bourdet, H. Frenay, A. Hauriou, "The Combat Manifesto" repr. in W. Lipgens, ed., *Documents on the History of European Integration, vol. 1* (Berlin and New York: Walter de Gruyter, 1985), p. 293.

5. J. H. Herz, "Idealist Internationalism and the Security Dilemma," *World Politics*, July 1950, p. 172.

6. E. Pezet and R. Pouring, "Defence of the federal principle," December 1943, in *World Politics*, July 1950, pp. 331-2.

7. R. Aron, "For the Western Alliance," *La France Libre* 15 January 1944 repr. in *Documents on the History of European Integration, vol. 2* (Berlin and New York: Walter de Gruyter, 1986), p. 311.

8. K. Hildebrand, *German Foreign Policy From Bismarck to Hitler* (London: Unwin Hyman, 1989), pp. 182-3.

9. H. von Moltke, "Initial Situation, Aims and Tasks," 24 April 1941 in *Documents on the History of European Integration, vol. 1*, p. 385: "If Britain is to be free to exercise leadership among the Anglo Saxons it must have peace on the European continent to its rear."

10. C. Goerdeler, "Germany's Future Tasks, 1-8 August 1944" in *Documents on the History of European Integration, vol. 1*, p. 446. Goerdeler was eventually arrested on 12 August 1944 and hanged on 2 February 1945.

11. The Ventotene Manifesto, August 1941 in *Documents on the History of European Integration, vol. 1*, pp. 471-484.

12. A. Spinelli, "The United States of Europe and various political trends, 1941-2" in *Documents on the History of European Integration, vol. 1*, pp. 488-489.

13. As suggested by S. George, *Britain and European Integration since 1945* (Oxford: Basil Blackwell, 1991), p. 2.

14. W. Lipgens, *A History of European Integration, vol. 1, 1945-1947: The Formation of the European Unity Movement* (Oxford: Clarendon Press, 1982).

15. Hildebrand, *German Foreign Policy From Bismarck to Hitler*, p. 197, no. 104; Stanley Hoffmann, "Reflections on the Nationstate in Western Europe Today," *Journal of Common Market Studies*, vol. 21, no. 3, 1982, pp. 21-37.

16. Hildebrand, op. cit., p. 363.

17. M. J. Hogan, "American Marshall Planners and the Search for a European Neocapitalism," *American Historical Review*, vol. 90, no. 1, February 1985, pp. 44-72; *The Marshall Plan* (Cambridge: Cambridge University Press, 1987).

18. Bullock, *Ernest Bevin*, p. 617; for a more general treatment of British policy towards Europe, see George, *Britain and European Integration since 1945*.

19. Ibid., "1947-9: the Best of Possible Worlds?," p. 626; Bullock, *Ernest Bevin*, p. 777.

20. Bullock, *Ernest Bevin*, pp. 768-769.

21. Ibid., p. 780. See also H. Pelling, *Britain and the Marshall Plan* (London and Basingstoke: The Macmillan Press, 1988).

22. A. Hartley, *Gaullism: The Rise and Fall of a Political Movement* (London: Routledge and Kegan Paul, 1972), pp. 122-123.

23. F. von Krosigk, "A Reconsideration of Federalism in the Scope of Present Discussion on European Integration," *Journal of Common Market Studies*, 9, 1970-71, p. 201; J. Monnet, "A Ferment of Change," *Journal of Common Market Studies*, 1, 2, 1963, p. 208

24. S. Burgess and G. Edwards, "The Six Plus One: British policymaking and the Question of European Economic Integration, 1955," *International Affairs*, vol. 64, no. 3, Summer 1988, pp. 393-413.

25. P-H. Laurent, "The Diplomacy of the Rome Treaty, 1956-7," *Journal of Contemporary History*, 7, 3-4, 1972, pp. 209-220.

26. D. Arter, *The Politics of European Integration in the Twentieth Century* (Aldershot: Dartmouth, 1993), p. 146.

27. Monnet, "A Ferment of Change," p. 209.

28. A. Buchan, "Europe and the Atlantic Alliance: Two Strategies or One," *Journal of Common Market Studies*, 1, 2, 1963, p. 241; R. J. Payne, *The West European Alllies, the Third World and US Foreign Policy* (New York: Greenwood Press, 1991), pp. 41-42.

29. Hartley, op. cit., pp. 206-207

30. See for example J. Jackson, "A tall man growing in stature," *The Times Higher Education Supplement*, 8 July, p. 194.

31. Ibid., pp. 507.

32. J. J. Servan Schreiber, *The American Challenge* (Harmondsworth: Penguin Books, 1969); J. Palmer, *Europe Without America* (Oxford: Oxford University Press, 1987), p. 62.

33. J. Linthorst Homan, "Which Europe?," *Journal of Common Market Studies*, 9, 1970-71, p. 91.

34. F. Stern, "Germany in a Semi-Gaullist Europe," *Foreign Affairs*, 1980 repr. in *Dreams and Delusions* (New York: Alfred A. Knopf, 1987), p. 204.

35. J. Pinder, "*Pragmatikos* and *Federalis*: Reflections on a Conference," *Government and Opposition*, vol. 20, no. 4, Winter 1985, pp. 473-487.

36. J. Galtung, *The European Community: A Superpower in the Making* (Oslo: Universitetsforlager and London: Allen and Unwin, 1973), pp. 154-157.

37. J. Mearsheimer, "Back to the Future: Instability in Europe After the Cold War," *International Security*, vol. 15, no. 1, Summer 1990, pp. 5-56.

38. M. Kundera, "The Tragedy of Central Europe," *New York Review of Books*, 26 April 1984. See also T. Garton Ash, "Does Central Europe Exist?" in *The Uses of Adversity* (Cambridge: Granta Books, 1898), pp. 161-191.

39. T. Garton Ash, *In Europe's Name: Germany and the Divided Continent* (London: Jonathan Cape, 1993), p. 407.

40. T. Judt, "*Ex Oriente Lux*? Post-Celebratory Speculations on the 'Lessons of '89' " in C. Crouch and D. Marquand, eds., *Towards Greater Europe? A Continent Without an Iron Curtain* (Oxford: Blackwell, 1992), pp. 91-104.

41. "Europe's Long Term Outlook Gloomy but . . ." *Financial Times*, 17 November 1994.

42. J. Peterson, *Europe and America in the 1990s* (Aldershot: Edward Elgar, 1993), pp. 205-6.

10

The Debate on Citizenship and European Union

Elizabeth Meehan

Introduction

Many people were and remain sceptical or cynical about citizenship of the European Union—and sometimes fearful that it will require a false homogeneity. 'There are no such animals as "European citizens." There are only French, German, or Italian citizens.' This was the view of Raymond Aron when, in 1974, he specifically addressed the question of whether multinational or European citizenship were possible.[1] In 1991, strongest resistance to the Maastricht Treaty in Denmark, the paragon among members of a citizens' state, focused on the Treaty's transnational citizenship proposals. The argument of this chapter is that there is some justification for the more inclusive language of European institutions, which before Maastricht, referred to "a People's Europe" and, in the Maastricht Treaty, entrenches the idea of "Citizens of the Union." It is also suggested, however, that inclusiveness does not depend on homogeneity.

To say that there is something in the language of European institutions is not to say that a version of Aron's concept of national citizenship is being transformed into citizenship of a new state, or "superstate" called "Europe." The point of the chapter is to suggest that a new understanding of citizenship is emerging that is neither national nor cosmopolitan. But it is multiple in the sense that the identities, rights and obligations, associated by Heater[2] with citizenship, are expressed through an increasingly complex configuration of common European Community institutions, states, national and transnational voluntary associations, regions and alliances of regions. Whether this framework is confederal, federal, quasi-federal has been much discussed, the usual conclusion being that the European Union is *sui generis*. It is not possible to foresee now the precise form that this new "public space"[3] citizens eventually will take. But, if unpredictable, its shape will not be accidental.

The new order comprises states and peoples which have some common experiences, interests and intellectual traditions and some differences. Sometimes, different national traditions are deliberately welded in new institutions. Sometimes, they seem to appear in their new form by default. Conversely, Community institutions and policies are sometimes the subject of difficult disputes about the proper concepts to use and the proper way to go about things. Then, outcomes depend upon what concessions may or may not be made when a plurality of different interests confront one another in the "public space" provided by the European Union.

What is certain is that the European Union already provides an additional framework, through which nationals of its member states can claim certain civil and social rights and that some political rights for individuals and sub-state regions have been initiated. Future developments may follow either of two possible directions or lurch between them. One possibility is that citizenship will continue to be primarily national but enriched with a European dimension. Or citizenship may become like that of the Roman Empire in which citizens were able to appeal to more than one set of enforceable standards when claiming their rights.[4]

The argument of this chapter—that something of the neo-imperial model exists even now—has to depend on the view that social rights, together with legal and political rights, form a triad which must be regarded as interlocked if we are to be able to speak of the existence of equal citizenship. This is a disputable position. Aron is not alone in holding that citizenship rights, properly defined, are restricted to legal and political rights. However, others have argued persuasively that the meaning of citizenship is not universal but dependent on historical, social and cultural contexts,[5] thus bearing W. B. Gallie's hallmarks of "an essentially contested concept."[6] This means that it is necessary to explore what citizenship has meant to participants in the European Union, how these meanings affect the outlooks of governments and what might be the expectations of those whose lives are regulated by both national and common institutions.

Since it is not possible in one chapter to review the meanings and practices of citizenship in all the member states, the possible extent of differences will be indicated by a brief comparison of Aron's narrow and Heater's broader understandings. The chapter then discusses the development of Community social policy and the entrenchment of legal and social rights in the European Union. It points out that these processes have given rise to channels for the exercise of secondary political rights. The chapter then moves to the initiation of primary political rights for individuals and a form of the right of self-determination for regions. In conclusion, it is argued that people have a more complicated sense of themselves than is acknowledged in narrow conceptions of citizenship and by the those who are sceptical or cynical about the prospects for European citizenship. This means that it is diversity, not homogeneity, that is crucial to the new "public space."

Competing Conceptions of Citizenship— National and Social Dimensions

Aron distinguishes between the rights of man and the rights of the citizen in the 1789 French Declaration on the Rights of Man and in the 1948 United Nations Universal Declaration of Human Rights, which also declares the rights of woman. Though a single belief—in the natural equality of human beings—justifies natural or human rights and citizenship rights, the two sets are not the same. To show this, Aron draws upon the Hegelian distinction between burghers and citizens.

The first are participants (or subjects, in Marx's adaptation of Hegel) in the economic life of civil society. Their roles may be associated with natural property rights, as in the eighteenth century, or with the right to have socioeconomic needs met, as in the twentieth century. Citizens are recognisable by the status conferred upon them in rules about the administration of justice and political participation. Human or burghers' rights may be recognised or denied, irrespective of political status. Citizenship rights may also be denied but they cannot be guaranteed except in the context of nationality and the state sometimes a homogeneous nationstate, sometimes a state of several nations which are culturally distinct but share the same legal nationality. Together, these distinctions inform his separation of regulation by the European Union (at the time of his writing, the European Communities) of the lives of its economic participants from the civil and political rights guaranteed by their different nationstates.

Aron makes the case that European citizenship is logically impossible and politically unlikely in four, main ways. First, as indicated, national and Community authorities regulate sets of rights of a different order from one another. Thus, secondly, European citizenship could not come about without a transfer of legal and political powers from the national to the common level (similar to the transfer of Scottish and English powers and rights to a single British regime.) Thirdly, Aron argues, citizens can insist that a nationstate respect their rights because the state can demand that citizens fulfil their duties to defend the state, whereas there is no inter- or multinational polity which has such authority. The fourth element in Aron's case is that there was, in 1974, no popular demand for a European federation simultaneously responsible for legal-political rights and economic regulation and which could command duties of citizens. Moreover, there was every sign that national leaders intended the Community to remain a regime in which burghers or economic subjects cooperated in the absence of a political federation.

Insofar as there was popular criticism of nationstates and the association of citizenship with legal nationality, it existed because of the treatment of nationalities submerged within contemporary boundaries. At the time of writing, Aron thought people were cynical about the possibility of resolving domestic problems through regulation at a still more remote level—though, as shown later, people who feel submerged now see opportunities for change in European Union. He was sceptical, himself, of the argument that burghers or economic subjects could be made more equal through, for example, workers' participatory rights, which form part of Community aspirations.

Though both Aron and Leca emphasise connections between nationality and citizenship, the link is mainly logical for the former and sociological for the latter. In building the logical case, Aron does what Leca says we must not. That is, he takes mainly one historical experience and context and ascribes to them a universal validity. A broader picture is drawn by Heater who provides empirical evidence which can corroborate claims that citizenship is a contestable concept, or, at least, that its meanings are contextual. He reminds us that:

> from very early in its history the term (citizenship) already contained a cluster of meanings,' (including) a defined legal or social status, a means of political identity, a focus of loyalty, a requirement of duties, an expectation of rights and a yardstick of good social behaviour.[7]

The history of citizenship, he also argues, shows that it is a very modern assumption that citizenship is necessarily and exclusively associated with the sovereign nationstate and possession of a particular legal nationality. The reasons for the modern overlap amongst sovereignty, the nationstate, nationality and citizenship stem from the rise of the state system and the strategic need for new states to control their borders[8]—and also served the human need to delineate the Other or the political/military purpose of encouraging this.[9] That linkages amongst state, nationality and citizens' rights are contingent, not analytically necessary, is evident not only from Heater's history of citizenship. It is also clear from a recent survey, showing that nationality is not essential for many rights in eleven member states of the European Union.[10] The survey also reveals inconsistency across states as to which rights do or do not depend on nationality—variations which are explicable by different historical contexts (for example, relations between the United Kingdom and in the Nordic/Scandinavian group of countries). That the connection can be broken when it seems appropriate to do so is confirmed in the Maastricht Treaty which entrenches citizenship of the Union while leaving rules about nationality to the member states.

Another indication that people tend to rethink conceptions and practices of citizenship to meet new circumstances lies in the periodic resurfacing of interest in citizenship in the Roman Empire. This occurred during the period of the British empire and, as indicated earlier, is being reconsidered by those analysts of modern Europe who are convinced that some tangible change is taking place—though not that transformation which Aron took to be the only logical yet politically impossible outcome. This theme will recur. In the meantime, the chapter concentrates on showing that workers' and welfare rights can, contrary to Aron, be considered part of citizenship rights and, therefore, that their regulation at the common level does represent, even prior to the Maastricht Treaty, an element of European citizenship. Heater draws attention to a remarkable continuity in the belief that citizenship includes what Aron counts as human rights—a belief which both predates and transcends the rise of the nationstate. One example is his discussion of John Stuart Mill's idea that workers' rights could be substitute in large societies for the direct democracy of the Greek city state—as a means of fulfilling the human need for participation and of developing civic virtues[11] and not merely for the purposes of pursuing self-interest.

The move towards common (now not fully so—see later discussion of the UK's "opt-out") standards of workers' rights in the European Union certainly embodies the idea that individual self-interest lies in avoiding disadvantages arising from migration and that this should be dealt with. But European policies also rest on the ethical idea that people should be able to participate in decisions that affect the undertakings in which they work and that workers, along with other "social partners," should be able to contribute to decisionmaking in and about the Union itself. The preambles to measures regulating work and social affairs often also refer to the need to construct a common moral order—if not, it must be granted, as an end in itself, at least as a way of inspiring loyalty to a new and wider regime.

Another area in which an historical approach provides a different way
of viewing current European developments stems from ideas about
wealth and welfare. Even if people in the eighteenth century did dis-
tinguish, as Aron suggests, between natural rights and citizenship in
abstract thought, practical political arrangements linked human circumstances and political status. Poverty made people second-class or
non-citizens. This was the consequence of two ideas; that only those
who are rational and able to be disinterested ought to participate in
politics and that these qualities were demonstrated by the accumulation of property. Together, these ideas were used to justify the denial
of rights for the poor and women. In the twentieth century it has
seemed obvious that there can be a different conclusion. This is that,
instead of excluding those without the means of independent subsist-
ence, deprived people can be provided with the material basis for being rational and, hence, enabled to participate in politics.[12] This is a
conclusion that can also be accepted by those whose primary concern
is not with the ethics of rights but the maintenance of public order and
international legitimacy.

Modern advocates of social citizenship are shown by Jordan[13] to be
of two types. One sort retains an individualistic understanding of human nature. The other echoes the classical idea of a moral order of
wellbeing and conviviality in which there are no private interests as
we have come to understand them—because personal wellbeing depends on the realisation of the public good. In the second version, social rights are not an instrument for the pursuit of private ends but are
both the cause and reflection of a solidaristic order—which, unlike its
Greek predecessors, claims not to include male property rights over
slaves and women.

Though the origins of a nationstate concept of citizenship coincided
with a period in which understandings focused on legal and political
rights, the creation and development of the European Union took place
at a time when it was accepted in a substantial body of political theory,
by citizens and even by governments that there was a connection—natural, logical, instrumental or expedient amongst civil, political and social rights. Common European regulation of social security and social
assistance for migrants and, regardless of migration, sex equality in in-
comes and income maintenance embody both individualistic and
collectivist elements.

On the one hand, European legal entitlements and permissive measures are designed to reduce national and sex discrimination against individuals in their exercise of economic and social opportunities in a
transnational regime. But, as in the case of workers' rights, traces of
the idea of a common moral order can be found in many references to

common standards of living, social cohesion and harmonious regional development. Even if not self-consciously intended by member state governments as a step towards a common citizenship, such measures and their further development cannot be discounted as a dimension of European citizenship—in a context where there is a popular belief that citizenship includes social rights.

Moreover, European social regulation confers a legally defined status on citizens, not only in the Maastricht Treaty, but from the early jurisprudence of the Court of Justice. Social policies have, thus, "spilled-over" into the legal and political sovereignty of member states and are now beginning to do the same in respect of the political rights of individual citizens and groups of them. Clearly, however, Aron was right to be sceptical of the likelihood of states becoming less significant to their inhabitants. It is the states themselves that comprise the apex of "government" of the European Union (unlike federal systems where union and state powers are separated) and governments remain the primary actors. But, as Heater shows, this need not necessarily rule out the possibility of trans-state citizenship rights. The Romans developed "a form of citizenship which was both pragmatic and extensible in application."[14] This meant that people of a variety of nationalities and senses of identity could share the common right of Roman citizenship which gave them opportunities to use dual or plural systems of justice. Obviously, the European Union is not an empire but, as the rest of this chapter discusses, it does mean that claimants of rights can appeal to standards other than those in national law and have a greater plurality than before of institutions through which to try to influence outcomes.

The Development of Social Policy in the European Community

The fundamental goals of the 1957 Treaty of Rome establishing the European Economic Community are its four freedoms; the freedom of movement of goods, services, capital and labour. This means that there must be no national discrimination in spheres governed by the Treaty. The legal and social rights of citizens of the member states stem largely, though not solely, from the freedom of movement of labour, including the providers of services. Some policies cover not only migrant workers but also call for certain standards within member states which apply to people who do not move.

Throughout the 1960s, the Commission and the Council of Ministers were at odds about whether Community policy should bring about common standards of material wellbeing and social protection or should be confined to ensuring that workers would not lose benefits as a result of migration. The Commission was in favour of harmonising material standards, while member states (then six) insisted that social policy was a matter of national sovereignty and that common regulation of social security and assistance should be confined to coordinating different national schemes so as to prevent individual detriment. Further social integration should be restricted to whatever might be necessary to promote economic objectives. By 1970, the Commission had had to agree to abandon its approach and to refrain from contacts with the "social partners" (then principally workers and employers; now including the voluntary sector), unless expressly authorised by the Council of Ministers. Almost immediately, however, governments realised that the Community needed a "human face," which could be provided by a more explicit social dimension. Thus, from the 1970s onwards common social policies began to develop.

The main agreements were reached first in the field of sex equality. A series of action programmes began and Directives were agreed, calling for equal pay for work of equal value and equal treatment in other aspects of employment. In the 1980s, the principle of equality was applied to private occupational pension schemes and state social security systems and extended to women who were self-employed. As a result of health and safety programmes authorised by the Single European Act, a Directive was agreed in 1992 to protect pregnant women from hazards at work and which specified rights of absence and maternity pay.

The question of workers' rights also emerged in the 1970s but did not bring about the fundamental innovations for which some people hoped. The first agreed action was to bring about common rights in situations of redundancy, mergers or the transfer of undertakings. The bigger aspect, the idea that workers should be able to participate in strategic decisionmaking in the firms where they worked, was hotly disputed because of substantial differences in the traditions of member states. Similarly, the idea that they might contribute more significantly to the development of Community policy did not take any tangible form at that time. These issues, however, continued to have an important place on the agenda of the Commission and some member states. Under the Presidency of Jacques Delors, a common framework of workers' participatory rights and a set of social rights for citizens were seen as important both in promoting the Single European Market and in mitigating adverse human consequences in the realisation of it.

Though European trades unionists, the European Parliament, some Commissioners and some states had in mind a directly applicable constitution of social rights, eventual proposals were weakened in order to try to maintain the support of the United Kingdom. Thus, in 1989, the European Council (minus the UK) signed a Solemn Declaration on social rights and the Commission[15] brought forward a set of proposal for

Directives and Recommendations for subsequent implementation in the states. In combination with part of the aims of the Single European Act many measures, including about twenty Directives on health and safety, have been passed. But, instead of promoting further common standards, member states have had to institutionalise fragmentation in the Maastricht Treaty.

The Maastricht Treaty was able to be ratified only on the basis of some forty "opt-out" protocols. Though the Treaty entrenches a universal legal status and introduces trans-state political rights, it also incorporates a Social Agreement from which the United Kingdom is exempt. The Treaty authorises the other eleven (now fourteen) member states to "borrow" Community institutions when they wish to promote the more fundamental workers' rights referred to above. The United Kingdom need not take part in such discussions and is not bound by any consequent rules. However, the people of the United Kingdom were included in the extensive consultation process that took place in 1993 in connection with the Green and White Papers[16] on the future of European social policy and the European Parliament is likely to recommend to the 1996 Intergovernmental Conference a universal constitution of rights. But it remains to be seen whether particular reforms can be brought about on a pre-Maastricht constitutional basis (thereby including the UK) or whether proposals will be of the type that will activate the Social Agreement. There is an argument that material forces will undermine this fragmentation and opposition parties in the United Kingdom have undertaken to "opt-in" if returned to power[17] but, for the time being, the social dimension of European citizenship is no longer fully universal.

Legal Status and Rights

It is central to Aron's argument about citizenship that legal status, particularly nationality, can be conferred only by states. And, as noted earlier, member states of the European Union still have exclusive power to determine who are their nationals.[18] Citizens of the Union, with access to common rights, are those people whom member states have deemed as their nationals. But it is also the case that the Court of Justice has some impact on aspects of the legal status of nationals of member states. It has also been less equivocal than the Council of Ministers about rights being inherent in social policy and has been explicit that there is a direct legal relationship between citizens and common institutions.

The idea that Community law creates rights and obligations in respect of individuals, as well as states, was first expressed in an early and path-breaking reference for a preliminary ruling (Case no. 26/62 *van Gend en Loos v Nederlandse Administratie der Belastingen*, [1962] ECR 1) and repeated several times subsequently.[19] The Dutch, Belgian and German governments all argued that alleged breaches of Treaty obligations (stemming, in this case, from bilateral tariff changes after the entry into force of the EEC Treaty) should be resolved by institutions. In contrast, the Court held that the Treaty was more than an agreement that created obligations among states but also gave rights to individuals. Moreover, it ruled, it was not only for all institutions, including national courts, to cooperate in ensuring the uniform application of Community law, but individuals, too, had a duty to cooperate in enforcement by using their legal rights. Such cases, then, give private individuals a role in defending the Community's "public interest" by contributing, through their cases, to the supervision of the actions of member states and Community institutions.[20]

In addition to developing a common European legal status which transcends the authority of states, the Court also, from time to time, modifies national rules about who counts as employed for the purpose of access to rights regulated by Community standards. It thus contributes to the emergence of a common, Community legal definition of an employed person. This is important because, until the "persons" referred to in the Single European Act and "citizens" in the Maastricht Treaty, Community social rights depended almost exclusively on employed or insured status.

Social Security and Assistance for Migrant Workers: Sex Equality at Work and in Social Security Schemes

Details of substantive developments in case law on the Regulations for migrant workers and their families have been discussed elsewhere.[21] Here, a general indication of the Court's approach is provided. It has continually reiterated that one of the fundamental principles of the Community is to maximise the freedom of workers to migrate and that this cannot be achieved if workers lose social security entitlements as a result of moving. It has repeatedly held that social security rights are inviolable and that social security should be construed broadly so as to encompass "both the satisfaction of an individual's primary needs and the guarantee of a given standard of living" (Case no. 139/82 *Piscetello v Instituto Razionale della Previdenza Sociale* [1983] ECR 1427). The Court struck down a particularly blatant exception for a French family allowance and has called upon member states to take steps to minimise capricious outcomes for individuals in the coordination of different national social security systems.

In giving effect to its values, the Court has extended the category of person entitled to benefit and has broadened the category of benefit to which he or she has a right. Workers have been able to claim insurance-based benefits, covered by Regulation 1408/71, denied to them because of the absence of their families, where no similar residence condition is imposed on workers and families who are nationals. Workers and family members have been able to claim need-based assistance under Regulation 1612/68 that is not explicitly referred to in the Regulation, on the ground that it constitutes a "social advantage" which should be applied without national discrimination. Workers have been able to augment their own insurance-based benefits by others with a need criterion if the latter are intended to supplement inadequate social security payments. Steiner[22] has argued that the Court's habit of remedying the defects of the one Regulation by reference to the tests and standards of the other, in order to give the fullest effect to the freedom of movement principle, has blurred customary distinctions between security and assistance so much that discrimination in almost any welfare benefit might be regarded as contravening Community law.

Though the particular plaintiff in the first three sex equality cases gained little herself, the rulings set out principles that were vital to subsequent disputes. The first of these was that Article 119 of the Treaty of Rome was directly effective in the member states (Case no. 43175 *Defrenne v Sabena* (no. 2) [1976] ECR 455). Secondly, the Court declared that sex equality was a fundamental right that must be upheld by all Community and national institutions (Case no. 149/77 *Defrenne v Sabena* (no. 3) [1978] ECR 1365). Both these rulings made it easier for claimants to seek satisfactory resolutions in their domestic courts without their cases always having to be referred to the ECJ. And, thirdly, though existing Community law allowed state pensions, and those linked to state schemes, to be free from the equality requirement, the Court held that pensions were not necessarily distinct from pay (Case no. 80/70 *Defrenne v Belgium* [1971] ECR 445). Later, after the entry into force of Directives on equal treatment in other conditions of employment and in state and occupational social security schemes, the Court ruled that permitted differences in the state pensionable ages of men and women could not justify different retirement ages. Retirement was a form of dismissal and, thus, subject to the principle of equality (Case no. *Marshall v. Southampton and South West Hampshire Area Health Authority* [1986 1 CMLR 688].

The positive and negative consequences of the last two rulings, and the details of others, are discussed elsewhere.[23] Again, this chapter provides only an indication of the role of the Court in giving substance to common standards. In general, the ECJ has encouraged convergence among the member states; for example, in definitions of pay and in narrowing exceptions permitted for reasons of authenticity, discretion or public security. The Court has reinforced moves towards equal treatment where women have been disadvantaged because of conventional assumptions about their domestic roles and the relationship between these and "suitable" forms of paid employment—for example, part time work, where rulings have increasingly called for equitable treatment. In cases of discrimination against pregnant women workers, the Court has upheld their rights forcefully arguing that, since pregnancy is unique to women, discrimination on grounds of pregnancy is the same as direct sex discrimination.

Notwithstanding the Court's activism in respect of the rights of Community nationals, the pre-Maastricht basis of European citizenship was subject to trenchant criticism. From the feminist perspective, it has been argued that the Community's gender-neutral terms such as "worker" and "head of household" replicate on a grander scale the structured inequality that is found within states, likewise disguised by the use of universalistic terms such as citizen and voter.[24] Nor can rights based on working status deal systematically with sexual violence and cultural stereotyping. Relevant to both sexes, the Community status of citizens-as-workers, instead of citizens-as-human-beings, has also attracted general criticism. For example, Spicker[25] points out that this means there can be no coherent Community health policy that deals with major scourges of humanity such as AIDS, drug addiction and environmental pollution. However, as noted earlier, developments in integration are now at a stage where the language of the Union is wider than the language of the Community. Discussion of this will recur. In the meantime, the chapter deals with channels which exist as the result of the social dimension through which people can exercise secondary political rights of association and consultation.

Channels for the Exercise of Secondary Political Rights

Many accounts of rights point out that benefits or entitlements may be empty symbols. In connection with civil rights in the United States, it has been argued that governments may pass laws designed to protect "victims" without any tangible distributive or redistributive consequences. In his seminal work, Edelman[26] argued that this happened because agencies were "captured" by the groups whose behaviour was supposed to be regulated in the interest of the intended beneficiaries. For example, railway magnates "captured" the interstate Commerce Commission which was to have protected the interests of travellers and the sellers of agricultural products in having fair prices. Sometimes, symbolic laws may satisfy the "victims" and sometimes they may create expectations for further action. For expectations to be transformed into tangible consequences, it is necessary for the "victims" to enter into a bargaining relationship with public administrators.[27] If such a policy-network is to succeed, administrators must play an interventionist part in respect of the "victims." What Blumrosen[28] calls "bland neutrality" by administrators as between, say, large corporations and racial minorities cannot lead to improvements for racial minority employees. Administrators need to counterbalance the preexisting inequality of power by helping the supposed beneficiaries of legislation with special help and information in the use of the law to secure their rights.

There is some evidence that the European Commission has tried to fulfil a role that is similar to that of American public administrators in the 1960s and 1970s. Despite the temporary injunction against such interaction at the end of the 1960s, the Commission continued to maintain links with national and cross-national trade unions and women's organisations. And Hoskyns,[29] for example, refers to the significance of sympathetic "insiders" for the inclusion in policy proposals of definitions that would expand rather than minimise equality.

The first contacts tended to be used by trades unionists to improve domestic situations more than serving as an acknowledgement of common values and the promotion of common rights.[30] Modern cooperation focuses on trans-Community networks of specialists and representatives of organised labour and women, for the sake of efficiency and the promotion of common policies.[31] For example, the Centre for Research on Women and the European Network of Women are consulted, like UNICE (Union of Industries of the European Community) and ETUC (European Trade Union Confederation), in order to encourage convergent social standards—with some success.[32] There is now an officially supported European Women's Lobby, composed of representatives of women from all member states, with consultative status.

A vast number of committees exists, composed of Commission staff and national nominees, to monitor policy implementation, a process which reveals defects and can lead to reforms. Visits to the Commission by groups and individuals from member states are encouraged may be given financial support. Much written information is disseminated in newsletters and journals such as Women of Europe and Social Europe. Information offices have been set up in the member states to deal specifically with rights (in addition to the general presence of the Commission in national capitals and major cities).[33] Networking, as well as publicity given to social policy cases in the ECJ, is having some impact on the cross-fertilisation of ideas and expectations. This is reported, for example, in connection with childcare facilities.[34]

The existence of such channels of influence means that Community nationals have some of the secondary political rights granted to aliens legally-resident in a hospitable country. This means that ordinary people have some opportunity to contribute to the definition of their own policy needs instead of being passive recipients of policies defined by others. This point is the subject of Hart's[35] comparison between the American Fair Labor Standards Act and the European Social Charter. She points out that in 1936, there was a similar criticism of the concept of worker in the United States—that it was assumed to mean a conventional model of male employment in manufacturing. Thus, agriculture and domestic service were not accepted as "work" and were deemed to be governed, not by contracts of employment, but by the conventions of familial relationships. As a result, neither black farm workers (mainly male) nor domestic workers (black and white females) were protected by the American "charter." But, she also points out, inspired by a political culture of constitutionalism and rights, the unprotected were able to use the pluralistic and permeable institutions of the United States to get their situations redefined. Though it took a long time, their success encourages Hart to be more optimistic than the critics referred to above about the impact of European social rights. Her optimism may find some vindication in the Maastricht Treaty's initiation of political rights for citizens, now unqualified by their working status.

Individual and Regional Political Rights

Two aspects of integration have facilitated the initiation of political rights for Community citizens. First, legal entitlements and social rights "spilled-over" into political rights. It began to be argued that, if it were true that the loss of social security entitlements and other social "advantages" inhibited the right of free movement, the same must be as true, or more so, of political rights. In addition, the resuscitation of the idea of citizen-as-human-being, familiar among the early federalists, coincided with movements towards political union.

In 1983, the European Council issued a Solemn Declaration on European Union and, in the following year, the European Parliament adopted a Draft Treaty of Union. Also in that year, the European Council set up an *ad hoc* committee, chaired by Pietro Adonnino, who reported in 1985.[36] The committee is remembered mostly for its recommendations on the cultural and social aspects of the People's Europe and on the symbols of politics, such as the Community emblem, anthem, flag and passport cover. Another of its consequences was the Citizen's Europe Advisory Service, with offices throughout the member states, where, as noted above, nationals can go to enquire about their legal and social rights.[37] But the Committee also dealt with political rights, asking the Council to invite Community institutions to introduce measures to bring into existence the citizen as a participant in the political process in the Community' and in the member states. Specific recommendations were made that were similar to some of those which now appear in the Maastricht Treaty on European Union. Between 1989 and 1991, the Commission and Parliament both made reports, and the latter passed Resolutions, to try to ensure that rights of "Union citizenship" would have substance.[38] Although the Parliament criticised the eventual Treaty in many important respects, it broadly welcomed the introduction of a number of proposals that include the two main dimensions of democratic political citizenship; the control of public powers and individual rights.

The former dimension includes increased powers for the Parliament in the formulation of common policies and new powers for the Court of Justice over member states not complying with Community law. Individual rights to contribute to the control of public powers are enhanced by the introduction of a Parliamentary Ombudsman, who may pursue citizens' allegations of maladministration in the Commission, and by the aim to achieve more "open government" in respect of the Commission. (The latter ambition, however, does not affect the deliberations of the Council of Ministers and does not apply to the intergovernmental "pillars" of the Treaty, through which policies on foreign affairs, policing, immigration and asylum will develop.)

The Treaty also calls upon member states to agree upon certain transnational voting rights. Any EU national, resident in another member state is to be able to vote in local elections and stand for local office. All EU nationals are to be able to vote in whichever member state they reside in European elections and to stand as candidates for the European Parliament. They are also to have the right to be protected outside the EU by the consular and diplomatic services of any member state.

The rights to vote and stand for office have been argued to be fundamentally flawed.[39] They can be derogated when governments have overriding, specific national problems or judge the public interest to be at stake. And these rights confer a second-class order of citizenship because they exclude the right to vote and stand for office in general elections. However, it should also be noted that, judging by the lengthy struggles for national citizenship, it may be too soon to rule out the likelihood of the extension of initial rights to national, general elections. And it is clear from the Court's judgements so far, that, derogations— which are possible in all Community policies—and defences based on them, are subjected to a strict standard of scrutiny. Such defences usually fall entirely or in part.

There is a widespread convention that citizenship is a quintessentially individualistic concept and, hence, problematic in dealing with collectivities of people; for example, marginalised social groups and dependent peoples. It may seem unusual, therefore, to discuss the political rights of regions in a chapter on citizenship. Nevertheless, questions about citizenship rest on a prior problem that is a collective one. This is the question of why people consent to be governed. Before the spread of ideas about universal respect for the equality of human beings and their rights to place private interests in the public realm, solutions to the problem of consent focused on the means of controlling public powers. This concern was also present in political liberalism in the sense that universal rights were thought of, not only in normative terms, but also as providing a larger number of people able to hold governments to account. Thus, thought of in terms of accountability and in the context of integration, individual citizens' rights may be congruent with the collective right of self-determination.

It is clear that many regions in the European Union are striving to protect their existing status or to bring about some new form of self-determination in which they can circumvent the powers of existing states to be the sole articulators of the national interest. These are not necessarily nationalists aspiring to statehood of their own. Many advocates of regional interests, though they do not wish to revolutionise existing constitutions, lack confidence that their needs are given due weight in what is advanced at the common level as the aggregate interest. Despite the differing ultimate goals, nationalists and regionalists are equally active in using the opportunities afforded by the European Union to promote their territories. They do so through a host of spontaneous and sponsored transnational networks dealing with economic and social development and regeneration. Very many regions have offices in Brussels. While their staffs have no constitutional status as representatives, daily contact and proximity enable their interests and views to be known.

Whereas governments, especially centralised ones, believe that the principle of subsidiarity in the Maastricht Treaty protects state sovereignty against the unnecessary exercise of common powers, regionalists (and the "social partners") believe that it entrenches the rights of people below the level of national government to take part in policy-making, implementation and evaluation. The regionalists' understanding of subsidiarity is consistent with a preexisting principle of decisionmaking in the Community and may be so with other provisions of the Treaty. "Partnership" in Community decisionmaking, which has grown in significance with the expansion of coordinated socioeconomic development, means that local and regional elected representatives and local "social partners" should be full participants, along with national and common authorities, in the full cycle of programmes in receipt of Community funds. The rights of regional representatives to take part in general policy-making at the common level has been institutionalised in the new Committee of the Regions. As in the case of individual rights, these rights for collectivities of people may be seen either as "window dressing" or as promising. It is worth noting, however, that, after initial misgivings about a new institution with rival claims to electoral legitimacy, the European Parliament eventually hailed the Committee of Regions—together with the growth of integrated regional policy—as a signal of the regions' right to self-determination.

Political Interests and Identities: Homogeneity and Diversity in the Public Space

Many people in positions of political leadership and observers of European integration suggest that a common citizenship depends on the prior existence of social homogeneity. Europe, on the other hand, is characterised by a cultural diversity, distinguished by national traditions, that is too laden with past conflicts for the requisite homogeneity to emerge spontaneously. Either this means that a European citizenship which is more than an empty symbol is unattainable. Or, the necessary homogeneity would have to be coerced into existence—which would defeat the liberal foundations of the Union. This view oversimplifies the ways in which people identify themselves and ignores an important, alternative way of thinking about the "public space" in which people may express their identities and advance their interests. There are both social and "sub-national" aspects to the argument that peoples' identities are neither solely competitively nationalistic nor eternally the same; in other words, like conceptions of citizenship, senses of identity are contextual.

It is plain from the cases taken to the Court of Justice that individual social identities and interests may override national loyalties. Many of the disputes giving rise to the jurisprudence on social rights discussed above involve conflicts with national public authorities and acknowledgement that there is a proper role for common, instead of national authorities. Even when support for the Maastricht Treaty was waning, British people were reported as overwhelmingly hoping that their government would be found guilty in the Court of failing to comply with common policies on water pollution. Throughout the Union, vast majorities of people think that it is proper and important for common institutions to deal with environmental issues.[40] Steelworkers in Italy and Germany, while recognising that they are in competition in terms of production, believe that they have common interests in common standards of health and safety and that they have a common interest in these standards being regulated by a common body of law.[41]

It is also clear that many people are not satisfied that their legal nationality is a fully suitable label. Political circumstances often give rise to the use of hyphenated self-descriptions; for example, Scottish and British, Black-American, Italian-American, French-Canadian, Bavarian-German, and so on. Moreover, the content of definitions and willingness to use particular labels both change over time; for example, whether or not the Anglo-Irish count as Irish and recent cavilling by Scots at the British part of their label. Increasingly, people are willing to add "European" to whichever other ways they identify themselves, especially, but not only, if they have moved. A Welsh migrant farming family described themselves in a radio interview as "Welsh-British-French-European!" Bedell[42] reports that there is a growing band of middle class British migrants in western Europe who enjoy a sense of being European, because infrastructures, amenities and education are treated, in their view, more seriously on the continent as components of citizenship.

Perhaps not surprisingly, the lead on identity politics has been taken in feminist political analysis and in the study of minority politics, but similar considerations are now being addressed in general democratic theory. Theories of equal citizenship for women show that, although women may identify with other women or groups of them, being a "good" woman is not the same as being a good citizen. Women may abjure "male" politics but they cannot choose to be immune from the impact of policies.[43] The achievement of policies which take account of women's interests needs women—sustained by identification with women's groups—to interact with other groups in the public space. If citizenship is to be equal in fact as well as form, the place in the public sphere for women's agendas must be as secure as for other groups. Similar arguments for democratic citizenship in general have been made by Mouffe and Walzer.[44] In both bodies of thought, democratic participation, freely entered into, needs not a neutral state but a political authority that takes positive steps to ensure that there is equal liberty for all in a pluralist public space.

Leca[45] points out that the fact that so many so-called national societies are multicultural and multiethnic means that it is imperative to have within even national polities the pluralist arrangements outlined above. This contrasts sharply with an implicit assumption in propositions that, in extrapolating from national experiences, it can be shown that homogeneity is a precondition for European citizenship. This assumption is that polities are always communitarian. If it were true that successful societies were necessarily *gemeinschaft* and never *gessellschaft*, there would, indeed, be grounds for cynicism, scepticism or fear about the European Union. As Tassin[46] argues, it cannot constitute a public space in a communitarian sense because, like a multiethnic state, it does not embody "a cohesive, common, original identity." But it is possible to think of the European Union as a *gessellschaft* society. As Tassin also argues, it can "a politically constituted public space" in which the plurality of political interests, feelings, wills, initiatives, judgements, decisions and actions come "face to face."

However, arguments in equal citizenship theories about the behaviour of the state are also relevant to the realisation of democracy in the European Union. In this respect, the Union is defective in ways that are not always thought of as part of the "democratic deficit" and which are aggravated, as its Parliament has pointed out, in the Maastricht Treaty. This is the growing tendency to reach multilateral, intergovernmental decisions instead of common ones, especially since the recognition of the European Council and, as indicated earlier, as a result of the new "pillars" of the Maastricht Treaty. This means that decisions are formulated and implemented without the safeguards of consultation and judicial review characteristic of common policies. Though governments may claim that such an approach is more democratic in the sense that important decisions are reached by elected politicians who are accountable at home, most of the policies that alarm bodies that defend civil liberties and human rights[47] have come, and are coming, about in this way. Policies on immigration and policing, for example, over which "Citizens of the Union" have virtually no influence, except— if they know about them—through their national governments, may have a profound impact upon the freedoms and "closures" of European citizenship.

In addition, some governments may be trying to minimize the tangible benefits of citizenship in the European public space by favouring enlargement. Large numbers of poor, new Union citizens from east central Europe, and perhaps Turkey, would mean that the material implications of common social standards would have to be so slight that they would be vacuous. And, the inclusion of unstable political communities could be used as a public interest justification for postponing indefinitely the entrenchment of primary political rights.[48]

Nevertheless, it is still possible to regard the Union as an additional arena for the realisation of democratic citizenship. As already indicated, it offers the opportunity for people to act on their social and regional identities and in pursuit of interests shared with people elsewhere, in addition to nationally-based channels. It is also the case that "social partners" and regionalists are increasingly assertive in using their right to make use of such opportunities—as is clear in responses to regional development initiatives and the consultation over future social policy. Instead of the cynicism about a more remote level of government, noted by Aron, is precisely the secondary rights of political participation afforded by that level of government that have fuelled the sense that primary rights should follow.

The existing and developing framework through which people may exercise their rights and duties and express their loyalties and dissent is a complex three-dimensional one.[49] Political actions are now carried out through a web of common institutions, states, regional and local authorities and voluntary associations on the domestic front and simultaneously, in national and/or transnational alliances, at the common level. Daunting to the newcomer, this web of channels of influence is not only an opportunity for the representation of particular interests. It also provides routes through which civil society in Europe can try, as Walzer and Mouffe argue, is essential to national civil societies, to challenge restrictions placed by public authorities on the areas in which associations of citizens may be active. Given the negative aspects of developments in Europe, as well as its opportunities, the participants in European civil society must not fail to continue to influence or challenge the way in which the European public space is being shaped.

Acknowledgement: The ideas in this chapter are developed more fully in my book, *Citizenship and the European Community*, published by Sage in 1993 and in an article, 'Citizenship and European Union' (provisional title), in a forthcoming special edition of *Publius*.

Footnotes

1. R. Aron, 'Is Multinational Citizenship Possible?,' *Social Research*, 41(4):1974, pp. 638-56.

2. D. Heater, *Citizenship. The Civic Ideal in World History, Politics and Education* (London, New York: Longman, 1990), p. 163.

3. E. Tassin, 'Europe: a Political Community?' in Mouffe, Chantal, ed., *Dimensions of Radical Democracy. Pluralism, Citizenship, Community* (London: Verso, 1992).

4. J. Leca, 'Nationalita e Cittadinanza nell'Europa delle Immigrazioni' in WAA, (Italian for various editors/authors) *Italia, Europa e Nuove Immigrazioni* (Torino: Edizione della Fondazione Giovanni Agnelli, 1990).

5. e.g.: H. van Gunsteren, 'Notes on a Theory of Citizenship' in P. Birnbaum, J. Lively and G. Parry, *Democracy, Consensus and Social Contract* (London and Beverly Hills: Sage/ECPR, 1978) J. Leca, op. cit.

6. Gallie is quoted in G. Close, 'Definitions of Citizenship' in J. P. Gardner, ed., *Hallmarks of Citizenship: A Green Paper* (London: The Institute for Citizenship and the British Institute of International and Comparative Law, undated).

7. Heater, op. cit.

8. A. Zolberg, 'Ethical Dilemmas of Immigration Policy in the New Europe.' Paper presented to conference on *Social Justice, Democratic Citizenship and Public Policy in the New Europe* (ECPR/Erasmus University, Rotterdam, 1991).

9. Leca, op. cit.; G. Delanty, *Inventing Europe: Idea, Identity, Reality* (Basingstoke: Macmillan, 1995).

10. J. P. Gardner, ed., *Hallmarks of Citizenship: A Green Paper* (London: The Institute for Citizenship and the British Institute of International and Comparative Law, undated).

11. Heater, op. cit., pp. 73-4.

12. D. S. King and J. Waldron 'Citizenship, Social Citizenship and the Defence of Welfare Provision,' *British Journal of Political Science* 18:1988, pp. 415-443.

13. B. Jordan, *The Common Good. Citizenship, Morality and Self Interest* (Oxford: Basil Blackwell, 1989).

14. Heater, op. cit., p. 16.

15. Commission of the European Communities, 'The Commission Proposes a Community Charter of Fundamental Social Rights,' Background Report ISEC/b25/89 (1989)a (London: Jean Monnet House).

Commission of the European Communities, 'Communication from the Commission Concerning Its Action Programme Relating to the Implementation of the Community Charter of Basic Social Rights for Workers.' COM(89)568 final (1989)b (Brussels: Commission of the European Communities).

16. Commission of the European Communities, 'European Social Policy. Options for the Future,' Consultative Document COM(93) (1993a), 17 November 1993 (Luxembourg: Office for Official Publications of the European Commission).

Commission of the European Communities, 'European Social Policy. A Way Forward for the Union,' White Paper, (1993b) (Luxembourg: Office for Official Publications of the European Communities).

17. E. Meehan, (forthcoming) 'Federalism, Citizenship and European Union' (provisional title). Special edition of Publius.

18. A. C. Evans and H. U. Jessurin d'Oliveira, *Nationality and Citizenship* (Florence: European University Institute, 1989).

19. J. Usher, *European Community Law and National Law. The Irreversible Transfer?* (London: University Association for Contemporary European Studies/George Allen and Unwin, 1981), pp. 20-24.

20. Usher, *ibid.*, p. 27.

21. e.g.: J. Steiner, (2nd ed.) *Textbook on EEC Law* (London: Blackstone Press, 1990). E. Meehan, *Citizenship and the European Community* (London: Sage, 1993).

22. J. Steiner, 'The Right to Welfare: Equality and Equity under Community Law,' European *Law Review*, 10: 21-41 1985, p. 40.

23. E. Collins and E. Meehan, 'Women's Rights in Employment and Related Areas' in C. McCrudden and G. Chambers, eds., *Individual Rights and the Law in Britain* (Oxford: Clarendon Press/Law Society, 1994).

24. The range of literature is reviewed in E. Meehan, 'European Community Policies on Sex Equality. A Bibliographic Essay,' *Women's Studies International Forum7* 15([1):1982, pp. 57-64.

25. P. Spicker, 'The Principle of Subsidiarity and the Social Policy of the European Community,' *Journal of European Social Policy*, 1(1):1991, pp. 3-14.

26. M. Edelman, *The Symbolic Uses of Politics* (Urbana, Illinois: University of Illinois Press, 1964).

27. Edelman, *ibid.*, J. Freeman, *The Politics of Women's Liberation* (New York: David McKay and Co, 1975).

28. A. W. Blumrosen, 'Toward Effective Administration of New Regulatory Statutes, Parts I and II,' *Administrative Law Review*, Winter and Spring: 90-120, 1977, pp. 209-37.

29. C. Hoskyns, 'Women, European Law and Transnational Politics,' *International Journal of the Sociology of the Law*, 1986, pp. 299-315; C. Hoskyns and L. Luckhaus, 'The European Community Directive on Equal Treatment in Social Security,' *Policy and Politics*, 17(4) 1989, pp. 321-336.

30. J. Holloway, *Social Policy Harmonisation in the European Community* (Farnborough: Gower, 1981).

31. W. Streeck and P. C. Schmitter 'From National Corporatism to Transnational Pluralism: Organized Interests in the Single European Market,' *Politics and Society* 19(2):1991, pp. 133-64.

32. Hoskyns, *op. cit.*

33. Commission of the European Communities, 'The Citizen's Europe Advisory Service,' Background Report ISEC/B5/90, 25.1.92, (London: Jean Monnet House, 1990).

34. P. Moss, 'Childcare and Equality of Opportunity' in L. Hantrais, S. Mangen and M. O'Brien, eds., *Caring and the Welfare State in the 1990s* (Aston University: The Cross-National Research Group, Cross-National Research Papers, 1990). J. Edwards and L. McKie, 'New Series: The Implications of 1992 for Social Policy,' *The European Community: A Vehicle for Promoting Equal Opportunities in Britain?*, Paper presented to the annual conference of the British Sociological Association, Kent, 1992.

35. V. Hart, 'The Right to a Fair Wage: American Experience and the European Community Charter of the Fundamental Social Rights of Workers' in V.

Hart and S. Stimpson, eds., *Writing a National Identity: Political, Economic and Cultural Perspectives on the Written Constitution* (Manchester: Manchester University Press, 1993).

36. Commission of the European Communities, 'People's Europe' (Adonnino Report), *Bulletin of the European Communities*, Supplement 7/85, 1985 (Luxembourg: Office for Official Publications of the European Communities).

37. Commission of the European Communities, 1990, *op. cit.*

38. European Parliament, *Documents on Political Union* (Dublin: European Parliament Office, 1992).

39. E. Moxon-Browne, 'The Concept of European Community Citizenship and the Development of Political Union,' Paper presented at ECPR Joint Sessions, Limerick, 1992.

40. R. Sinnott, *John Whyte Memorial Lecture*, The Queen's University of Belfast; a preview of a cross-national research project on attitudes to governance carried out under the auspices of the European University Institute, Florence, 1992.

41. European Consortium for Political Research (ECPR) (1991) unpublished proceedings of a special meeting on social rights and citizenship.

42. G. Bedell, 'Britons Join the Continental Drift,' *Independent on Sunday*, 17 February, 1991.

43. A. Phillips, 'Citizenship and Feminist Politics' in G. Andrews, ed., *Citizenship* (London: Lawrence and Wishart, 1991). M. Dietz, 'Context is All: Feminism and Theories of Citizenship' in C. Mouffe, ed., *Dimensions of Radical Democracy: Pluralism, Citizenship, Community* (London: Verso, 1992).

44. C. Mouffe, 'Democratic Citizenship and the Political Community' in C. Mouffe, ed., *Dimensions of Radical Democracy. Pluralism, Citizenship, Community* (London: Verso, 1992). M. Walzer, 'The Civil Society Argument' in C. Mouffe, ed., *Dimensions of Radical Democracy: Pluralism, Citizenship, Community* (London: Verso, 1992).

45. J. Leca, 'Questions on Citizenship' in C. Mouffe, ed., *Dimensions of Radical Democracy: Pluralism, Citizenship and Community* (London: Verso, 1992).

46. Tassin, *op. cit.*, pp. 188-9.

47. M. Spencer, *1992 and All That: Civil Liberties in the Balance* (London: Civil Liberties Trust, 1990).

48. Moxon-Browne, *op. cit.*

49. S. Baine, J. Benington and J. Russell, *Changing Europe. Challenges Facing the Voluntary and Community Sectors in the 1990s* (London: NCVO Publications and Community Development Foundation, 1992).

About the Book

Surveying the ideals and visions held by the founders of the European Community, this timely book also assesses the concepts and theories surrounding the European Union today. This volume is the first to explore the theoretical cleavages among Monnet, Spinelli, the federalists, and the functionalists together with the views of the Socialist, Labour, Social Democratic, Conservative, and Christian Democratic parties on the challenges of a United States of Europe. The contributors combine their theoretical analyses with extensive use of archival material, party programs, and speeches to provide an authoritative and comprehensive study of value to all scholars interested in European integration.

225

About the Editors
and Contributors

Philomena Murray is Senior Lecturer in Political Science at the University of Melbourne and President of the Contemporary European Studies Association of Australia. She was a diplomat from 1984 to 1989, in Dublin and Paris and has worked in European Community institutions in Brussels. In 1991, she was awarded a large ARC (Australian Research Council) Grant, for her forthcoming book: *The European Community—A Supranational Polity.* She has written on European integration, major actors in European Union and on the party groups of the European Parliament and is co-editor of *Europe in the 1990s: Australia's Options,* CESAA, 1994.

Paul Rich is Principle Lecturer in the Department of Politics and Public Policy at the University of Luton and formerly Senior Research Fellow in the Department of Political Science at the University of Melbourne. He is the author of numerous articles on British and South African politics and has written *White Power and the Liberal Conscience* (1984), *Race and Empire in British Politics* (1986), *Hope and Despair: English Speaking Intellectuals and South African Politics, 1896-1976* (1993) and is joint editor of *Race, Government and Politics in Britain* (1986) and editor of *The Dynamics of Change in Southern Africa* (1994). He has recently completed a study for Cambridge University Press entitled *State Power and Black Politics in South Africa, 1912-1951* and is currently engaged in a study of comparative regional integration.

Richard Dunphy is currently Lecturer in European politics at the University of Dundee, Scotland. He has previously lectured in European Studies at University College Cork. He was born in 1960 in Northern Ireland, educated at Trinity College Dublin, the National University of Ireland, and the European University Institute, Florence, from which he received his Ph.D. in 1988. He is the author of *The Making of Fianna Fail Power in Ireland, 1923-48* (Oxford University Press, forthcoming), and is currently working on a study of Left-wing parties and European integration. He has published articles on aspects of Irish and European politics.

Martin Holland is currently Senior Lecturer at the University of Canterbury, New Zealand, and formerly a Jean Monnet Fellow at the European University Institute (1987) and an Alexander von Humbolt Fellow at the Arnold Bergstraesser Institut (1993). His most recent Community titles include *The Future of European Political Cooperation* (1991), *European Community Integration* (1993) and *European Foreign Policy in Transition* (1994).

Elizabeth Meehan is Professor of Politics at the Queen's University of Belfast. She also holds the Jean Monnet Chair in European Social Policy. Before moving to Belfast, she lectured in Politics at Bath University and was a Hallsworth Fellow at Manchester University. She writes about both women's rights and European integration, her main recent publication being *Citizenship and the European Community* (1993).

Cornelia Navari is Lecturer in the Department of Political Science and International Studies at the University of Birmingham, UK. Her works include *The Condition of States* (1991) and *Chatham House and British Foreign Policy During the Interwar Period* (1994) and articles on ideas of international relations in the twentieth century. She has contributed a chapter on "David Mitrany and International Functionalism," *Thinkers of the Twenty Years' Crisis*, eds., Peter Wilson and David Long (forthcoming); "The Origins of the Briand Plan," *Diplomacy and Statecraft*, 3,4, 1992; "The Great Illusion revisited, the International Theory of Norman Angell," *Review of International Studies*, 15, 3, 1989.

Peter Wilson is Lecturer in International Relations at the London School of Economics and Political Science. He is the author of several articles on international relations theory and is currently completing a study of the international thought of the Fabian writer, Leonard Woolf. He is co-editor (with David Long) of *Thinkers of the Twenty Years' Crisis* (forthcoming).

Index

For Product Safety Concerns and Information please contact our EU representative GPSR@taylorandfrancis.com Taylor & Francis Verlag GmbH, Kaufingerstraße 24, 80331 München, Germany

Printed and bound by CPI Group (UK) Ltd, Croydon, CR0 4YY
31/12/2025
02027630-0008